Critical Muslim 29

Futures

Critical Muslim is published quarterly by C. Hurst & Co. (Publishers) Ltd. on behalf of and in conjunction with Critical Muslim Ltd. and the Muslim Institute, London.

All editorial correspondence to Muslim Institute, CAN Mezzanine, 49–51 East Road, London N1 6AH, United Kingdom.
E-mail: editorial@criticalmuslim.com

C. Hurst & Co (Publishers) Ltd.,41 Great Russell Street, London WC1B 3PL

ISBN: 978-1-78738-149-0 ISSN: 2048-8475

To subscribe or place an order by credit/debit card or cheque (pounds sterling only) please contact Kathleen May at the Hurst address above or e-mail kathleen@hurstpub.co.uk

Tel: 020 7255 2201

A one-year subscription, inclusive of postage (four issues), costs £50 (UK), £65 (Europe) and £75 (rest of the world), this includes full access to the *Critical Muslim* series and archive online. Digital only subscription is £3.30 per month.

A Cataloguing-in-Publication data record for this book is available from the British Library

Critical Muslim

<u>Subscribe to Critical Muslim</u>

Now in its eighth year in print, *Critical Muslim* is also available online. Users can access the site for just £3.30 per month – or for those with a print subscription it is included as part of the package. In return, you'll get access to everything in the series (including our entire archive), and a clean, accessible reading experience for desktop computers and handheld devices — entirely free of advertising.

<table>
<tr><td><u>Full subscription</u></td><td><u>Digital Only</u></td></tr>
<tr><td>The print edition of *Critical Muslim* is published quarterly in January, April, July and October. As a subscriber to the print edition, you'll receive new issues directly to your door, as well as full access to our digital archive.</td><td>Immediate online access to *Critical Muslim*

Browse the full *Critical Muslim* archive

Cancel any time</td></tr>
<tr><td>United Kingdom £50/year
Europe £65/year
Rest of the World £75/year</td><td>£3.30 per month</td></tr>
</table>

www.criticalmuslim.io

CM29

January–March 2019

CONTENTS

FUTURES

ARTS AND LETTERS

REVIEWS

ET CETERA

FUTURES

INTRODUCTION:
POSTNORMAL HORIZONS

Ziauddin Sardar

It is all about gestures. Or more specifically, about 'hand movement', which according to an advertisement for Volkswagen, makes you 'smarter and more popular'. This is why the German car manufacturer has devoted enormous financial resources to develop 'gesture control' — you will be able to drive future VWs simply by waving your hands. 'How much can we say with our hands? What does the future look like?' The advertisement asks. And concludes, with a clarion declaration: Volkswagen is 'Making the Future Real'. We are also provided with a convenient code to 'Shazam' 'to see the future with Volkswagen'. Seeing, as they say, is believing.

Is it? Is the future 'real'? Can it be made 'real'? The best answer in these best of all possible postnormal times cannot be black or white. It is both: yes and no; and maybe and perhaps. In one sense, there is nothing real about the future: it simply does not exist. It is always a time that has yet to be reached. Moreover, the future will not exist even in the future for the future exists only when it becomes the present at which point it ceases to be the future. As the future does not actually exist, it has to be invented; to put it another way, images, metaphors, ideas about the future have to be generated and projected. Where do these images, metaphors and ideas come from? Mostly from the (recent) past and the present. Collectively, they frame our thoughts and actions about the future; and we are influenced not just by our notions of what happened in the past, and what is happening now, but also by our images of what may yet happen in the future. Thus, while the future is elusive and uncertain, it is also a domain over which we can exercise some influence. That's exactly why VW frames its advertisement in the image of a technological future.

We cannot change the past; we can only interpret and reinterpret history; but we can't actually change it. We cannot change the present either: that requires instantaneous change which is – as yet – impossible. But our inability to have some understanding of the future combined with the pictures and representations of what we want the future to be does provide us with some ability to usher in those futures we desire. It is in that sense that the future becomes 'real'. Whether we want VW – which is, after all, the company that developed a 'defeat device' that allowed its cars to produce forty times more pollution than the legal limit – to make the future 'real' is another question all together.

'The future' has become all things to all people; it is the best place to find whatever you are looking for. It is the location of western technocratic dreams. It is the site where you turn for love, peace and goodwill to all humanity. It is where all reforms take place. It is where we may meet the end of civilisation as we know it. It is where some wish to come face to face with singularity: the point where man and machine infuse, humans transcend biology, superintelligence is created and transhumanists triumph (around 2045 by the reckoning of Google futurist and inventor Ray Kurzweil). All of which suggests that there is no such thing as 'the future'. There are numerous futures – alternatives that technocrats and luddites, corporations and politicians, right-wing philanthropists and left-wing idealists envisage and try to shape.

But here is the rub: 'the future' is, strictly speaking, not a future at all! It is simply the present extrapolated onto the coming years. It is the extended present that corporations and technocrats, and legions of American futurists and consultants, sell as 'the future', a commodity gift wrapped as technological nirvana. That's what most of the 'predictions' from pop futurists amount to.

Simply extending the present into the future is also a way of colonising the future. The ideology of colonialism is not confined to history; it has a strong futures component. As Christopher Jones, who has spent a lifetime working as a futurist, notes, trend analysis is a basic pillar of futures studies. Trends, by definition, 'are the general direction that some phenomenon is changing or developing'. But there is no guarantee that 'general direction' will continue. Trends are not destiny – they can change, they can be changed, emerging phenomenon may disturb and distort them, and sometimes they can be thrown totally off course by 'wild cards' or outliers, which we call 'Black Swans'. So scores of assumptions are being made when trends are projected onto the future and used as a basis for 'predictions'. Such predictions can have a self-fulfilling effect too. On the whole, they express a deep desire for business as usual: for oppressive structures to be maintained, for consumerist culture to march on to its inevitable glory, for society to be led by the nose, by technology controlled by a handful of global corporations.

There is, however, another way that the future is colonised. As Sohail Inayatullah points out, 'the future is not merely a place but a feeling' – a sentiment that can be enhanced through narratives. Inyatullah has developed what he calls Casual Layered Analysis (CLA) to dissect and interrogate narratives about the future. His intention is to move people away from what we may call narratives of unthinking futures to narratives of transformative futures. The point Inyatullah makes so strongly is that feelings and emotions provoked by images, metaphors and accustomed narratives of the future have a powerful hold on our perception of the future. As such, I would argue, they can become an instrument not just of colonisation of the future but also of enslaving our imagination. In a workshop I conducted in Istanbul a few years ago, I asked the participants – mostly Masters and PhD students – to imagine and describe what Istanbul would look like in twenty years' time. Almost without fail, they regurgitated images from well-known Hollywood products: *Blade Runner*, *The Fifth Element* and *Star Trek*.

But such familiar futures are not confined to imagination: they are often given concrete form. In my 1985 book, *Islamic Futures*, I presented a familiar futures scenario for Mecca:

> This scenario takes the present development to its absurd, but logical conclusion. The holy city of Makkah continues to see development until every segment of the city is transformed: two-thirds of the city consists of roads saturated with traffic, the remaining part has tower blocks, each one higher than the next. The same developments happen in Muna. The mountains surrounding Makkah and Muna are flattened and given over to highways. To cope with the increasing traffic congestion during hajj, a whole complex of flyovers and spaghetti junctions are built. Consumer shops, fast-food dispensers and petrol pumps occupy every inch of available space. Exhaust fumes in the air make it very difficult to breathe. Lead from the polluted air ensures that even the hardy date palm cannot grow. Makkah and its environment is now

transformed into a perpendicular metropolis; it is a city like any other American city: say, like Columbus, Ohio.

Perhaps I got the city wrong. I should have gone for Houston, Texas. But Mecca today is a product of a colonised familiar future. As is Kuala Lumpur: a product of Malaysia's '2020 Vision', which was distinguished by a total absence of any originality. Both Mecca and Kuala Lumpur are a product of borrowed futures, or what Inayatullah elsewhere calls 'used futures'. The Saudi Vision 2030, with its 50 islands of global upmarket tourism, too is an artefact of a colonised imagination. Pride of place is given to NEOM city project, which

> will focus on nine specialised investment sectors and living conditions that will drive the future of human civilisation, energy and water, mobility, biotech, food, technological & digital sciences, advanced manufacturing, media, and entertainment with liveability as its foundation.

God save us all! Both Kuala Lumpur and Mecca, and the NEOM city project, pay no attention to what Maya van Leemput, who incorporates futures in her multi-media art practice, calls 'lived experiences' of the inhabitants, which ought to be the source of images of futures of cities. There is little concern for diversity not just in terms of culture but also architecture, for historical continuity, ecological well-being, or indeed for imagination that is free from the suffocating hold of superannuated used futures.

We need to go beyond the extended present and familiar futures approaches to break the power of the present and open up all our futures to other possibilities. The future is the only arena where real change is possible; but we have to ensure that change takes place within the boundaries of sustainability, it has to be change that we desire and envisage, that leads to a just and equitable, ecologically balanced world.

During my twelve-year stint as editor of *Futures* (1999–2011), the primary scholarly journal of futures studies, I learned two things. First, I came to the realisation that most papers submitted to the journal could be divided, like computer code, into ones and zeros – or optimists and pessimists. The optimists study the future from the perspective of the past and the present. No matter what methods they use – trends analysis and extrapolation, scenario building, cross matrix analysis and even highly sophisticated procedures such as modelling or morphological analysis – the end result in most cases is more of the same. Except better, faster, bigger, smaller, cheaper. They tend to be scientists and technocrats who work for corporations or the government; and come, on the whole, from industrialised countries. One can say that they give us the western establishment view of the future. They see change in mainly quantitative terms. These futures are designed to stimulate demand for more and more. Amongst the optimists we also find the idealists, ecologists and new age visionaries who wish for cleaner, greener futures and develop elaborate projections of utopian future worlds. They then sit back and hope that the universe has the sense and the good will to transform their visions into future realities. The New Age visionaries – who conventionally came from California before it was taken over by Silicon Valley but now also come from Australia – want to paint the future canvas with love, harmony and not-so-free sex. This is where the leftover dreams of the 1960s and 1970s meet (what's left over of the) postmodern pastiche.

The pessimists use the same methods as the optimists to reach diametrically opposite conclusions. Except they concentrate on the downside of technology and focus on destructive trends. Most futurists of pessimist inclinations tend to be social scientists, philosophers, artists and rather left-wing. All pessimistic futures essentially boil down to what we may call the Terminator scenario. Here, runaway technology produces a dark, dreary and dingy future. The world is controlled by megalomaniac corporations, privacy has evaporated, and cyborgs police the streets. These two alternative futures are, themselves, simply a convergence on a dichotomy, one confirmed by the editor of *The Faber Book of Utopias*, John Carey. Researching this book, published in 2000, he found that human utopias fell into one of two classifications: technological or green, if in many versions of each.

Needless to say, I do not subscribe to any of these views of the future. I belong to a group of futurists who believe that futures are not a priori given, who see the duality between optimistic and pessimistic futurists as largely irrelevant. We appreciate that some methods of predicting and forecasting the future can easily be used to foreclose futures of all others. We note that highly sophisticated techniques, and they have become more and more sophisticated with the rise of Big Data, machine learning, bots and Artificial Intelligence, simply end up by projecting the (selected) past and the (often-privileged) present on to a linear future. In contrast, we seek a more pragmatic approach that empowers people and opens up futures to pluralistic and democratic potentials and possibilities. Some of my colleagues and other fellow travellers have contributed to this issue of *Critical Muslim*.

Second, I learned that the present itself is not static. It is always changing. Indeed, change itself is constantly changing, and accelerating. The present has changed so drastically and so rapidly that many things we took for granted as norms and normal make little sense. Conventional does not work. Established paradigms are cracking under the pressure of change. Customary and cherished values seem irrelevant. Time-honoured ways of doing things lead to consistent failure. So the present has gone post-normal; and we find ourselves in

> a time when little out there can be trusted or gives us confidence. The espiritu del tiempo, the spirit of our age, is characterised by uncertainty, rapid change, realignment of power, upheaval and chaotic behaviour. We live in an in-between period where old orthodoxies are dying, new ones have yet to be born, and very few things seem to make sense. Ours is a transitional age, a time without the confidence that we can return to any past we have known and with no confidence in any path to a desirable, attainable or sustainable future. It is a time when all choices seem perilous, likely to lead to ruin, if not entirely over the edge of the abyss. In our time it is possible to dream all dreams of visionary futures but almost impossible to believe we have the capability or commitment to make any of them a reality. We live in a state of flux beset by indecision: what is for the best, which is worse? We are disempowered by the risks, cowed into timidity by fear of the choices we might be inclined or persuaded to contemplate.

Or, as the Italian journalist Ezio Mauro put it, we are 'hanging between the "no longer" and the "not yet" and thus we are necessarily unstable'.

The zeitgeist of our epoch is well captured by the description of a Prada perfume in the British Airways in-flight duty-free catalogue I flicked through recently. 'Infusion D'Iris', we are told, 'is inspired by a search for balance and harmony in a chaotic and contradictory world'. Whether a ridiculously priced olfactory concoction can bring harmony to the world is a question best left unanswered. But the present is certainly rampant with contradictions and exhibits all the signs of being constantly on the edge of chaos. Contradictions are ubiquitous: politics everywhere is fragmented, nations and societies are divided as never before, competing interests and groups exist in social media bubbles denouncing and fighting each other. Indeed, the fact that the world is now deeply interconnected has increased contradictions – which cannot be resolved – many manifolds. But the world has also become complex. We cannot, as we used to, isolated problems and solve them for now they are interlinked and interconnected in a web of complexity. Most of our problems – political, scientific, technological, social, cultural, geographical – have become 'wicked', that is, they are connected to a host of other problems, incomplete, full of contradictions and constantly in flux in a rapidly changing environment. There are no simple solutions as complex problems require complex approaches. Throw in some positive feedback in a complex and contradictory environment and the end result is chaos. Thus, the accent in postnormal times is firmly on the 3Cs: contradictions, complexity and chaos.

There are driving forces behind the 3Cs. In a world of accelerating change, it is hardly surprising that things happen very rapidly. A single tweet can go viral and have an intended or unintended impact precipitously. Things also tend to happen at the level of the whole world while at the same time reaching individuals and communities in the remotest parts of the planet. And, not infrequently, a number of things happen concurrently. Thus 4Ss – Speed, Scope, Scale, Simultaneity – constantly feed the 3Cs. As news, opinions, statements, messages, blogs, tweets, posts on various social media, as well as actions, policies, and political, social and cultural declarations simultaneously whirl speedily around the globe reaching every nook and cranny, they increase contradictions, enhance complexity and habitually lead to chaotic events.

If the present is becoming postnormal, then, to use the title of the 2013 Exit Calm album, 'the future isn't what it used to be'. It too is creeping towards postnormality. So binary, bipolar opposites – artificial or natural, optimistic or pessimist, utopian or dystopian – approaches to making sense of a plethora of alternative futures are now irrelevant. The future is not one, a priori given tomorrow. A better way of understanding futures is to see them as three, distinct, unfolding tomorrows, which may sometimes be sequential but more often occur simultaneously. The first tomorrow is the extended present, a product of deeply embedded trends. The second tomorrow is that of familiar futures, an outcome of recognisable images borrowed from films, television, novels and advertisements, metaphors that have gained common currency and conventional narratives lassoed on the frame of galloping change. So far so recognisable. The third tomorrow, however, is a radical place: it is the unthought futures – futures beyond the conventional and the predictable. Unthought futures are not unthinkable; it is just that we do not think about them largely because they are located outside our conventional framework of thought and action, or, if you like, dominant paradigms. Unthought futures require us to question our basic assumptions and axioms, and move towards truly uncharted futures territory. It is the unthought that breaks the shackles of extended present and familiar futures and leads toward genuinely decolonised futures.

Ironically, futures are also the unthought of contemporary Islam. In other words, futures is conspicuously absent from modern Muslim thought as though the basic assumptions of Islam do not permit reflection and consideration of the future. When I first started exploring and writing about futures in the late 1970s, I was dumbfounded to discover that the only mention of the future in Islamic literature occurred in relation either to prophesies or to the Day of Judgement – as though there was nothing between now and the Hereafter. The 'Unseen' seems to be located firmly beyond the grave; and, it seems quite clear to me that some highly pious individuals had died and then returned so that they could, in vivid detail, describe the *Spectacle of Death Including Glimpses of Life Beyond the Grave*. More recently, future has been associated with what has come to be known as the *ijaz* literature devoted to the dubious and disingenuous pursuit of alleged miracles, codes and prophecies of the Qur'an.

In sharp contrast, the Qur'an specifically asks the believers to be conscious of their history as well as their future: 'Beware of that which is before you and that which will be after you, in order that you may receive Mercy' (36:45). As Mirza Sarajkić notes, 'when we approach and read the Qur'an from a futures perspective we discover that it is the book of futures par excellence. By its content and context, it is thoroughly oriented towards the futures'. However, both classical and modern commentators and interpreters of the Qur'an 'have followed a centuries old set pattern. Key Qur'anic terms relating to the future have been given certain meanings at the expense of other potential meanings, and both classical and the modern commentators have firmly stuck to those meanings'. Sarajkić points out that the term for the unseen (*ghayb*), can mean the Hereafter but it also means 'the unknown', 'that which is currently absent and not visible but which can indeed be present and be visible in the distant time horizon'. The Qur'an uses a number of different terms for futures: *al-ġadd*, tomorrow; *ghayb*, the unseen future waiting to be known; *akhirah*, the ultimate future; *nazara*, reflections on futures. Moreover, the future in the Qur'an is always plural and impregnated with God's signs and signals which can be studied and explored. Sarajkić analyses a number of verses – 'O you who believe! Be aware of God, and let every soul reflect what it has forwarded for tomorrow, and be aware of God' (59:18); 'the future belongs to those who are aware/conscious' (7:128) – from a fresh, futures perspective to reveal a text that constantly urges the believers to reflect on all our tomorrows. Sarajkić's conclusion is categorical: 'there is little doubt that the Qur'an regards thinking, studying, and exploring alternative futures systematically and seriously as an intellectual responsibility of highest order for the Muslim community'.

There is indeed a tradition of futures thought and reflection in Islamic history. And it starts with the Prophet Muhammad himself. Consider, for example, the detailed planning over a number of years involved in the *hijra*, the migration from Mecca to Medina. The *hijra* itself was made on the anticipation of a more viable future for the then small Muslim community and involved exceptionally detailed planning – including escape routes, laying false tracks, providing adequate food and provisions for the journey, moving individual families to Medina over two years, to even moving Ali, the Prophet's cousin, into his house. Think also of the Constitution of Medina and how much futures thinking went into creating an all-inclusive document that forged Muslims (immigrants as well as residents of Medina), Jews, Christian and pagans into a unified community of the future; and provided rights and attributed responsibilities to each community. Abu Bakr the first Caliph, foresaw the expansion of Muslim lands and realised that future needs could not be fulfilled with the existing system of administration. He therefore developed a new, and profoundly flexible, system of administration and management which could adjust to future needs. Umar, the second Caliph, realised that the future survival of the Muslim ummah was dependent on available resources, and that all resources could not be consumed by one generation. He refused to distribute the conquered lands of Syria, Iraq, Iran and Egypt amongst the conquerors. In doing so, he went against the Sunnah – example – of the Prophet, explicit wishes of his companions, and even risked conflict. He declared that the newly required resources were for 'succeeding generations', and set them aside as future resources for the rapidly expanding Muslim community.

Future consciousness is also embedded in a host of Islamic concepts. The notion of *ijtihad* (sustained and reasoned struggle), for example, is concerned primarily with change and with shaping and reshaping futures. The concept of *khilafah* (trusteeship of human beings) adds another dimension of accountability and futures. The planet and its environment is a trust from God that has to be managed appropriately and passed on to future generations. The institution of *waqfs* (pious foundations), that can be traced back to the time of Umar, and adopted in the West (minus the spiritual dimension) centuries later, is specifically focussed on conserving and preserving resources for generations to come. Indeed, futures concerns are an integral part of the original objectives – *maqasids* – of the Sharia as evident in the future oriented logic of the, now long forgotten, institutions of *haram* and *hima*. *Haram* were inviolate zones around cities in which development was prohibited by the Sharia to ensure that the city does not suffer from pollution, that flora and fauna are conserved, and the city survives the future. *Hima* were reserves for the conversation of wildlife and forests designed to prevent deforestation and sustain the ecology of a region.

Classical Muslim philosophers and thinkers show a keen awareness of the future. For example, ibn Sina (980–1037) imagined a future world based on the liberated intellect where rationality was supreme. Ibn Rushd (1126–1198) argued that, apart from God, only human intellect was eternal and the future should be guided by it. His friend and colleague, ibn Taufyl (1105–1185), wrote what is considered to be the first philosophical novel, *The Life of Hayy*, and placed his protagonist, who spontaneously emerges from the slime, on a desert island in an attempt to show just how such a world can be created. Ibn Khaldun (1332–1406), who according to a new biography by Robert Irwin was quite obsessed with the future, provided a theory of the rise and fall of civilisations and how history moves in cycles.

The future is, of course, a consequence of both the past and the present. Or, to put it another way: futures thinking requires prospective, the inclusion of knowledge from history and an appreciation of changing contemporary reality. Recognition of the importance of studying and exploring futures for Muslim societies ought to begin with a futures readings of sacred texts and the rich intellectual history of Islam. The eleventh century philosopher and theologian, al-Ghazzali, divided knowledge, from an Islamic perspective, into two branches: *fardl-ayn*, or individually requisite knowledge, which is essential for all individuals to survive, such as social ethics, morality, civic law; and *fardul kifaya*, or socially requisite knowledge, vital for the survival of the community as a whole, such as agriculture, medicine, and engineering. Every community must have some members who pursue the main disciplines of socially requisite knowledge. If no one undertakes the endeavour, say no one studies medicine for example, the whole community suffers. Futures studies is now a preeminent *fardul kifaya*: to study and explore alternative futures, to envision and shape their own futures, has now become an obligation (*fard*) for all Muslim communities everywhere.

The obligation has acquired urgency because the postnormal horizons before us actually threaten the very survival of Muslim societies. Both physical endurance and the very identity of Muslims as Muslims is in danger. The Muslim world – spreading from Morocco in the West to Indonesia in the East - is often described as 'the middle belt'. It is the middle belt of the Earth that will initially face the severest impact of climate change. Already the temperatures in parts of the Middle East and South Asia have reached above 50 degrees celsius. If the trends continue, the coming decades will make it impossible for human beings to live in these regions. A whole generation of new environmental refugees will be created. Currently, three out of four refugees in the world are Muslim. By 2035, this ratio could change to four out of five. Consider another statistic from the front page of the *Guardian*: 'One in four Europeans vote populist'. The number of Europeans living under governments with a populist cabinet, the report tells us, has increased thirteen-fold: from 12.5 million in 1998 to 170.3 million in 2018. That is, half of Europe now has an extreme right-wing administration. This is not a temporary blip: the populists, according to the *Sunday Times*, have western democracies in a vice like 'grip'. And contrary to popular myth, they are not 'alienated white underclass', angry pensioners and the unemployed in 'Europe's wasteland'. Populism 'cast its net surprisingly widely across society, scooping votes from full-time workers, middle-class conservatives, the self-employed, people on average or high incomes, and even the young'. How long before Europe completes the historical cycle and returns to its fascist past, aided and abetted by racist AI?

We are forced to rethink most of what modernity and postmodernism made prevalent. Modernisation, constant growth, even the notion of perpetual efficiency now belongs to the wastebasket of history. Even the idea of culture has become unhinged.

If the future is a cultural fact, as some artists and anthropologists seem to suggest, then, Richard Appignanesi tells us, we better be aware that culture – at least in its western manifestation – is decaying if not already dead. The postnormal times are also a postculture period where the key virtues of modernity and postmodernism have become deadly. The nation state has become a 'criminal phantom', democracy is 'without foundation beyond self-authorisation', the media is hysterical, 'western power is enslaved by its own technological facility' and hyperreality 'cancels our existential sense of time passing normally'.

The evaporating normality is also making its mark on futures studies itself. As Jordi Serra, perhaps the most prominent futurist in Spain whose series of thirteen, fifty-minute television shows on futures *(El dia de dema,* 'The Day of Tomorrow') was recently broadcast on Catalan television, suggests the promise of conventional futures studies that 'it is possible to envision, forecast and build preferred futures is not entirely true'. Postnormal times are far too complex and chaotic for such simplistic assumptions. Serra emphasises, along with other contributors to this issue of *Critical Muslim,* that both quantitative and qualitative methods are needed simultaneously for a better understanding of futures. Science is not enough. Imagination, art, and literature have a strong role to play in our understanding of postnormal horizons. So we are forced to concede that 'futures cannot be about managing, let alone, controlling the future'. While the future cannot be managed or controlled, it can be navigated.

However, postnormal times cannot be overseen by old academic disciplines, locked inside water-tight compartments, or timeworn skills and competences. Sustainable futures demand multi, inter, and trans disciplinary approaches. Some disciplines, such as economics and 'development studies' need radical transformations. Others need to be rethought; area studies, for example, make little sense in a complex, interconnected world where no 'area' exists in splendid isolation for 'experts' to ruminate on! Still others, such as anthropology, should be consigned to history. And a plethora of new inter and transdisciplinary – for want of a better word - 'disciplines' have to be created. Similarly, critical thinking by itself is not good enough, we need a range of new competencies: in futures and anticipatory thinking, inter and trans disciplinary work, coping with incomplete and complex information, appreciating and handling uncertainty, recognising ignorance in its various forms, understanding how phenomenon move towards postnormality (postnormal creep). Futurist and founder of the website 'Work Futures', Stowe Boyd, suggests the skills of freestyling, the ability to adjust to a changing situation; emergent leadership, 'the ability to steer things in the right direction without the authority to do so through social competence'; complex ethics and 'postnormal creativity' – 'in postnormal times creativity may paradoxically become normal: an everyone, everyday, everywhere, process'.

Finally, one may ask, who are we doing futures for? The answer is provided by Cesar Villanueva who has used futures for conflict resolution and building peace. As I have witnessed, he has worked with fishermen, victims of typhoons and disasters, and war torn communities. 'We engage in futures', Villanueva writes, 'not just for ourselves but for our communities, the country, and the world community at large. All four are subject to typhoons be it personal, structural, social, even spiritual'. We trust in God. But according to the Prophet's advice, we also have to tie our camel – to the sturdy pole of sustainable futures to ensure that it remains pluralistic and open for all potentials and possibilities. Let's begin, as the VW ad suggests, with a few gestures!

FUTURES IN THE QUR'AN

Mirza Sarajkić

What does the Qur'an have to say about studying and exploring alternative futures? In certain circles, the question itself is regarded as somewhat out of the ordinary if not downright blasphemous. The future is the domain of the Unseen; it belongs to God. Any attempt to predict the future is to play God. In other circles, the future is all about 'prophesy' – witness the sheer number of tomes dedicated to this phenomenon with titles like *The Prophecies of the Holy Qur'an*, *Israel and the Prophecies of the Holy Qur'an*, and *The Prophecy and Warnings Shines Through the Mystifying Codes of the Holy Qur'an*. Most of this is mindboggling, irrational material that serves as psychotherapy for a decaying culture. Its basic function is to drain the believers of all agency and turn religion – or more specifically theology – into a toxic brew.

A true appreciation of how the Qur'an talks about the future, and how it encourages a systematic study of futures, has been conspicuously lacking for a very simple, but powerful, reason: commentaries and interpretations of the Qur'an have followed a centuries old set pattern. Key Qur'anic terms relating to the future have been given certain meanings at the expense of other potential meanings, and both classical and the modern commentators have firmly stuck to those meanings. For example, the unseen (*ghayb*), can refer to the Hereafter; it is God – 'the One who knows the seen and the unseen'. But *ghayb* also means 'the unknown', that which is currently absent and not visible but which can indeed be present and be visible in the distant time horizon. When we approach and read the Qur'an from a futures perspective we discover that it is the book of futures par excellence. By its content and context, it is thoroughly oriented towards the futures.

Muslims believe that the Qur'an was revealed to take them out of a corrupt present, the time of Prophet Muhammad, and guide them towards brighter and more just futures. The Qur'an describes itself as 'Divine Guidance' (*hudā*) or 'spiritual light' (*nur*) to those 'who are conscious' - *muttaqīn* – about their futures as well as the futures of the worlds (2:3, 16:54, 45:11, 20:123). The plural form for these terms in the Qur'an is highly significant (68:52, 12:104, 21:107). Even in conventional theology, the future in the Qur'an is not singular but plural. The Qur'an provides guidance to 'people of faith' and prepares them for the *akhirah* – the final future or the Hereafter, next world and other world as Muslims repeatedly translate and understand this term. This is actually quintessential of Islamic worldviews in which a human being has the gift of life on this world in order to make a difference through ethical excellence and selfless commitment to the betterment of all humanity, eventually leading, by the grace of God, to a 'blissful hereafter'. But the Hereafter can also be 'hellish' (42:7) if a path of moral corruption and evil deeds is followed. So even when the basic tenets of faith are concerned, future is not singular.

I would argue that the fundamental orientation of the Qur'an is undeniably futuristic. There are numerous verses that directly highlight the significance of futures. There are verses that encourage visioning, there are verses that present various scenarios as tools of reflection, and there are even verses that can be seen as 'backcasting' – a planning method that starts from a given future and works backwards to identify policies and actions – with a little use of the imagination.

Consider, for example, the following verse: 'O you who believe! Be aware of God, and let every soul reflect what it has forwarded for tomorrow, and be aware of God. God knows all the details of your deeds' (59:18). There are several important features in this verse. First, it comes in the form of command. God is asking, indeed demanding, from the believers to reflect on the future. Future in this verse is described as tomorrow (*al-ġadd*); one of many different terms used for futures, confirming the Qur'anic tendency to speak about future in plural. Second, the very verb used in the verse is also telling. God orders the believers to reflect (*naẓara*) on the future; the choice of the verb focuses the believers' mind towards a precise action: reflection. *Naẓara* does not refer only to regular thinking but more detailed and sophisticated elaboration, or, if you like, theories about futures. Indeed, the word for theory in Arabic is exactly *naẓar*; *ilm al-nazar* – knowledge of theory – is used in Arabic to define the science of sophisticated reflection, and is frequently used in Islamic philosophy. As such, God is demanding from the people of faith to deeply reflect on and ponder what futures may bring, what consequences and opportunities they may usher, and what actions we may need to avoid or tackle the consequences and what we ought to make of the opportunities. One may ask: why is this degree of intellectual gravity and systematic rigour needed when it comes to the future? One answer can be given from the general perspective and context of the Qur'anic approach: the ultimate future (*akhirah*) is the apex of all our futures so what happens in the immediate, near and far futures also has an impact on our ultimate future. How our actions impact futures we consciously or unwittingly shape, what we leave behind for futures generations, has ultimate bearing on how we shape our *akhirah*. So God is asking the believers to seriously think about the future consequences of their actions in the present. People of faith are invited to reflect upon all the futures that at the end of the road merges into the final one – *akhira*. Third, what the verse says about *taqwa*, normally translated as God consciousness, is equally exciting and revealing. This verse is among many in the Qur'an in which believers are asked to be cognisant and constantly aware of God (*tawqa*). *Taqwa* is truly the highest state that people of faith should strive for and it is clearly designated as sublime nobility in the eyes of God (49:13). In 59:18, *taqwa* is firmly bound to the notion of the future. People of faith, the verse is implying, should strive to constantly remember God, keep Him on their minds and act and behave accordingly. They can achieve *taqwa* by deep reflection (*nazar*) about futures and what they do and contribute to the future. So reaching the sublime status of *taqwa* lies through the study and exploration of the future: in order to be *'aware of God'*, you have to act to ensure that your current actions do not harm the future and *reflect what you have forwarded for tomorrow*. It is important to note that the dictum on reflection on futures is situated between two demands to be aware of God: the second 'be aware of God' intensifies the message of the verse which can be summed up, after examining all its context, as the following divine advice: in order to reach the pinnacle of spiritual nobility you are obliged to have your own theory/philosophy of the future.

This perception of the future as intellectual and spiritual obligation of the believer is reinforced in a number of verses, such as:

'the future *belongs to those who are aware/conscious'* (7:128).

'These are some stories from the past that we reveal to you. Neither you, nor your people knew them before this. So be patient. The future *belongs to the mindful/awake'* (11:49).

'Did he look into the future, or did he receive a promise from the Most Merciful?' (19:78).

The verses, relating to the future, have their respective contexts and meanings; and they use different descriptions in Arabic (*ʿāqiba, ġayb,* etc.). But their general gist is the same: you have to be awake to future possibilities!

The basic semantic unit of the Qur'an is sign (*āya*), usually translated as verse. The Qur'an is a cluster of divine signs in the form of sentences or verses as this Arabic term is most commonly understood. Nevertheless, divine signs are not confined only to one form or one place. Rather, we are surrounded by them. God's signs are everywhere, emanating from Him. As the Qur'an says:

'We will show them our signs on the horizons, and in their very souls, until it becomes clear to them that it is the truth. Is it not sufficient that your Lord is witness over everything?' (41:53).

The main message of this verse is that futures are imbued with signs and signals. One of the most important tasks for people of faith is to expect, detect and try to recognise these future signs. This was a common feature of prophets, who envisioned a better and just future, as the chosen ones among the believers. Actually, visioning the future is presented as an important characteristic of notable individuals or main actors in the Qur'an. One can find a number of examples but I will focus on the story of Khidr and Prophet Musa, told in 18: 62-82.

In Islamic tradition Khidr is seen as a prophet, a messenger, even an angel. But the Qur'an describes him as a 'Servant of God':

'a man to whom We had granted Our mercy and whom We had given knowledge of our own' (18: 65).

Moses meets Khidr 'where two seas meet' and asks to accompany him in his journeys to gain from his knowledge and experience. The Servant of God replies:

'You will not be able to bear with me patiently' (18: 67).

Moses insists.

'How could you be patient in matters beyond your knowledge?' (18:68), Khidr asks.

But Moses is persistent; and promises to be patient. The two travel and come across a boat. The Servant of God makes a hole in the boat.

Moses is shocked: 'how could you make a hole in it? Do you want to drown its passengers?'.

The Man reminds Moses: 'did I not say that you will not be able to bear with me patiently?'

They travel further and meet a boy. The Servant of God kills him. Moses is stunned and cries out in dismay:

'what a terrible thing to do?' (18:74).

He is reminded once again of his promise. Then they proceed to a town where they ask for food but are denied hospitality. They come across a crumbling wall. Khidr repairs the wall. Moses says:

'if you had wished you could have taken payment for doing that' (18: 77).

The Servant of God now declares:

'this is where you and I part company' (18: 78). He explains the meaning of things to Moses:

> the boat belonged to some needy people and I damaged it because I knew that coming after them was a king who was seizing every (serviceable) boat by force. The young boy had parents who were people of faith, and so, fearing he would trouble them through wickedness and disbelief, we wished their Lord would give them another child – pure and more compassionate – in his place. The wall belonged to two young orphans in the town and there was buried treasure beneath it belonging to them. Their father had been a righteous man, so your Lord intended them to reach maturity and then dig up their treasure as a mercy from your Lord. (18: 79-82)

The Khidr narrative is clearly meant to be read as an allegory. But it is important to note that the knowledge (*ilm*) that he possessed was based on reasoning (*rušd*) (18:66). On their journey, Moses could not understand Khidr's reasoning and found his actions troubling. He was looking at these events solely from the perspective of the present; as such, his assessment turned out to be shallow and wrong. In contrast, Khidr was reading the signs or 'sounding the future'; his actions were based on deep and sophisticated future visioning which ultimately resulted in promoting justice. Classical commentators predominantly focussed on the origins of Khidr, whether he was a prophet or an angel, and issues related to Musa's self-assumption of his knowledge. Those issues have metaphysical importance but the striking point of this story lies in refined crystallisation of present/future orientation of two notable actors in Qur'anic narrative. Khidr is doubtlessly depicted as a man deeply engaged in the process of decoding future signs. His reasoning is future oriented; he is meticulously reading possible tomorrows and his actions are based on his understanding how the future will unfold. He is positioned in the Qur'an as *Magister Magnus* to those who represent the spiritual elite in Qur'anic narrative. The essence of the story is obvious: the future matters more than just spiritual concerns.

This point is well illustrated in the 2017 Turkish science fiction film, *Bugday* (Gain), directed by Semih Kaplanoglu. The film is set in a post-apocalyptic world where genetically modified food has destroyed all crops, much of the earth's surface is contaminated, and the vast majority of people are kept outside the deadly electromagnetic zapping towers that protect a select few from unwanted intruders. Inside the enclave, Professor Erol Erin and his teams work effortlessly to try and save humanity from the catastrophic crop failures. Erin discovers that a potential solution may lie in the contentious theory of 'genetic chaos' proposed by the rogue scientist Cemil Akman, who has disappeared. Erin sets out to find Akman, travelling to the barren regions outside the city borders. When Erin eventually finds Akman, he turns out to be a Khidr-like figure. The two go on a journey where Erin becomes the unquestioning student of Akman. Here, the film takes on a metaphysical turn, perhaps in a nod to classical mystical interpretations, with much discussion of guilt and ego, visions and dreams. However, it is noteworthy that the film depicts the enigmatic Khidr/Akman as a scientist who had foreseen the consequences of his research in genetic engineering through rational means. As the Qur'an tells us later on in the same chapter, even though you may think you are doing good work, your efforts may be misguided (18:103).

Given that the notion of futures subtly pervades the text of the Qur'an, it is not surprising that it contains various ideas which could be seen as equivalent to contemporary concepts in futures studies. Consider, for example, the notion of scenarios. The Qur'anic versions are designed as sophisticated guidelines for the people of faith to prepare themselves for different futures while remaining within ethical boundaries. Some of these scenarios are embedded into the stories of prophets and prominent individuals portrayed in the Qur'an. Other possible scenarios have perennial character and potential because they are not limited to particular time horizons. Scenarios in the Qur'an regularly begin with the word 'perhaps' or *asā*. Here are three examples:

They said, 'We were persecuted before you came to us, and after you came to us.'

He said, 'Perhaps your Lord will destroy your enemy, and make you successors in the land; then He will see how you behave' (7:129).

Say, 'Perhaps some of what you are impatient for has drawn near' (27:72).

'Perhaps God will restrain the might of those who disbelieve' (4:84).

These verses are challenging believers to think about potential futures, which might be very unpredictable, desirable, unexpected and sometimes even unthought ones. Close reading of these verses reveals an exceptional narrative play that beg certain natural questions. In the first and the third verse, the scenario is partially fixed as if God is asking: What is the rest of the scenario if all your wishes and prayers are answered without any effort or contribution from you? Have you ever envisaged how you would rule the world? Have you thought about future outcomes and have you prepared for them? The second verse raises the question: what are you going to do if 'what you are impatient for' actually happens? Are you prepared for this eventuality? But, of course, 'what you are impatient for', could equally be an optimistic or pessimistic, good or a bad, scenario. So you are required to think clearly about what you may impatiently desire from your future.

The Qur'an also contains scenarios which we can describe in the language of postnormal times theory as 'unthought futures' that are often expressed in the mode of God's will (*sawfa*). These challenge the inertia, the feeling of self-sufficiency and sense of moral superiority of the believers. Emblematic examples can be found in chapters 5 and 56. Here is an example: 'We have decreed death among you, and We will not be outstripped. In replacing you with your likes, and transforming you into what you do not know' (56:60-61). If ripped out of its context, the messages of this verse appears to foreshadow a *Westworld* scenario. But essentially what we are being told is that the believers do not have a monopoly on God's affection; they can be written out of the future, if it is God's will. But that outcome depends on how the believers themselves act, behave and shape their future.

What I find particularly fascinating is how the Qur'an utilises backcasting to force the reader to think creatively about the future. In a number of places the Qur'an talks of catastrophic events or the fate of a community in the Hereafter. Scenes from calamities that befall a community are than unravelled in series of previous steps/phases/processes that eventually lead to the final phase. In some places the Qur'an describes the fate of a people in the Hereafter followed by whole sequence of the situations that preceded their afterlife misfortune. The afterlife of the wicked are contrasted with the blessed who are portrayed in their everlasting joy. Images of their bliss are followed by the series of their noble actions that – along with God's mercy – led them to this sublime state. The classical commentators transformed the message of these verses into eschatology concerned largely with descriptions of Heaven and Hell, End of Days and such like. But the point to note is that the Qur'an is talking in these verses, which are about future events and the Hereafter future, in the *past* tense. They may or may not allegorically describe particular ultimate futures, but they certainly suggest that all futures are embedded in a web of past and present actions. You are invited to reflect how you arrived in the present; and then think about the future you desire and how you will navigate your way towards it. In some cases, the Qur'an suggests, people can retrace – or backcast if you like – their actions, readjust their moral and ethical coordinates, and then move towards more just futures:

'Corruption has appeared on land and sea, because of what people's hands have earned, in order to make them taste some of what they have done, so that they might return' (30:41.

'We scattered them into communities on earth. Some of them righteous, and some of them short of that. And We tested them with fortunes and misfortunes, so that they may rewind their actions' (7:168).

The second verse continues to talk about future generations who did not learn the lessons of previous generations and 'took the fleeting gains of this lower world' – or, placed their own interests above those of the coming generations. If you continue on this path, continue to ignore future consequences of your actions, allow the destructive trends to endure, you reach a point from which there is no return:

'Deaf, dumb, blind. They will never return' (2:180).

It is a pity, I think, that both classical and modern Muslim scholars look at the future oriented verses in the Qur'an solely in terms of eschatology. But we can read the Qur'an with contemporary eyes, bringing our own fresh thought to our engagement with the Sacred Text. We do not, for example, have to read the opening verses of Chapter 30 – 'The Byzantines' – as 'a prophesy' or 'miracle of the Qur'an' as it is so often portrayed. These verses mention the heavy defeat of the Christian Emperor, Heraclius (610–641) and victory of Persians king Khosrow II (570–630) in 614. They go on to announce – predict – a big comeback of Heraclius' army in the near future, which actually took place around 628: 'The Byzantines have been defeated in [their] nearest land. They will reverse their defeat with a victory in a few years' time' (30:2-2-3). We can take this verse as a prediction that came true. There is no need to build an enormous eschatological edifice around it. What we do need to do is to examine the verse in the full light of history and see what lessons it could contain. The initial defeat of the Byzantines was viewed by the Meccan pagans, the enemies of the then fledgling Muslim community, as a victory for paganism. The Muslims were disheartened. The victory of Persians was so massive that it was out of the question that Byzantines could come back in the Middle East as a major power. That was frustrating for the first generation of Muslims in Mecca whose horizons of the futures were almost shut down. The Qur'an consoles them by pointing out that the fortune of the Byzantines would be reversed. The Byzantines came back – in the form of a 'black swan' as the postnormal futurists like to say. In turn, the Muslims themselves became a 'black swan': from being an outlier in a remote desert they defeated the Roman empire. What we learn is that outliers cannot be ignored; they have the potential to transform the future!

The opening verses are followed by a long passage that invite the reader to reflect on the signs of God – 'the heavens and the earth and everything between them'; travel around the world and witness the diversity of people and languages, examine the rise and fall of civilisations, and marvel at the rich flora and fauna and the complex ecology of the planet. This, the Qur'an is saying, is the abode of your terrestrial journey; conserve it and you conserve your futures. Those who perished before you. 'God did not wrong them; they wronged themselves' (30:9)

I hope I have convinced the believers that the Qur'an has a great deal to say about the future; and, in the Qur'an, it is always in the plural – futures. My interpretation of some of the verses differs from most of the canonical medieval exegesis of the Qur'an – or, rather, fills in the gap that have been left untouched for quite some time for many reasons. The main one being the rigid approach to the Qur'an and its classical interpretation that is sacralised and universally adopted with rare efforts to update, deconstruct or gain a fresh appreciation. But a reading of the Qur'an from a futures perspective, with full appreciation of the context, reveals a plethora of new insights. There is little doubt that the Qur'an regards thinking, studying, and exploring alternative futures systematically and seriously as an intellectual responsibility of the highest order for the Muslim community. 'Do the people of these towns', the Qur'an asks, 'feel secure that Our punishment will not come upon them by night, while they sleep [intellectually inert, unprepared for the future]? (7:97).

FUTURES IN FIVE SCENES

Jordi Serra del Pino

Scene one

1995: at the entrance of a building I was living in at that time
'Jordi, what does this mean?'
Ms Garcia was pointing at a new sign I have just put in my mailbox:

> Jordi Serra del Pino
> Prospectivista

My name was not the mystery. No, the question referred to the 'prospectivista' – the Catalan word for futurist. Mrs. Garcia was one of my neighbours, an old lady that had been very friendly with my wife and I since we moved into the building. Not only that, she had some influence in the community and I wanted to let her know that Futures (prospective) was a respectable practice. In retrospect, I think that I also wanted to impress her, let her know what a great thing Futures was and that she was lucky enough to have a trained futurist in her own building. Her look showed true curiosity and, maybe, a spark of anticipation. I started explaining Futures to her. I tried to sound erudite yet accessible; but, before too long, I began to realise that I was losing her. I decided to raise the stakes by improving (or so I thought) the quality of my explanation, but her body language was clear, I was a sinking ship. And there I was, desperately trying to find the most sophisticated examples to make my case, when she decided to put me out of my misery. With a movement of her hand she stopped me while asking a second question.

'Just tell me this, do you throw tarot cards?'

That was the proverbial torpedo to my flotation line, I was not sinking, I had already sunk.

'No Mrs. Garcia, I do not throw tarot cards.'

Her look now was a mixture of disappointment and compassion. At that moment I comprehended that, for her, I would have been a lot more interesting, not to say exciting, if I would have been a fortune teller. It was quite obvious that she had paid no attention to my speech. Her expectations were more in line of knowing if I could tell her if her daughter would find a suitable husband, or if her husband would overcome his breathing problems.

It was quite a blow. It was the first time that I understood, despite many people's interest in the future, that they might not have an equal interest in Futures. The implications of this realisation chased me, and gave me a great deal to think about. Only years later I would understand that this had been a key moment in my professional career.

Scene 2

1999: in a radio studio

I had foolishly accepted to be on a talk show discussing the year 2000 and how the future may look in the forthcoming century. For some reason the host decided that it could be interesting to combine a futurist and a witch. And I am not making any derogative labelling here, the woman whose name I have forgotten was very keen on introducing herself as a witch. After some preliminary comment I began to realise that the debate would go south quite fast. It started when the host asked us what the differences between our respective approaches to the study of the future were, and my response started the hostilities. I had just started to say...

'Well, to begin with, Futures is a science...'

'How dare you say that my work is not scientific?'

The interjection came from the witch, she was fuming. Although I did not really state that her work was not scientific, the implication was clear. I decided to ease the tension.

'Fine, then, if what you do is also science, how is it done? How do you do your science?'

'Ah, my friend, what I have is a gift, if you possess the gift of witchcraft you can do it, if you don't have it you can't. All the women in my family have shared this gift and that is why I can do my witch science.'

I tried to explain that, by definition, science has to be open and accessible for anybody; that any kind of person, regardless of his personal features and skills can learn it and develop it. That, this was, precisely, why Futures can be learned the same way you can learn physics or sociology. Yet, there she was claiming that whatever she was doing was conditioned by the previous possession of a particular set of capacities that could not be taught, only inherited. I thought that my argument was definitive, but she refused to accept it and maintained that her work was as scientific as anyone else's. By then, I began to see that she was not really concerned by her, should I say professional activity, falling under the category of science or not. The real issue had more to do with respectability, or even, credibility. She assumed that my claim that her profession was not based on science was an attempt to undermine her, maybe even a subtle way to steal some of her clients. My experience with Mrs. Garcia had made it clear to me that some people would never ask for my services but would gladly visit her; and, I assure you, I was really hoping that none of my clients would go to a witch to explore alternative futures. However, my issue with her witchcraft was not the accuracy of her predictions but two other things.

First, that she was basically predicting the future. The idea of prediction is very problematic for me. For starters, it is one of the most disempowering concepts. Basically, a prediction is a statement of total certainty about a future event, something like, 'next week you will find a good job'. This kind of statement has two implications that are contrary to the tenets of Futures Studies. One, the future is predetermined and, somehow, whoever does the prediction has mastered its causal mechanisms; therefore, the future ceases to be a myriad of possibilities and becomes fate. Two, when predicting, the future is reduced to one sole happening, it becomes singular. But for futurists it is essential that the future remains plural because only when the future is plural, human choice matters. That is why we work with forecasts, probabilistic statements, instead of predictions. Thus, a prediction destroys both any notion of freedom in the future and the relevance of human agency.

Second, and more important, knowing what may happen is not enough if it is not properly contextualised. If you are told that you will suffer a serious accident tomorrow, you may decide to stay at home in bed all day. But if the accident happens at your home, while staying in bed, it will have done you no good. For a futurist knowing what may occur is an accessory, what is really substantial is to understand why and how it may occur. Only this knowledge will help us to make better decisions, sometimes to the point of altering what you originally believed could happen.

So, I had no issue with the witch's approach. I simply considered (and I still do) that these kinds of outcomes are either disempowering or useless in order to make better decisions about the future. Yet, there was something I learned that day, science was part of the question regarding people's different approaches to the future and Futures. In fact, many people do not cut any slack to Futures being scientific when thinking about the future.

Scene 3

2009: Responding to 'What is in a name'
I had been invited to participate in a rejoinder. The then editor of *Futures*, the monthly journal of policy, planning and futures studies, Ziauddin Sardar wrote a paper, 'The Namesake: futures, futures studies, futurology, futuristic, foresight - what's in a name?', where he picked and developed an online debate on the World Futures Studies Federation list serve, about the implications of the different labels we use in the field. Basically, why some of us talk of Futures, while others refer to Foresight or go by Prospective. Sardar rightly dismissed the label 'futurism', which is associated with an early twentieth century movement with art that leaned

towards fascism. He pointed out that foresight is often used by business organisations and management consultants. And he also questioned the term 'futurology' as it suggests that the study of futures is an exact science, or a single monolithic discipline. In contrast, he emphasised the plurality of our field: it emphasises multiple futures and is intrinsically multi-, inter- and transdisciplinary. Hence, futures studies is the ideal nomenclature. Sardar also used the paper to introduce his personal take on the scientific nature of futures studies. Basically, he argued, science may be too restrictive a framework for futures to fully develop. Futures often deals with 'wicked problems' that cannot be isolated and reduced to one or two variables but require multiple perspectives to understand. As such, futures studies needs input from social science, humanities and the arts.

While I could agree with most of the nuances carried by the different tags, I could not avoid feeling uncomfortable with the notion of an unscientific futures. Of course, part of that had to do with the fact that my background in futures is partially from the Continental European School, with a heavy influence of French thinkers such as industrialist and philosopher Gaston Berger. Within this approach the scientific claim of futures (prospective) is taken for granted. But it also had to do with a deeper issue, my personal struggle to let people know that futures was a serious affair and a respectable professional career. My first contact with futures took place in a Barcelona association, the 'Catalan Futures Centre' (Centre Català de Prospectiva), which was originally called 'Futurology Friend's Club' (Club d'Amics de la Futurologia). However, they had to change their name very soon as the Club became associated with divination arts, like Occult and Tarot. The fact is that in Spain a futurologist is normally someone who pretends to have mastered some hermetic knowledge to uncover the secrets of the future. The term futurology simply does not apply to anything vaguely resembling a scientific endeavour. Personally, and beyond my clash with the radio witch, I have lost count of the number of times I had to explain that futures (prospective) has nothing to do with this kind of futurology.

I guess that all along I had considered science the single thing that distinguishes me from fortune tellers. By sticking to science, I was asserting that my notion of futures was on solid ground, and I had the methods that allowed others to have their say in what they would like the future to be. My adherence to the plurality of possible futures was a fundamental principle of my activity. Not only that, by following a scientific procedure to develop my work, I was also letting others gain insight over my practice and my outcomes. In short, I was claiming that what I do could not be further away from fake futurology.

And yet, maybe Sardar was spot on and science is too much of a corset to explore the future in all its richness and diversity. Maybe that is why the unscientific stance to the future is more appealing to people like my former neighbour Mrs. Garcia. Science could be an adequate response to the predictive approach, but it is also true that science has helped to commodify the future in many aspects. Therefore, the answer would be to find a futures perspective that could combine simultaneously a scientific and intuitive line of work, if such a thing was possible!

Scene 4

2011: My Participation in the 2nd Crazy Futures meeting in Bucharest
Within a few months after 'The Namesake', Sardar published another seminal paper: 'Welcome to Postnormal Times'. He was also involved in organising annual workshops in Bucharest, in association with the Romanian Ministry of Higher Education. The workshops brought academic and professional futurists together with doctoral and masters students from all over Romania to discuss and debate futures theories and methods and to come up with the zaniest futures the participants could possibly imagine – hence the title: 'Crazy Futures'. Thye provided a great opportunity to debate why futures was falling short. Sometimes, we would say that the data or information we were using was not very good, or just not good enough. In other cases, we would agree that some of our methods need a serious overhaul and all the different approaches, theoretical and methodological, were just not good enough.

But 'Welcome to Postnormal Times' proposed an intriguing alternative premise: nowadays reality is different, unprecedented, because change has changed. Of course, someone could object that almost every generation has had the perception that its time is like no other, that either they are enduring the worst moment in history or the most promising one (maybe even both simultaneously). Yet, the point is that present day societies have some first-time specificities. To begin with, the world has never been as complex as it is today, not only because there has never been as many people on Earth as there are now, but mostly because the human population is interconnected to a degree like none other in the past; and let us keep in mind that one of the features of a complex system is the presence of many components interacting in multiple ways. From this perspective, there can be little doubt that we are living in the most complex moment in human history. But there is a second element, Chaos. Again, chaos is hardly new on Earth but, precisely for the extraordinary increase in the number of humans, as well as their actions and interrelations, the potential for chaotic behaviour has increased exponentially. And thus, we see constantly how minor happenings transcend their local context to become global events with impact that look totally out of proportion; the speed and reach information and communication technologies have conferred to our actions has boosted this feature to, one more time, an unparalleled level in history. And third, as Sardar points out, a world that has become complex and chaotic ends up frequently being very contradictory: initiatives intended for a good purpose end up provoking just the opposite, emerging discourses that are inconsistent with existing ones, advances in knowledge in some fields reveal phenomenal ignorance in others. But mostly the growing evidence that some of these contradictions cannot be resolved because simple, binary approaches fall short in a world riddled with complexity and chaos.

Yet, the most essential feature of Postnormal Times is that it is a transitional epoch. As Sardar puts it we are in 'an in-between period where old orthodoxies are dying, new ones have yet to be born, and very few things seem to make sense.' Whatever we choose to name it, this is not an end state, we are moving towards a new era of which we comprehend very little. Therefore, it may be unwise to try to build very solid structures as we just do not know what they have to be, what purpose they have to accomplish, for how long they have to stand.

There was an interesting mention in the 'Welcome to Postnormal Times' that really caught my attention. The whole postnormal thing was coming from a previous paper, a 1993 article by Jerome Ravetz and Silvio Funtowicz, entitled 'A new Science for a Postnormal Age'. In that paper Ravetz and Funtowicz argued that something does not seem to work with science, indeed, it has not been working for a while. Scientists have been unable to reach consensus on critical issues such as climate change. And it does not really matter if this disagreement has been due to the fact that some scientist believe that we still lack conclusive evidence or because they have let other factors bias their scientific criteria and judement. Whether it is one case or the other (or worse, both) science has failed. Science's promise was to shed a light that would cast away ignorance and uncertainty. If science would state something, we would know and, therefore, there would be no doubt; and, in those cases in which we would not know, its rigorous application would lead us to an unquestionable conclusion. And yet, it has taken decades to reach a minimum consensus on the matter of climate change and, despite the fact that its first effects are already punching us in the face, some still question its existence. In short, we live in a moment in which a scientific fact does not carry more weight than any other kind of fact (I can almost hear the witch in the background telling me 'I told ya!'). However, Ravetz and Funtowicz were not advocating giving up on science. On the contrary. They proposed to create a new kind of science, one better equipped for such occasions 'where facts are uncertain, values in dispute, stakes high and decisions urgent'. In a nutshell, they reasoned that normal science was almost solely concerned with the product of any given research; essentially, the end result of the research is consistent with the methods applied. For them, that is just the beginning, the first P, the Product, but we need to consider additional elements: the Procedure, how the research has been conducted is relevant in itself; the Persons, the personality and idiosyncrasy of the researcher is pertinent; and finally, the Principles, the values, philias and phobias that were brought (consciously or unconsciously) into the research. Thus, we pass from focussing on one P to four Ps, giving us little choice but accepting that scientific evidence is also contextual.

Could it be then that the witch and I were not so far from each other? If so, the relevance I had been giving to science all these years could it be just another form of hubris. Maybe the lesson I failed to learn from my encounter with Mrs. Garcia is that the future is too powerful a notion to be captured with a single stance. For years I have been saying that the approach to the future has to be, necessarily, transdisciplinary; that no disciple alone can grasp on itself the future and, nonetheless, I had limited myself to a single (mental) approach. Very postnormal indeed!

Scene 5

2017: in a voting station during First Referendum in Catalonia in October
This was the day Catalonia held a referendum to decide if it should be independent from Spain. The Spanish state had decreed that the referendum was illegal and cannot happen. Around 18,000 policemen had been deployed to prevent it from taking place.

It was Sunday, and I got up at 5.00am to go to the polling station. I was part of a group that had been taking turns protecting the polling station during the whole weekend, like other people in many stations all over Catalonia. There were about fifty of us. We want to vote because it is the only way we have found the ability to say how we would like the future of Catalonia to be. Many of us believed that we were making history, I couldn't help but feel, deep in my guts, that we were building the future. At 7.00am we got out of the building to organise the access to the station to discover that hundreds of people were already queuing outside. It started to rain but nobody moved. Volunteers were requested to sit in the tables and manage the voting procedure, and I decide to enlist myself. Finally, the ballot boxes arrived and there was a first burst of joy, they were quite ugly, but they could not look more beautiful to us. We made the final preparations and got ready for the voting. Then things began to get nasty, footage of the police attacking other stations began to arrive and, all of a sudden, we became conscious of the situation turning ugly. We were scared but mostly we were shocked and raged by the brutality of the police charges. Almost immediately the hacker assaults started, to prevent the referendum from occurring. Uncertainty began to take its toll on us. It could not be that. Being this close and still not being able to have the referendum! The line of people waiting to vote kept on growing, the elderly, sick or disabled were taken into the station and everybody was holding their breath. Finally, a decision was taken, we changed the system and began to register voters manually, the central referendum authority had a backup census and could check for irregularities afterwards. A second outburst of jubilation spread when we announced that we can carry on with the referendum. For a while we just focussed on the feeling of joy, some people cried when they voted, others thanked us for being there, some asked permission to take a selfie but all shared a sense of communion. Whatever happens in the future we will always remember that, facing incredible odds and all sorts of hurdles, we stood and fought for our dreams and hopes.

It was a very long day. We punctuated the high moments with those of fear and indignation. A couple of times we even applied the panic protocol to hide the ballot boxes. I also had my dark moment when I learned that my son and wife were beaten (not severely though) while protecting another station. And I have to admit that, for a while, all I wanted was to face the agents that hit my family and hit them back. Nevertheless, we managed to finish the referendum peacefully in our station, count the votes and sign the official records. It was 9.30pm when we got out of the station to announce the results, the street was still full of people, the yes had won overwhelmingly and there was a final rush of joy. We jumped, danced, sang, hugged each other, cried and clapped. We had won, in more than one sense of the word, we had won. I returned physically, psychologically and emotionally exhausted. I had been talking for years about the importance of getting involved in the construction of the future, but I could not have imagined that it could be such a straining endeavour.

So yes, we won but, at the same time we did not. Catalonia became the first postnormal state in the world. According to Wikipedia, Catalonia was a republic for just 9 hours. To be honest, I cannot really explain what happened afterwards. I know the basic facts, but I cannot say why we failed to fully implement the republic. My guess is that the Catalan leaders feared an escalation from the Spanish government response leading deaths and injuries on the streets. And judging from the repression that unfolded in the following days it is hard to think otherwise. Nowadays we have several people in jail facing manufactured charges that may keep them imprisoned for the rest of their lives, others have had to go into exile and over a thousand other persons have been charged. The Spanish state, with the king at the forefront, has decided that preserving the unity of Spain is more important than the rule of law and democratic principles. The authoritarian face Spain has been known for in the past resurfaces again; and although it is clear that Spain has the force to prevent Catalan gaining independence (with the European Union looking at the other side) it seems obvious that it may provoke its own collapse as well. So, if anybody asks me now if Catalonia is a republic or a region, I just reply that it is a postnormal country, because it simultaneously is a republic, a region, none of them and both. You cannot be more postnormal than that!

But I have also learned two important lessons from what happened then and the following months.

The first one being that the old futures promise that it is possible to envision, forecast and build preferred futures is not entirely true. Maybe it was at some point, maybe it was true that by generating enough consensus and by coordinating the present actions some futures were built in the past. But I do believe that the world today is far too complex and chaotic for such a linear approach to work. Nowadays, the number of connections and interactions with a chaotic potential are very high, so high, that planning may become an exercise in futility and frustration. However, I am not saying that I have given up on planning or the future. Looking at tomorrow as a plethora of possibilities with a myriad of outcomes and implications, while considering the diverse alternative itineraries we could travel, is far too deep in my nature. I am a futurist, this is not just a job or something I do, it is an essential part of my being and that is why the second lesson is so painful.

The reasons why I have been so devoted to futures have been wrong. Deeply wrong. Futures is one of the last products of the promise of modernity: science will produce the knowledge that will let us master our destiny. If we think about it, we can see how science was already providing a way to rule nature and space, it was just a matter of time before it would do the same with time itself. World War Two supplied the momentum, something like that could not happen again perhaps not in the same way; therefore, we needed a better way to manage the future. And it makes perfect sense that we approached the analysis of the future the same way we did in other fields, using all the tricks in our intellectual bag: we resort to linearity, duality, induction, empiricism and the whole lot. They had worked beautifully in other endeavours, just consider all that we had achieved, the future would be no different. Yet the future proved to be hard to objectify and to commodify. To begin with it could not be turned into a single entity. Even when there would be a strong pressure to move to a specific future there would be the need to generate (or keep) an alternative, if nothing else, to prove that this alternative would be a disaster. No, futures realised very soon that the only way to make human choice relevant was to have a plurality of future possibilities, or, as the French call it, futuribles. Second, we also discovered that there would be occasion in which the future was better explained, captured or anticipated by non-scientific means. Thus, imagination, art, utopias, science fiction, pulp literature, comic books, movies and televsion series have frequently provided greater insights into the future than science. So, it is now that I realise that the tension between scientific futures and 'the future', and my clashes with Mrs. Garcia and the witch, were the symptoms of a deeper issue. Futures cannot be a purely scientific enterprise and, more to the point, it has never been. So yes, maybe futures was modernity's last son, but it was more a bastard than a legitimate offspring. From the very beginning, it has been tainted with some non-scientific (pre-, alter- or post-modernity) contributions and that is what makes it unique and problematic. It does not really work as a science, but it does not want to be something else. Futures has to find a way to reconcile its mixed heritage to make the most of its scientific and un-scientific legacy.

Nonetheless, there is something that needs to be done imperatively. It has to rethink its purpose. Futures cannot be about managing, let alone, controlling the future. If the postnormal hypothesis is true, the future cannot be managed or controlled, but it can be navigated. And precisely because we are living in postnormal times, anticipation is more critical than ever. Ravetz and Funtowicz were absolutely right: facts are uncertain, values in dispute, stakes high and decisions urgent. And the only way to improve our odds is to get better at anticipating, to enhance our capacity to spot potential storms over the horizon and, also, to find safe ports in the uncertain, complex and chaotic sea we have to sail to make our navigation less turbulent and more promising. But in a postnormal context our modern lineage may be more part of the problem than that of the solution. We have to come to terms with the fact that modernity, progress and the associated worldview have a great deal of responsibility in the creation of most of the predicament we currently find ourselves in. Consequently, it would be quite naive to expect that the factors that created the situation could be capable of coming up with a viable true alternative. Within the postnormal thinking this would be a good example of the deepest level of ignorance, what we call invincible ignorance. The kind of ignorance that is not a result of what we do not know but, precisely, of what we think we know. To quote the former American Secretary of State, Donald Rumsfeld, these would be the unknown unknowns. And we cannot beat invincible ignorance by trying to learn more (or better), even by trying to expand one's conscience. No, we can only defeat invincible ignorance by unlearning. That is, by questioning the assumptions of our worldview, by challenging the foundations of our knowledge, by lighting the implicit premises in our understanding of the cosmos. And this is precisely what I am trying to do these days. The painful part is that Mrs. Garcia and her question were right; or, as we like to say within the postnormal framework, they were partially right. My scientific background could be the single main factor blurring my understanding of the future. Hence, I have to question my status as a futures/future 'expert' and, by doing this, hopefully, strive to be a better, maybe truer, futurist.

But I do not feel bad about it. Actually, I guess I should consider myself lucky. After all these years tangoing with the future, I get to see it under a totally different light. And this also means that I get another chance to start anew, to begin a new journey. What I have learned all these years has brought me here and, once again, the future offers me the possibility of an exciting adventure. All things considered, it is not a bad deal. Wouldn't you agree?

TOUCHING THE FUTURE

Christopher B Jones

It was the nature of the field itself that first appealed to my elemental nature. My fascination with volcanoes, islands, mountain building, plate tectonics, and climate. That was one personal context that led me to the Alternative Futures masters program in Political Science at the University of Hawaii at Manoa. I began graduate school in 1980 and have been involved both with the department and futures studies ever since. My mentor for both my Masters and PhD dissertation was the distinguished futurist Jim Dator, a parent of the field, who established one of the few existing futures studies programs in the world. I was fortunate to be exposed to the academic side of futures studies: ten years in the Hawaii system, three years on the faculty of the Studies of the Future Masters of Science Program at the University of Houston Clear Lake, involvement with the World Futures Studies Federation, and exposure to the emerging literature, leaders, and scholars in the field. I was able to work or collaborate with many of the leaders in the field over the last four decades. Thus, I am an academically trained futurist, with one of the first doctorates in futures studies.

But what is futures studies? Quite simply, it is the systematic and scholarly exploration of alternative futures. It comes in other rubrics as well: foresight, strategic foresight, futurology, prospective, and sometimes simply futures. There is dispute within futures studies regarding whether it is a discipline or not; but most futurists see it as a field of inquiry. Like most academic pursuits, futures studies has theories, methods, landmark texts and studies, and established figures – stretching all the way back to its inception in the aftermath of the Second World War.

There is a growing consensus within the field about some of the assumptions that we hold about the future and futurists. One key assumption is that the future cannot be predicted. Other than the movements of the sun and stars, human futures are seen as unpredictable due to the complexities of driving forces and behaviour of humans and the environment. While some aspects of human behaviour can be predicted, counterintuitive or unanticipated consequences from technological, social, economic, and environmental events and developments are legion. Borrowing from the language of climatology and weather, good futurists may make forecasts, but they should never make predictions.

A second major and related assumption is that there is no singular future, but an array of alternative futures. Most academic futurists would grant that there is not a single future out there, but probable, possible, and preferred futures. One popular tool to illustrate the idea is the *futures cone* that graphically displays the range of possible and probable futures.

The notion of alternative futures, particularly preferred futures and the idea that we can realise those, was one of the ideas that attracted me to the Hawaii Masters program. The development of futures studies owes a great deal to the work of Fred Polak, another father of the field, who theorised the role of images in alternative futures. Polak argued that the future is largely a result of our individual and collective images of the future: a consequence of the collective images of the future that we have, and the actions that we take based on those images. Dator conceptualised four generic futures based on literature and popular media: Business As Usual, Stagnation and Collapse, Disciplined, and Transformational. But there were many more alternatives possible within the alternative futures universe. For example, the postnormal times theory has three generic futures: extended present, familiar futures, and unthought futures. My dissertation included deep ecology, radical feminist, and spiritual transformation alternative futures.

While futures studies has theories, it has no single theoretical framework. The field has a range of ideological perspectives and borrows freely from other disciplines. However, it's fair to say that the theory environment of the Political Science Department and the Alternative Futures Program was more disposed to critical theory; many contemporary tools and approaches in future studies have been informed by both postmodernism and structuralism, emerging from neo-Marxism, radical feminism, and deep ecology. Poststructuralism has clearly left its mark on futures studies as well as the humanities and social sciences in higher education in the United States.

Students in the Hawaii program were encouraged to engage in critical thinking and analysis, to become aware of our own biases and assumptions, and consider the Big Picture. My graduate school cohort was influenced by visitors to the university including Emmanuel Wallerstein, William Irwin Thompson, Johan Galtung, and other global thought leaders. Our critical outlook was informed by Dator's instruction to us that in order to understand the next ten years, we needed a good understanding of the past hundred years. Many of us were influenced by historical dialectics, by hegemonic studies, long-wave economic cycles, and deep structures of power such as patriarchy. My worldview was informed by the broad sweep of space and time in science fiction and by popular culture images of the future. Hawaii offered a unique standpoint between East and West, the cultures of Oceania, and a Pacific Shift worldview.

My theory of social change was based on communication theory, in terms of how people accept change. Given that the current era is characterised by rapid change driven by a number of factors, the question of change seemed to be focused on the individual and adaptation to change, along the lines of Alvin Toffler's *Future Shock*. But there are many kinds of change, and one kind of positive social change appeared to be the improvement of human rights over time, and social justice and equality. Over time, my view of social change has been tempered to the extent that every change appears to have impacts, winners and losers, and that the underlying dynamic of progress or growth may itself be problematic. The scope of change is also a key factor, the temporal context, from minutes to eons means that change needs to be seen contextually in terms of impacts over time. For millions of years our human ancestors likely existed on this planet with very little significant change other than the ebb and flow of village life as hunter-gatherers. We are now living in times of accelerating change, but that appears to be atypical compared to the broad sweep of our species' history. I am increasingly convinced that conflict is a leading driver of change: Dator taught us that as the world becomes increasingly globalised, technologically powerful, and diverse culturally, socially, and politically, it will see increased conflict. More recently, postnormal times theory helps better explain the acceleration of change, the uncertainty, and the impacts of complexity, chaos, and contradiction on politics and daily life.

Methodologies

Two basic methods in the field are trend and emerging issues analysis, seen as essential elements of strategic planning, strategic foresight, and futures studies frameworks. Scholars and practitioners have a variety of frameworks and trends and emerging issues belong in the formative stages of exploring the fabric of the future. For example, Wendy Schultz, an elemental force in futures studies, identifies five critical activities in foresight: identifying and monitoring change, critiquing the impacts of change, imagining alternative futures, envisioning preferred futures, and then planning, teambuilding, and implementing desirable features. Sohail Inayatullah, who pioneered the methodology of causal layered analysis (CLA), identifies the six pillars model of futures studies: mapping tools, anticipating, timing, deepening the future, creating alternatives, and transforming. Both see trend analysis as iterative and integral to the foresight process. Schultz sees it as a fundamental and recursive process and Inayatullah situates trends and emerging issues in the *anticipating* pillar and as the Litany layer in CLA.

Futures studies is a mixed methods phenomenon, a discipline or field characterised by both quantitative and qualitative methodologies and tools. While we may not be able to predict the future, futures methodologies have helped better explain and understand the topography of the future and the evolving present. Arguably, futures studies represents the first global effort to consider and better anticipate changes wrought by technology, society, and globalisation. Examples of quantitative futures work include straight trend extrapolation, Mic-Mac modeling, and the Delphi process. Qualitative tools are extensive: scenario building, visioning, and emerging issues analysis. Quantitative and qualitative tools are often combined, and mixed methods approaches are seen in academic futures journals. Overall, foresight and futures studies have made their impact on planning at the international level, particularly with regard to climate change, but planning at the city, regional, and national level that includes some futures studies methodologies and components do give hope that we are beginning to steer our way into our collective futures, rather than bumble our way into the future.

My research and scholarly work has been primarily qualitative, although much of the work I have done is also informed by quantitative concerns, such as the litany of the global *problematique*: species extinction, sea level rise, global warming, and other metrics of human impact on the environment. There are metrics for positive indicators, as well, such as the success of the battle against smallpox, reduction in human starvation and warfare, and rise of a large middle class in the developing world (recognising that all of these will have their own unanticipated consequences). My futures research work has primarily used qualitative trend analysis, emerging issues analysis, wildcards, scenario development, and visioning methodologies. Ultimately, to my mind, this all has to do with sense making, with finding meaning in the data collection, analysis, and synthesis of the changing world around us. While it often occurs in proprietary (corporate) and defence intellectual space, the domain of governments, intergovernmental organisations, and NGOs, the futures enterprise should also be an aspect of basic citizenship, something that schoolchildren, teens, and adults should all participate in, within organisations in their communities and polities.

So, why are trends 'grist for the mill'? Trends, by definition, are the general direction that some phenomenon is changing or developing. In an industrial society, trends have significant consequences for planning ahead. Resource extraction, manufacturing, and energy use, among many things, are measured and the changes in those phenomena have impacts in a chain of causality on other systems, developments, and the social and political responses to those changes. Trends can be local or global, can measure goods and services, but also attitudes, opinions, and cultural patterns. Some trends are hard to quantify, while others are more precise.

Trends can also be categorised, in the aggregate, as for example, *Megatrends*. Robust strategic planning processes usually include social, technological, economic, environmental, and political (STEEP) trends to contextualise the analysis and decision-making at the corporate or governmental level. Dator's tsunamis take the trends to their next level: the need to consider the consequences of these global driving forces as they impact our lives at all levels of analysis. Where do trends lurk?

Governments and the UN are a primary source of trend data, as well as trade industry reports, and increasingly available as Big Data on the Internet. Google Ngrams, for example, are a way to measure trending ideas. Data centres are popping up across the developing world to make public data more accessible to both decision-makers and the public.

Emerging issues are those nascent trends that are just beginning to be seen. Given that all trends begin as emerging issues, by the 1960s think tanks and government planners began focusing attention on what is known as environmental scanning or horizon scanning to help identify emerging issues in their infancy and developed strategies to monitor and assess the significance and impact of emerging issues. Put simply, horizon scanning requires reading and monitoring all available literature on a particular subject. The metaphor of the automobile is used as a metaphor for horizon scanning: one does not drive into the future by looking through the rear-view mirror, but by scanning the oncoming environment for potential threats or opportunities.

My first research project at University of Hawaii was as a team member for a Mexico City think tank doing a content analysis of major US periodicals. We were provided with newspaper clippings on Mexico from selected US markets, and a rubric to assess whether the content was positive, negative, or neutral in its tone or politics. We tracked the column inches. The results were proprietary, but I learned a lot about reading between the lines, about cultural assumptions, and about working at a distance with an overseas think tank.

Later, I gained much research experience as an early intern at the Institute for Alternative Futures (IAF), a Washington DC area think tank headed by Clement Bezold. One of my very first tasks was to help reorganise the organisation's library overflowing a large closet. The library contained a large number of books that represented the field at the time, and off prints, photocopies, mimeograph copies of research reports from RAND Corporation, SRI international, and UN agencies. There were topical file organisers across a wide range of topics. The library also had journals and newsletters from the field, international development journals, and a growing subsection on healthcare and pharmaceuticals. (In recent years, IAF research has focused on healthcare and social welfare futures.) I learned much from absorbing some of the content of the library while I was there, but also about typology and categorisation.

One section of the library focused on trends and trend assessment, and there were a number of recent publications from the Office of Technology Assessment (OTA) and the Congressional Clearinghouse for the Future, both of which had been recently established by Congress. OTA started with a staff in the hundreds, with significant funding, but was later abolished by Newt Gingrich (who claimed to be a futurist) when he became Speaker of the House.

My job as a researcher on a contract for the US Geological Survey (USGS) was to explore emerging issues for inland waters. It had to survey the literature and research and identify the key driving forces and emerging issues related to US water ways. It was my first major effort in developing and using a global typography, and to see the distinction between what was emerging - weak signals - and more robust, developed trends. Data collection involved a systematic search through the IAF library, and trips to the local library in Alexandria and the Library of Congress. I collected reports and publications from government agencies, the USGS itself, the NOAA, NASA, environmental advocacy groups, and DC think tanks. I scanned newspapers, journals, and science periodicals, such as *Science News* to which IAF subscribed. After collecting all this data, reading or skimming it, I summarised and/or captured the trends, issues, and developments related to inland waters, typed them up (high technology then was the Selectric typewriter). I then, using scissors, cutting the page into strips of paper, separated each of the issues and trends, and began to organise them, using rubber cement to fix them to a large piece of newsprint. I organised the trends into clusters or categories, around the central theme of emerging issues in inland waterways, sub themes emerged: competing uses, pollution, agriculture, health and disease, litigation and politics, ecology, and others. After review and some reorganisation with the project team, the trends and emerging issues fell into place on our emerging map.

I learned a great deal about trend and issue analysis, working in a team, and the results of the study were well received by the client. One surprising lesson for me was on typology and our lengthy discussions about the appropriate categories to use to organise our trends and issues mapping. The categories sometimes seemed to do violence to the ideas, when trends or issues did not neatly fit into one, or overlapped two. We discussed whether it was best to follow the classic STEEP categories, or use the themes that seemed to emerge organically. The mandate of the client was to focus only on US waters, but it was obvious that some issues related to water, things like acid rain/precipitation, were cross-border issues. There were a number of emerging issues/trends that were identified as technically beyond the scope of the project because they originated in Canada. I found that frustrating, but the silver lining was that I was beginning to see things more systemically, and began to understand that systems thinking was part of the solution to many of the problems that seem to be facing the planet.

My biggest internship takeaway was the power of emerging issues analysis, and the relationship between emergent issues or events and longer-term trends that they may or may not evolve into. That has continued to inform my personal and professional life and my commitment to environmental scanning, the identification of weak signals, and how those feed into alternative futures possibilities.

The decade that followed included the completion of my Masters on the alternative futures of space development, and then a PhD that explored the myth and politics of the Gaia hypothesis - both of which used emerging issues, trends, and wildcards to generate alternative scenarios of possible and preferred futures.

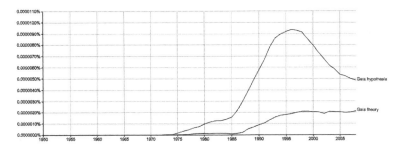

A Google Books Ngram (figure) shows that the phrases 'Gaia hypothesis' and 'Gaia theory' emerged in the late 1970s, and the former peaked in the mid-1990s, while the latter has plateaued. What was emergent, has become a trend.

Dator was highly influential in my thinking and training, and was a role model for environmental scanning in the pre-computer era. Multiple times during the year, Dator would close his office door (routinely, always open when he was not in class) and spend the day in Hamilton Library skimming and scanning periodicals. He told us to do the same, and to make the search for emerging issues an ongoing monitoring process in our personal futures. Emerging issues are often found on the fringes. In the pre-Internet era, trends inhabited traditional publishing, trade journals, government statistics, and science journals. Emerging trends were more likely to be found first in newspaper reporting rather than scholarly journals, and also in popular magazines before becoming academic subjects. In the policy area, emerging issues could be found in state legislation before reaching federal attention (particularly harbingers like California), and in new legislative bills before they become law. In many states, bills are reintroduced year after year before they finally get enough support for adoption. Bills early in this cycle would be emerging issues, by definition.

Given the proliferation of technology and social media, the task of environmental scanning, and identifying emerging issues has become both easier, technically, but more complicated given the proliferation of technologies and growing diversity in social and cultural space. Consulting groups, such as the Herman Group and Shaping Tomorrow offer environmental scanning services and newsletters, and arguably any organisation should maintain its own trend and emerging issues monitoring and analysis program. *Fast Company, Wired, MIT Review* and other periodicals continue to be rich sources of both trends and emerging issues in technology. Web-based services, such as Futurism, also monitor and report on science and technology innovations and impacts on our images of the future.

Even with the proliferation of Internet news and information sources, especially the spread of Creative Commons scientific research and publication, periodicals are still a rich source of technological, cultural, and social emerging issues. One technique adapted from Dator's library scanning we have used in numerous workshops to train students to do emerging issues analysis, is to collect a large number of current magazines, purchased at a bookstore, across a wide range of genre and categories. In the workshop, participants choose from among these, and skim tables of contents and articles for anything that looks new or novel. That is the first criteria for identifying an emerging issue. At the University of Houston, Schultz developed a workshop tool to assess emerging issues, assessing the item's perceived: novelty, significance, and likely impact. In these workshops, we also asked other questions, for example about alignment of the trend with specific alternative futures. And given that trends do not develop in a vacuum: what are contingent factors or trends that could enhance or temper the emerging change or issue?

During the decade, I was involved as a researcher in another dozen or so projects involving high technology, telecommunications, sea level rise, solid waste, the futures of bureaucracy, the courts, and Antarctica, and climate change. Virtually all of the foresight projects that went through the Hawaii Research Center for Future Studies (HRCFS) contained some form of environmental scanning, often with brainstorming exercises to explore secondary and tertiary impacts of emerging trends. Collaborative qualitative research for the Hawaii Judiciary, managed by Inayatullah, explored a number of emerging issues and trends, such as the rights of robots, digital courts, and high technology and the courts.

Wildcards and the PNT Menagerie

Wildcards are low probability, high impact events or developments. Now more popularly known as Black Swan events, wildcards have been an important part of the discussion about alternative futures, because they have the potential for disruptive change. Wildcards have been called 'blue sky events' as well, because they seemingly come out of nowhere – at least in some cases. Although there were some observers and experts that forecast trouble for the former Soviet Union, few experts anticipated the rapid dissolution of the Soviet Empire and the end of the Iron Curtain. For most people, this was a wildcard event. The aeroplane attack on the World Trade Center on 9/11 was a similar wildcard event, although fiction writer Tom Clancy imagined an aeroplane suicide attack on the US Capitol in 1994.

Other events and developments may have surprising effects like wildcards, what Ziauddin Sardar and colleagues describe as black elephants and black jellyfish – to join the black swan in a post-normal times menagerie. A black elephant is a highly probable and widely forecast event or development that is ignored or downplayed by the dominant culture or political ideology. An example of the black elephant is global warming, because despite the scientific consensus, climate change deniers create uncertainty about dramatic action to reverse climate change. Black Jellyfish are low probability, high impact events or developments driven by positive feedback loops and convergent trends. The menagerie become a useful and important part of the toolbox to understand the changing dynamics on a global scale. That speaks to the underlying task of competent emerging issues analysis and trend analysis to relate it to alternative futures scenarios, integral futures, and causal layered analysis to provide the context for those emerging issues and trends.

Alternative futures scenario-building, back-casting, and in-casting exercises are necessary to help crystallise the often contradictory, competing, and converging trends. Also, recognising the oversized role of global driving forces, that is macro trends, is also critical to understand the changing dynamics of trends given that none developed in a vacuum. The emergence of post-normal times theory, for example, requires that the context or paradigm for change at the largest scales is changing, which may complicate technology assessment, for example, when the scientific paradigms, political environment, and culture are increasingly characterised by chaos, complexity, and contradiction.

An important feature to appreciate is timing: we need to keep in mind that changes and events occur over different levels and scales of time. Human timescales are measured in decades in terms of longevity, gestation changes occur over nine months, and our heart rate can change in less than a minute. Defence systems are designed to last for twenty or more years. The stock market updates in less than a second. Quarterly reports and election cycles suggest changes over months and years. Planetary systems, however, evolved in tens of thousands and hundreds of thousands of years. The geochemical carbon cycle is millions of years long. Which brings us to the Gaia theory, a Big Picture view of planetary evolution, as an idea, a meme, but also as a theoretical standpoint to understand long scale change.

Many trends are cyclical, such as periods of growth and recession in stock markets, as are geological cycles, ice ages, and even cosmic cycles. I took an interest in ice ages in my early twenties, and was fascinated to see that our challenge with anthropomorphic global warming coincided with the end stage of the current interglacial period. During my undergraduate years, it was well-established that the last 2 million years or so were characterised by ice cycles that last roughly 100,000 years, but that are separated by warmer 'interglacial' periods that typically last 12 to 20,000 years. The regularity of these periods was intriguing, and research led to the work of Milutin Milankovitch, a Serbian mathematician who proposed that orbital forcing due to a wobble of the Earth's tilt on its axis was the likely culprit for glaciations. The Milankovitch effect has become a popular explanation for this apparent resetting of the planet's thermostat every hundred millennia or so. Shortly after learning of this likely solution to understanding ice cycles, I read Lovelock's first book.

Lovelock has continued to deepen and refine the theory, and has crafted strong arguments with his critics. The basic idea is that Earth has a planetary regulatory system, called Gaia, that took shape not long after life evolved on the planet, but has nevertheless managed to maintain 'optimal conditions' for life on earth. Gaia has maintained a fairly narrow temperature range, and oxygen and atmospheric balance for hundreds of millions of years. What makes this remarkable is the fact that over the course of life on the planet, solar insulation – that is the total radiant energy output of our sun – has increased, according to astronomers, by 30 per cent. And yet, life on planet Earth has managed to maintain a fairly constant temperature. Moreover, without some greenhouse effect, life would not exist. However, that temperature has changed, it has been both warmer and cooler over the last 3 billion years, but has managed to adapt to solar and cosmic (dust) change. What Lovelock believed that should alarm us now is that Gaia may be resetting to a higher state of thermodynamic equilibrium, similar to or higher than the Carboniferous Period, more than 300 million years ago, when the planet's average temperature was 6°C warmer. Climate scientists have warned of the catastrophic consequences to human civilisation of even 2°C average warming.

Some large-scale trends may be 'baked in' – significant trends that will likely create ever more chaos and contradiction. Our species' insatiable appetite for fossil fuels, growing energy needs and baked in trends, such as the sixth extinction cycle (emerging issue: insect apocalypse), carbon dioxide and greenhouse gas emission growth, and accelerated warming that will likely continue to generate more frequent and more severe weather events, sea level rise, and drought. The ripple effects of the coming climate catastrophes will reverberate within the economy, with ever-greater potential for conflict over water and resources, due to coastal migration and infrastructure collapse, and ultimately to politics and government.

However, there are also numerous positive trends, social movements, and global connectivity, networking, and consciousness. Globalisation, while having weaknesses and challenges, is also a unifying force and the notion of a global village is a meme. Visioning preferred futures, work on sustainable construction, energy, and agriculture, de-growth, post-anthropocene workshops, and post normal studies, and participatory futures work in general do offer some paths away from Apocalypse. Technological innovation may supply some answers, but may just as easily contribute to the greater complexity and chaos in the technosphere. Solar energy, renewables, and alternatives to fossil fuels are making headway.

Civilisations and societies both come and go over the long haul of history, and we would do well to show some humility as a species, as a global society, and recall how fragile human structures of myth and fiction can be. Most of the alternative futures floating around the planet are Enlightenment futures, based on the current scientific paradigm that dominates science, technology, and much of popular culture across the planet. Within the West there is a deeper discourse about the tension between scientism and other epistemologies, and as the West continues to decline as a dominant global culture, we need to look to Islamic, Confucian, Buddhist, Taoist, and indigenous epistemologies to inform positive futures narratives.

Back to the Elements

A question I constantly ask my doctoral students: so what? What is the meaning of trend analysis and emerging issues research? What is the significance of horizon scanning, foresight, and these specific tools? The beauty of causal layered analysis is that it allows us to step back and look at all the details, all the litany, and try to see them in a bigger context. The trends and emerging issues are sometimes just 'factoids' that fill the airwaves that demand attention from our consciousness, but may obscure the underlying forces of change or serious challenges that would better deserve our attention. At one level, trends are a game of Trivial Pursuit, where someone can have most of the answers but still not see the Big Picture.

Put another way, trends and emerging issues and wildcards are but pieces of the puzzle, where context is everything. Other methodologies, such as scenario building, visioning preferred futures and CLA are required to round out the role of trends in the broader global context, that Big Picture. We also need to keep some humility as the dominant species on the planet, to be more fully aware of our timescales in terms of our species, planetary, and cosmic evolution. Historian Yuval Noah Harari has made a compelling case that Homo sapiens became the dominant species on the planet due to our ability to create myths that allow strangers to cooperate. But he also argues that the million years or more of our existence as hunter gatherers/scavengers was the true golden age, that agriculture and civilisation have degraded human health, longevity, and apparently the size of our brains. Hunter-gatherers may have been smarter, but I do not think that we are likely to revert to Stone Age economics and a hunter-gatherer society. We might recognise some of our wandering ways in contemporary human behaviour (Elon Musk's plan to die on Mars, one in ten Americans moves every year).

The long-term trend of our technological society may be harmful in other ways. One answer to the Fermi paradox, of why humans do not appear to have contacted intelligent alien civilisations, maybe because, as science fiction author Liu Cixin argued, nascent technological civilisations tend to be extinguished by more advanced civilisations (the dark forest metaphor). There are certainly other black swan existential threats, as I have noted elsewhere. But, it should be clear to the reader that I am persuaded that physical reality, our natural environment particularly, will be the most important long-term driver of technology, economics, and politics. It is our elemental futures that will force us to come to terms with the damage that our technology and economic ideas are doing to ourselves and planet.

The vast preponderance of evidence, the trends, and emerging issues in ecology and environment suggests serious troubles ahead for individuals, communities, and nation-states in coping with accelerating warming. Ironically, the million plus years that our species spent in hunter-gatherer phase coincides with the generally (geologically speaking) cooler ice age, characterised by glacial periods of roughly 100,000 years. We appear to be on the cusp of a new epoch. Will we fail, as have countless complex societies during the historical period? Are we Gaia's solution to a problem (global cooling) and a catalyst for hot times? Will we succeed in being the masters of our planet and evolution? The trends cannot answer those questions, but they will be part of the response.

FUTURES THROUGH STORIES

Sohail Inayatullah

Narratives, which are often based on metaphors, are important. Indeed decisive in policymaking and strategy. 'The metaphor', Spanish philosopher, José Ortega y Gasset, once wrote, 'is perhaps one of man's most fruitful potentialities.... Its efficacy verges on magic'. How one uses metaphor can define the results that are created. As we know from many studies, if crime is described as a friend then there is greater likelihood of subjects arguing for jails and punishment. If we present crime as a social problem, then the intended policy result is more likely to be increased funding for education and poverty eradication. In the USA, if one argues for welfare, then interest in the legislative bill drops dramatically. If one suggests charity for the poor, then it goes up. The welfare discourse creates the image of the person who does not work hard, indeed, games the system; the other of the innocent poor.

During the Brexit referendum campaign, the Leavers focused on 'taking charge' and it is 'not fair', thus evoking a strategy of empowerment. Stories do not describe reality, they create reality. Stories create us. They matter. We should not be surprised at how well campaigners do as they argue for 'law and order' – this is code for spending on the military and safety for those who feel threatened by changing demographics supported by 'liberal elites'. In the recent 2018 mid-term American elections, Trump focused on the caravan of asylum seekers moving toward the US. He wished to evoke himself as the protector of the nation against the unclean outsiders in contrast to weak Democrats, who would allow them in and thus endanger society. Immigration is one of the clearest battlegrounds of a story.

Indeed, most battles and visions are metaphorical. Each perspective tells a different story. Every world religion has been based on challenging the dominant narrative and creating a new story. And there is no way out, in the sense of a world outside a story, even if some argue for a meta story of stories, for even that becomes a story.

We can, however, explore the stories we tell ourselves. We can ask if we are being used by these stories or if these stories are serving us. Stories thus become assets for personal and collective change. By inquiring into stories, we can only reduce their impact on us – that is, we can be choosing – active agents – instead of letting the narrative define us.

So let me begin this essay with my own narrative and then shift to methods that can help us create new personal, institutional and global narratives.

Narratives and Futures Studies

It is usual for a speaker to be introduced, his or her brief biography is read, before the speech is given. On a number of occasion after I have spoken I am asked: 'how old are you?'. Or: 'Do you ever sleep?'

When I unpacked this - why was I working so hard – I found a number of layered reasons. Systemically, it was the migrant story, trying to make it first in the USA, and then later in Australia. My operating worldview was a world of hierarchy – a clear sense of which activities were above and which were below. The core metaphor was climbing up the ladder, a step at a time, while eyeing that those at the top of the ladder were not trying to push one back down or getting rid of the ladder all together.

But where did this need to climb up emerge? When was the worldview framed? For me, I remember my primary school teacher in fourth grade at the state school in Bloomington, Indiana, asking me: 'Do you know why Pakistan is so poor?' I responded I did not. At the feeling level, I wondered why she had singled me out. She then said; 'Because you people are lazy'. This set up a lifelong pattern of proving her wrong. It has only been in the past ten years when I have begun to question the second order implications of this narrative. While hard work has led to external benefits, over the past decade, I have moved to work-life balance with time for family, time for nature, and friends. Work continues, but now it is not the ladder per se, but the bench at the beach park. This is code for: nature, play, time with loved ones, plus being able to work in relaxed environments. I remember my children years ago, holding a protest at my home office, yelling out:

'No more email, no more email'. A few days later I removed myself from all listserves – these were fun for debates but time consuming and were taking me away from what really mattered. Recently, my wife had suggested that I was still bringing work to the beach (my beach bench had become a work bench); perhaps it was time to have short or long periods without the bench or ladder. Essentially, this is undoing the ladder and hard work toward other frames of reference – just swimming at the beach – a flatter connecting and more enjoyable experience.

Narratives as mentioned earlier are powerful ways to frame what one is doing, what is emerging, and what one intends to do. One can frame this in terms of horizons. Horizon one is the current practice; horizon two, the emerging practice, and horizon three, the desired future. In my own professional life, this has shifted from planting seeds, to nurturing young trees to creating a forest of foresight. This narrative emerged when I was asked by UNESCO to apply for the UNESCO Chair in Futures Studies. The application process was somewhat of a catalogue of activities. I was in search of a conceptual framework. Once I saw futures in my own life as a narrative then the process became significantly easier.

While clearly the memories from primary school set up the pattern of hard work, the first stage of my professional career can be best described as the apprentice, learning how to garden. I spent a year as a graduate assistant in Statistics. From there, I moved to the Hawaii Judiciary, where I spent a decade engaged in foresight. I was first an intern, then a futures planner, then the senior policy analyst in the Office of Planning and Statistics. It would only be in 2005 or so that I understood what I had been doing. The great American New Age psychologist and founder of the Foundation for Mind Research, Jean Houston asked me at a workshop we were conducting about my life history. Then she said: 'ah ah, the Judiciary was your apprenticeship'. I instantly understood. Her medieval categorisation worked as it gave me insights as the courts were where I learned the practice of futures studies and institutional change.

During the final years of my apprenticeship, I returned to the University and finished a doctorate on macrohistory and the works of Indian philosopher, P.R. Sarkar, comparing his theories to ibn Khaldun, Karl Marx, Pitirim Sorokin, Auguste Comte, and others. There was then a period of three years of wandering, figuring the next phase of life.

Eventually, I moved to Australia to work at a University and began to engage in the spread of macrohistory and futures studies.

Then, when I was asked about my auto-biographical framework, I would suggest seed planting. It was only decades later when I was writing the UNESCO application, that I realised I was thinking of the eighteenth century American nurseryman Johnny Appleseed. He was an idiosyncratic vegetarian who was planting apple seeds all over the Midwest of the USA. But Appleseed did not just throw seeds randomly. He created nurseries where ever he went. This certainly became the next phase of my life - the shift from giving lectures and workshops throughout Australia and the Asia-Pacific as seed planting to finding particular young trees to nurture. These became specific clients or sites of futures innovation; they were organisations and institutions like Tamkang University, the Australian Federal Police, the Australian Federal Department of Agriculture, particularly bio-security, local city councils and local government throughout Southeast Queensland and Victoria, Malaysian universities such as University Science Malaysia (USM) and the Malaysian leadership academy, the Pearls of Policing, the University of the Sunshine Coast, Queensland government, and Mt Eliza Executive Education. I would run visioning workshops, short courses, and supervise doctoral students. Individuals and projects were nurtured. Over a period of fifteen years, I could see the nurseries gaining in strength, the networks through their own volition, expanding.

However, for the UNESCO position, for my next phase, something more was needed. The narrative shift was the creation of a forest of foresight – an ecology of futures. In this project, the seed planter becomes far less important, as the forest maintains itself. It is sustainable. Picking or choosing which are the best foresight projects – the tallest or most robust trees – becomes far less important than ensuring the ecology of the forest as a whole not just survives but thrives. It is this narrative that led to the birthing of the Asia-Pacific Futures Network. We have no presidents or secretaries rather it is a flow of information, courses, and conferences. The network grows the forest - is the forest.

But this is not all about nurturing trees and the eco-system. Within this story, much needs to be pruned. There can be horrible low quality futures studies work. Many are individuals who do not have the passion, but are 'johnny come latelies' consultants, there for the quick buck. They provide forecasts with false precision. Instead of questioning the future, or challenging the framing of the question, they reinforce current assumptions. For example, in the transport planning context, is the issue merely forecasting private car demand and enhancing speed or creating new models of public and private mobility and connectivity? A questioning process would create new pathways for innovation. Forecasting merely provides data to the question within its current terms - it does not extend the terms of reference.

Moreover, they fall into the trap of futurist as knower of the future. Instead of coming to terms with uncertainty and enhancing agency, 'the answer' is provided. More important for me is helping individuals and organisations embark on a deeper learning journey. The consultant or forecasting brand of foresight and futurist needs to be challenged as to the scientific rigour of their utterances and their unexamined assumptions. There can also be individuals with a fetish for promoting their own particular brand or to gain access to funds instead of understanding that UNESCO is there to twine networks, to enhance complexity, and ensure robustness – to link all the philosophical tents, not to privilege particular epistemological positions. Thus, quality control is a must. Some trees need to be cut down so the forest can regrow - some theoretical perspectives are nonsensical, litany based. For example, there is a group of foresight experts who wish to live forever. While I understand this pushes the boundaries of longevity science, what they disown is their own fear of death – the future creates anxiety and fear for them. Instead of owning this fear, they search for the 'silver bullet' and hope they will stay alive for another forty years. And when the singularity – the supposed invention of superintelligent technology that transforms humanity – comes, they hope they can live forever in a downloaded form. They are unable to see that they are living the traditional religious narrative; the singularity is merely the avatar returning so that eternal life for the chosen is possible. One creates a technological heaven; another a mystical heaven. Both are often unable to see the deeper myths that underlie their utterances.

Futures can be seen in itself as layered. The easiest and greatest demand is for tools and methods to help forecast or manage complexity or gain a working map of how the world is changing. While important, many merely seek to add tools instead of seeing how they can be used to make a strategic difference. The next layer is futures for strategy, to help individuals, organisations, institutions, nations and other collectivities use the future to optimise their goals, to enhance productivity or meet changing citizen needs. This is empowering and certainly a worthy endeavour. However, futures done well becomes post-strategic. What I have learned is that strategy is often within the current framework. Certainly within the framework of the dominant organisational ego. It is more, more, and more. Transformative futures seeks to go beyond strategy by ensuring the selves that seek to optimise are understood: disowned selves questioned. Instead of the strategic plan, anticipatory action learning results. Solutions are not a list of official actions but emerge from 'where the energy is' – where there is passion and excitement for change. Transformative futures is learning based. It also seeks to integrate rational and emotional dimensions. The future is not merely a place but a feeling, a possibility of change. It has an expansion dimension, a deeply inclusive dimension, and integrates as much as possible different dimensions of what it means to be human – technological and spiritual, if you will. But for transformation to even have the possibility, as a futurist, I have to be upfront with my biases and positions. I need to often leave my role as an expert, a professor, at the door. Rather, what I have learned is that our role is transmutation, to not be the smartest in the room, but to help bring out the intelligence in everyone else in the room. It is their show, we are there to facilitate emergence. For me, two metaphors are critical. The first is the Whirling Dervish, the Sufi mystic, holding the space, the centre, even as the world dances around her/him. He/she remains fixed on the beauty within and without. The second is microvita, or the hypothesis that what is, is pockets of consciousness that are both material and mind. Futures done well, authentically, can lead to the moment of collective insight when magic, even the sacred, enters the room.

Thus, the new narrative of the forest of foresight creates, cooperates and when needed prunes that which is not needed or has become overly dominant (putting the entire forest at risk). It also seeks to move the ecology of foresight from being focused on tools and methods, to strategies (what is called strategic foresight) to inner and outer transformation, to emergence in the context of enhanced agency. The forest can become a magical place for deep change.

Casual Layered Analysis

While my metaphors may be interesting for some readers, for others this is merely idiosyncratic. However, the basis question is how can others use stories to access their life choices and create alternative persoɪal and societal futures. We need a clear methodology to do this.

For the last thirty years, I have been using Causal Layered Analysis (CLA). CLA links narrative with strategy, with the litany of reality. It attempts to ensure that 'culture does not eat strategy for breakfast'. CLA both maps narratives as well as seeks to move from the current narrative to a transformed narrative. It intends to add depth to the futures discourse, which are often based on scenarios. Scenarios create other possibilities, they broaden our engagement with contingency and novelty. CLA, however, deepens, going to other layers of reality to create solutions to problems that do not go away.

CLA is defined by its four levels. These are the litany, social/systemic causes, discourse/worldview, and myth/metaphor. The first level, the litany, is the official unquestioned future. It is the tip of the iceberg, the quantifiable measure of reality. These can be headlines, quantitative reports or key performance indicators.

The second level is the systemic. It is person invariant. It consists of the social, technological, economic, environmental and political causes and solutions of the litany. The data of the litany is explained and questioned – mapped and analysed – at this second level. Social science solutions as well as those suggested by managers and engineers appear at this level. The third level is the discourse/worldview. Deeper, unconsciously held ideological and discursive assumptions are unpacked at this level. Instead of the lack of history of the litany or the short-term historical of the system, deep history is used to identify causes and possibilities. As well, how different stakeholders construct the litany and system is explored. The fourth level is the myth/metaphor, the unconscious emotive dimensions of the issue. This is the level of poets and writers, as well as of marketing experts. They seek not detail, but broad brushes of possible realities.

The challenge is to conduct research and praxis that move up and down these layers of analysis to ensure that different ways of knowing are included. Different perspectives (including those of stakeholders, ideologies and epistemes) are in particular brought in the third and fourth levels – at the levels of worldview and myth/metaphor. This allows for breadth. These differences are then used to reconstruct the more visible levels – social policy and litany. Thus, in the transformed future, the system that supports and the litanies that empirically measure the new reality are transformed.

Conceptual movement through depth and breadth, allows for the creation of authentic alternative futures and integrated transformation. CLA begins and ends by questioning the past, present, and future, and thus in creating alternative and preferred futures.

Case Studies

I seek to change the core metaphor and narrative with groups I work with and link it to strategy. For example, Brett Casey from Queensland Deaf Services suggests we should shift from hearing/seeing deafness as a loss of hearing to deafness as 'gaining of deafness'. By gaining deafness it is now an asset, signing as a new language. Based on this approach he seeks to design and create a new integrated deafness suburb in Australia. His narrative approach moves the person with hearing loss not as a victim of losing one's community, but as a victor gaining a new community, and eventually, in integration. Inclusion results from his shift in the story. But it is not just the story shift but a new measureable result – the new city/suburb – that is critical, otherwise empty words result.

A participant in a futures workshop in Melbourne who is engaged in left leaning social justice causes seeks to transform the metaphor of his law firm from David/Goliath to the Polio vaccine. In the new future, instead of being reactive and waiting for distressing cases to come to them, they engage, lobby, legislate, change public opinion so as to prevent inequity. This changes the nature of their law firm. One African organisation focused on creating employment opportunities for the youth bulge moved their story from 'pummelled by the present' to ' a flock of eagles.' What this meant is that they returned to purpose and vision instead of the daily battle with administrative issues that tired them. Since the time of the futures intervention, they have become part of their nation's broader work strategy. While they are still engaged in front line efforts of jobs, they have moved to an intervention and strategy of creating meaning and dignity.

Metaphors work and then because of changing external conditions cease to be relevant. It is at that time new stories are needed. In libraries, the traditional metaphor of the collector in charge of the collection is no longer as relevant because of the spread of Google and now AI. Librarians are in search of new narratives. There are many: one that stands is the innovator in the new knowledge gardens. This moves the librarian from the known to the unknown, to actively creating desired futures, mapping out the new gardens (AI, micro-manufacturing, libraries as publishers, libraries as places for community making, direct brain downloads). The new metaphor with the new discourse – narrative – suggests experimentation, new sources of funding, a new strategy for human resources. It marks a shift in deep culture. Traditional librarians certainly will have to transform what they do, and how they think about who they are, and can be.

One CEO of a leading Olympics swimming nation who took a recent CLA course focused on changing the core metaphor of his strategy. He was focused on the last millisecond, the moment if a gold is won or not. Strategy for him had been about preparing for that moment. However, the futures process broadened his approach. While he had been successful at helping his nation win Olympic medals, the life of these Olympians after the games was far less stellar – spouse abuse, alcoholism, drug use were common issues they faced after leaving the limelight. He realised he was overly focused on the last second, instead of their overall life. He changed his metaphor to the water park – not just the Olympic pool and events after the victory, but other events after the games – their broader full life path.

Another large energy company when asked about their current story, suggested the 'pretender.' They have lofty vision statements, but none of these are real – they are too far removed from their current culture. In the narrative foresight process, a new story emerged – that of the energy genie. The genie would use big data, connect that data with customers so they had real time access to their energy use, and over time create integrated energy cooperatives and networks. The genie eventually would create energy anytime and anywhere.

Narrative thus helps create new realities. But this does not mean all stories coexist. Rather, one story wins out over other stories. This can be because of its memetic advantage (more efficient, greater insight, relevance, resonance) or because of political interests. During the global financial crises, there were numerous competing stories attempting to make sense of the new reality: was the 'financial crisis' a housing crisis because of bad debt (lazy citizens) or bad banking (a few bad apples that were stretching the rules) or because of the rise of Asia (more hard working, better savers, hungrier) or globalisation (contagion). How one frames the story, leads to different conclusions. Given the conceptual and political power of the narrative of 'too big to fail', the winner was 'wall street' and not 'main street'.

Narrative is Very Personal

CLA can be applied not just to the external but also to the inner world of meanings and lived experiences – the litany of self-representation, the system of identities, the discourses of the architecture of the mind, and foundational myths and metaphors that define the construction of identity, of being and becoming, of the reality of trauma and the possibility of transcendence. CLA explores current stories that we tell ourselves and seeks to create new narratives for individuals that more effectively represent their desired futures.

One South African apartheid fighter changed his metaphor from the 'knight in shining armour' to the road builder. His new environment did not require an adversarial approach, rather, strategies that created bridges and were localised were far more important. He did not willingly move in this direction. It was based on his experience that his earlier conditioning led to a particular narrative which was far less useful now.

These new metaphors then shape personal reality in novel ways. The old story that was created through an interaction with people and the environment is no longer functional and new metaphors are required. One participant in a workshop changed her house story:

> I changed my metaphor in the last weeks: From rooted, 'settled' and a bit lethargic, living in an old massive house in 'Real Street' to transformative,

transcendent and light, moving to 'Luna Street' into a glass house – surrounded by air, bamboo and glass.

But this was not just about the house, but her own reality, focused on what is, shifted to focus on what can be. That is, the house itself was a metaphor for her life. Her approach in her international organisation has also changed, moving from focused on just her own office and division to now attempting to shift the direction of the entire organisation, indeed, even institutional change.

CLA of the Self

Individuals can thus go through the CLA process to find their new narrative and vision. The litany becomes the words we say about ourselves over and over, in our minds and to others. The system is the rules we use to organise identity and expression. This is the map of our mind - do we believe it is neural pathways, or the Freudian id, ego and superego, or the Maslow layers of actualisation, or the Hal and Sidra Stone approach focused on the multiplicity of selves? The worldview is the origin of the issue. This is the historical roots of the issue. At the metaphorical level is 'the story of our life'. Through a questioning process, we can thus use CLA to create a new life story with a new life strategy, if the previous one is no longer seen as functioning or beneficial.

The challenge, as with all foresight work, is to move from fragmentation to the preferred future, the integrated way forward. By identifying the issues (the internal research question) and the double binds that restrict their solutions, individuals create alternative maps of their consciousness and then move toward a new metaphor, a new life narrative, and consequently an alternative future. The questions we use to lead individuals to new transformative narratives are:

1. What are the things I say over and over about the way the external world is? What are the things I say over and over about how I feel about the world?
2. What is disowned in this process, what do I push away, which selves are seen as less important? What external behaviour in others

irritate and upset me? Can this provide insight into the disowned selves?

3. What are the origins of the issue? Are there any trigger events that have created this overarching inner worldview about the ways things are or should be?

4. Is there a core metaphor that describes this situation?

5. What might be a new story, a new metaphor that can reduce or transform the double-bind?

6. How can this new metaphor be supported by behaviour and practice?

These questions thus begin from the litany to the system to the worldview and then to the current metaphor. The new metaphor, then is solidified by a new system and a new litany. It finds support going forward.

In the past five years, I have used the work of the late yogic monk of the Indian social and spiritual organisation Ananda Marga, to explore the role of the post-rational in this process. Dada argued that the new story when it emerges rationally, while useful, does not articulate the deepest part of who we are. And thus, now after creating metaphor, we link it to mantra. The mantra is based on the person's own worldview ie Allah hu or Ya Allah for Muslims, Om for those in the Vedic tradition. Om mani padme hum for Buddhists, and for those who reject these traditions, simply the words, breathe, breathe. In this altered state, I've noticed a new image emerging, leading to a new story. For example, one south Asian woman in an inner CLA workshop focused on the feeling of loneliness: she went from being a lonely tree to a tree in the forest. While this was an important narrative shift in that she was now in a community, the metaphor was still passive. In the meditative state, she suddenly became a butterfly with other butterflies. Strategically, the goal for her would be to seek out situations where she was with others, engaged in activities that involved movement and beauty.

Limits of My Story

Let me conclude by returning to my story. Why is futures studies attractive? There are a number of factors. First, growing up in numerous countries and civilisations, it became very clear to me that claims for the naturalness of universality were overblown. Nations and civilisations exist in a field – each are in relationship with each other, sometimes violent, exclusive, other times peaceful and inclusive. Each nation and civilisation has in its core text those that it sees as 'evil' and outsiders, that it must fight against. It also became clear that the current world system was deeply flawed – the nation-state capitalist system does not work for all. Futures became a way for me to legitimise dreaming of a different world – a possible world, and as we have learned, one of the factors in creating probability is to argue that one's vision is in fact likely.

And thus phase one was seeding change. Phase two has been growing these young trees, including myself. Phase three has been the forest of futures imaginations, possibilities and strategies. This is expressed in my life in courses, workshops, strategy sessions, books, articles, videos, mentoring. Phase four should be obvious – being part of the process to create a different world – far more equitable, where money is constantly moving, cities are green and smart, governance is truly global, there is gender equity, and the deep culture integrates the material with the spiritual.

All stories have limits? What are the limits to my above narrative?

When discussing my own University of Hawaii professors who deeply influenced me, I know they eventually became Banyan trees, providing support for younger scholars. They are now solid, grounded in the past, providing shade for others, and still growing, branches growing toward the sun. But if they take too much of the earth's nutrients they will not let others trees grow. The younger trees then need to lift their roots and move, indeed, they need to abandon the ecological metaphor for the story of movement, of migration. They need to become voyagers and create new ecologies of foresight.

While useful as an overall metaphor of the field of Futures Studies, in actual foresight interventions/labs/workshops, the tree is perhaps not the best metaphor. This is because in pedagogical settings, I need to be active, intellectually and emotionally responsive, meeting and anticipating the needs of participants. As well, these workshops are in institutional settings, the castle, if you will. And the question is not just the external arena, the forest, but the role of the futurist, scholar, agent of change within the environment.

In traditional pedagogy, the professor was both the priest (the holder of knowledge) and the knight (the holder of power) ensuring that the best got in, and the dregs were thrown out. Futures work, however, is far more inclusive. Indeed, it requires many intelligences to do well – emotional, spiritual, and intellectual, for example. Also, instead of merely stating reality, futures thinking is about changing thinking, and creating new narratives. It requires participants to leave the castle or cathedral or mosque or temple, using action learning to create new social change movements, or products, or processes. The workshop begins in the castle, but then moves to the nearby fields and markets, and eventually goes to further unknown places. It is the grand voyage to the unknown, to the co-creation of new worlds.

Thus, while the futurist may need to be the knight/priest, other narratives are required that ensure new directions. Certainly, with the advent of the web, 'the lecture' the priestly aspect of teaching, if you will, is no longer so important. Long sermons are not needed. Convincing others, while always pivotal, does not occur through life in the castle or monastery, but in the regions that surround. As the noted Indian intellectual Ashis Nandy argued decades ago, it is the shaman who is a far more appropriate analogy for the futurist.

Continuing in this vein, a far more satisfying metaphor is the wizard on top of the castle. In this story, the wizard has access to the knowledge of the priest, the sword of the knight, and has a view of the surrounding areas (the markets) – he or she can help the client, the student, the workshop participant – see far and wide. He or she can help them use their knowledge in dramatically new ways. The wizard understands the rules of the castle (and cathedral and monastery/temple) but seeks to help those within both transform the world they live in (optimise), be ready for disasters (worst case scenario planning, contingency, create new worlds (novelty) and help them find their true vision and their true narrative.

The wizard tells the story of past, present, and future, and helps all move from their current condition to their desired future.

And, this should be obvious, none of this is possible without the support of friends – the witch in the forest, for example, other archetypes – kings and queens, wizards, priests, in other places and other worlds.

And the futurist understands the weaknesses of all narratives, including that of the wizard. He/she uses them, but does his or her best to not use them. The wizard metaphor creates epistemological privilege: the wizard may not be critically self-reflective, who uses normative power inappropriately. The castle narrative creates commoners and those trying to breach the walls. Each story creates new realities and possibilities and disowns others. There are wands to create new realities, but there is no wand to escape dialectics, contradictions, built into all of our stories. Thus I can not conclude with a simple list of things to do or think about. Rather, I can only pass it to you.

I hope you can create a narrative that helps create the futures you desire in the context of the greater we and the challenges we and each one of our many selves face.

POSTCULTURE

Richard Appignanesi

The Indian-American sociologist, Arjun Appadurai, argues that we should consider 'the human preoccupations that shape the future as a cultural fact'. By conceiving the future as specific cultural form, 'we will be better able to place within this scheme more particular ideas about prophecy, well-being, emergency, crisis, and regulations'. This begs the question: what is culture?

Do not trust anyone who speaks of culture without first defining it. Pronouncements on culture seldom if ever survive the test of this golden rule. The reason is apparent. Any attempt to define culture at once founders on the reefs of eclectic plurality. Culture is not reserved only for ethnographic designation. There is a pop culture, another of high culture, a New Age culture, a culinary culture, a culture of violence, a culture of rogue bankers, and so forth into endless particularist multitude. It demonstrates taxonomy chiefly by the rival incompatible differences within itself. The word culture attaches itself promiscuously to every sort of manifestation. We might pointlessly object to many of these usages of culture as being superficial, misapplied or invalid. It might indeed be true but fruitless to say that culture has entirely succumbed to nominalism. We will yet have to satisfy the golden rule of trustworthy definition. Where in all this termitary of cultures is the culture which can bear universal sense? Is there some unacknowledged template of culture which answers universally to all its unruly factions?

It would seem there is none. How can there be a single definition of culture when it disintegrates even at micro-level? Nor are we better served at the macro-level. Judeo-Christian, Islamic and other such grand narrative cultures decompose into the bloodiest, irreconcilable schisms routinely witnessed in actuality. Of course, these macro-cultures ought rightly to be called civilisations, a term often paired with culture. Civility once had the sense we now invest in culture; but there is more at stake in this change than a preferred mode of expression.

Culture emerged from the original twin connotations of the Latin word *cultus*, meaning both to 'till the soil' and 'worship'. Culture and ritual are the obvious conjunct prerequisites – I would say technologies – essential to the material and spiritual foundations of civilisation. Cultivation of nature implies a transcendent dissociation from it in urban culture as a tributary of ever-expanding civilisation. By the time of Roman philosopher and statesman, Cicero, culture had already taken its accepted sense of personal cultivation which sets one's proper civility apart from the plebeian mob and the yonder barbarian. It is a culture of the urbane; the cult of transcendent self-tillage. Roman classical civilisation made evident a distinction between the inner spirit of culture and the vulgate public one, a separation between the moral and material domains of culture; and for the first time specified its opposition to the falseness of civilisation. Civilisation was judged unnatural, degenerate, a fall from the original Golden Age of humanity. Culture has proceeded ever since in this familiar vein of nostalgia for a genuinely restored 'state of nature' while committed technologically to its extirpation. But this is already culture privatised by civilisation and endowed with an aura of utopian antiquity, our unattainable future-past, so to speak.

One thing not normally associated with this immemorial nostalgia for naturally organic culture is the dread foreknowledge that culture stands temporarily as the most fragile human ecology. The anxiety is experienced defensively by migrants who sense their culture will not endure transport to another. One's domestic culture discloses its frailty at the very moment of exposure to wider horizons. It is brought home to those who have left it that their culture destines them to a persecutory burden. Migrants, of which I count myself one by origin, know very well, and often bitterly resent, that their culture of provenance has failed them, and has left them orphaned exiles and refugees. Their place in a host culture is that of guest accommodated in terms of ambivalent sufferance against which it is folly for them to transgress. My Italian forbears in their small Montreal enclave gave me to understand, early and not in so many words, the debt of gratitude we owed our hosts. I had from them the other sense of forbear, the lesson of forbearance. Being 'nearly American' on the soil of America offers best rescue to the immigrant who responds to the gift of allegiance and is transformed by it, so they felt. I set aside for now the uncertainty: was their identity thereby severely diminished, even lost?

The question remains of culture's singular integrity which can survive distinct and even inimical frontier-line differences. I need not belabour the point that culture is divisive. One can only speak of culture by speaking from an already stationed culture. Culture assumes its identity negatively by not being someone else's. Its meaning can forgo definition because it is presumed obvious by instantiation. Culture thereby gains its fissile nature and its disposition to irredentism. Odd though it might at first seem, multiculturalism could be said an understanding of what culture is – if we are alert to the irony that it cannot be a policy of benign remedy or a politically correct solution to intercultural hostilities, but a mere redundant statement of the very problem itself of culture, its alienable nature.

We are perhaps a little nearer to understanding that a definition of culture resides precisely in its power of indefinability. A definition of culture may well be that which is lost to the desiderata of global civilisation. Such a likelihood, with its explicit threat of homogenisation posed to culture's native reserves of diversity, might help explain why civilisation is now a term in disfavour among theoreticians committed to salvaging culture exactly from that progressive cost of fast-forward adaptation to global civilisation. There is inadmissible certainty in this camp that the end result of a techno-evolutionary civilisational process will leave only a taxidermic simulacrum of culture. Ecumenical credence is therefore invested in culture when it is instead more likely that civilisation alone can provide the stimulant to ecumenical accommodation. Jubilation, if this were absolutely so; but it is not. Civilisation and culture do not make for a comfortable hand-in-glove fit. On the contrary, the erosion of culture's fabric bares through to the visible manipulations of globalised civilisation. Culture does not require civilisation for its initiative but depends on the skills of community patterned on memory. It textures the existential uncertainties of what we call tradition. Culture is that which is left over after civilisation's failure to face the impermanence of human endeavour. The problem can be condensed in a telling equation:

civilisation produces the citizen: culture creates the communal subject.

Both representations are opposed by and to the bare historically irreducible human being (not to be confused with the nominal human individual).

I lean here on Heidegger's naming of *Dasein* (being-there) which is the human entity – 'that Being for which Being is a problem' – who is partly possessed by and yet distinct from the categories of science. This existential being-in-the-world resists captivity in the abstractions of theory. The facts of history turn inwards in actual existing beings and become wayward natures. Jean-Paul Sartre tells us that our needs, our passions, our most abstract thoughts are *'always outside of themselves toward'* (his emphasis), and by toward he intends an 'impulse toward objectification'. Existence does not mean 'a stable substance which rests in itself, but rather a perpetual disequilibrium, a wrenching away from itself with all its body'. What does existence in culture purport, then? 'The world is outside; language and culture are not inside the individual like stamps registered by his nervous system. It is the individual who is inside culture and inside language; that is, inside a special section of the field of instruments.' Culture, in our ability to manifest it at all, restricts our horizon of consciousness. It impedes consciousness of the total life-world.

Sartre does not foreclose pessimistically on culture as only rigidly restrictive. He is saying that culture perforce externalises our own limits on what is deemed culturally permissible and can thereby appear an impediment, a blind-spot obstacle to our fulfilment in the total life-world. But he has also indicated that culture is not 'in' us, not an essentially inhering loop from which we cannot escape: which clearly suggests that it must to some conscious degree also be electively optative. There is always some potential spur to conscious intention which permits us at any moment to opt out of cultural restriction. It will of course require maverick privilege to do so; but even so, we still need to know what sharpness to one's conscious intention must be delivered before that 'inspired' privilege can be brought to manoeuvre. Optative or restrictive – these two opposed and incompatible prospects of culture are in their own way future-orientated. But the future – whereto?

Let us step back for a moment and take a benign view of our current electronic regime. Digital culture appears blessed to its evangelists by its resources of instantaneity which promise an ecumenical utopia. Users embedded in that culture are themselves being evolved by it into multitasking and cognitively enhanced sifters of universal information. The good news is twofold: a potential leap forward in consciousness evolution and a collectivity of networked intelligences far more apt than ever to ameliorate the world. Optimism of this sort is still attempting to run on the depleted fossil fuel of culture.

Matthew Arnold's Victorian idea of liberal education had supposed that knowledge of the best in culture is per se discriminatory of what makes for one's betterment in society. Is it a 'dead white man's' outmoded notion? Today's neoliberal view of cyberculture differs absolutely from the past. It is no longer individual self-cultivation of knowledge which interests the networker who is by definition collaborative. The user is immanent or in the current lingo 'plugged in' to the cybersystem of collective knowledge. There can be no calculable effect of 'self-improvement' on consumers of knowledge but only their absorption in an ever-widening loop of online information. Nor is it sensible to speak of a real 'interface' with a replicant system whose outer reaches are trans-individual and a-temporal. Here the bad news starts.

We are liable to forget that cyberculture happens also to host criminal deceit, the dark net of perversity, the cellular contagion of Salafi-jihadist terrorism. The suicidal Islamist might appear exceptional, disconnected from the normal world, and yet instantly available online to collaborative imitations. Resemblance to communal life by such publicly occult means of conjuration – what else is that but a new form of shamanism. Paul Virilio names this sort of magic, far more pernicious in its digital regalia, hyperterrorism. Hysteria will inevitably preside as the result of audio-visual paralysis. Virilio: 'The saying goes that "hysteria is the enemy of Time". If so, the real time of terror relayed in a loop is most definitely "hysterical" and it is the time of globalisation as a whole, whether economic, political or strategic. The time required for reflection has been outdone; the time of the conditioned reflex is the order of the day of grand terrorism.' Culture is fatally vulnerable to the seduction of digitally hyperrealised community. I am not insensitive to the benefits that cyberculture has conferred upon the world, the advances in science and industry, the blessings that far outweigh the egregious evils – taking the adjective to mean in its archaic duality, as it should, 'shockingly bad or good', for such is the two-sided case of cyberculture, that it is modernity's *pharmakon*, simultaneously poison and remedy.

Existence can for the first time in history imagine itself immaterially socialised in virtual reality. This is certainly a 'first' in history and is allied to the illusion of an 'end' of history prevailing among an ill-assorted cast of neoconservatives, Christian and Islamist ideologues. It has also induced a global façade of universal culture – which does not mean that culture is everywhere turning the same but is everywhere claiming its 'human rights' to inalienable difference by appeal to the spectre of universal validation. Universality of this kind rests on a paradoxical situation. Cultural diversity can pursue its objective of ecumenical tolerance in apparent quarantine from a universal civilisation of technological levelment. But they are both effectively complicit and twinned in the fashionable code name, hyperreality. I prefer simply to call it postculture. Nor does my postulate spell the 'end' of culture. Rather, it suggests a spectral after-life of culture, a wearisome life-like prolongation gauged by a pervasive sense of terror – a terror, note well, from which the actualisation of terrorism derives and benefits. I stress here, to be clear, that the 'terror' I speak of concerns the invasive undercurrent tinnitus of panic in the everyday – a 'culture of panic', if you will – of which terrorism in its jihadist occasions is but an epiphenomenon. Tele-communication takes priority in what Virilio calls the 'interoperability of weaponry' today: 'Now, with the Information Revolution, calibration of public opinion and politically correct standardisation no longer go far enough. They must be topped up with the emotional synchronisation of the hordes, a process in which terror must be instantaneously felt by all, everywhere at once, here and there, on the scale of a global totalitarianism.'

But I have left out of my account the aboriginality of culture in which presumably its definition is found. Consider this idea proposed by Jean-Paul Sartre: 'What we call freedom is the irreducibility of the cultural order to the natural order.' Sartre introduces us to an infrangible line of maintenance which separates culture from nature. This is our horizon of freedom which has no causal, material or any empirical support of evidence. It is for this very reason an irreducible line of consciousness which situates us in being unnatural. To speak colourfully, I might say that human being is nature's one admission of unnatural perversion.

Sartre has also provided a minimally negative definition of culture. He specifies that culture in consequence does not permit a 'return to nature'. The re-entry of nature into culture can only occur by artifice of ideology. Ideological revisionism of this sort is easily spotted at work, digging below the parapet line of culture to expose the natural foundations of human behaviour. It will claim to have struck a fundamental invariable unconscious, either the psychical one of Freudian doctrine or the genetic other of socio-biology, to which culture is a mere secondary additive. These reductionist ideologies do not consider that our access to nature is granted to us solely by way of what culture has made of it. This is true of the Kalahari Bushman as it is for the Wall Street stockbroker, whatever their differences of adaptation. They have each fabricated a 'nature' which the technologies of their culture strive to render 'suitable to purpose'. Culture is precisely this equipping of nature. We have possession of conscious insight into nature which is unrecognisable to nature itself. There is indeed strictly no nature at all except in its cultivation by ideology. Nature does not know existence as a problem. Human being is alone the entity for whom being is a problem. And we have given to that inexistent problem the consciousness of nature. And our bonus is culture.

So, where do we finally stand with culture? Wittgenstein advised submitting certain words to mental hygiene: 'Sometimes an expression has to be withdrawn from language and sent for cleaning – and then it can be put back into circulation'. 'Culture' has to be withdrawn and put into dry-cleaning for renovation. Meanwhile, I suggest that we mark culture's suspension from use by affixing 'post' to it. Postculture, like a receipt from the cleaners, will serve to question our trust. Who is charged with the cleaning?

Vice and Virtue

Postculture risks being another declamatory term of fashion. To my knowledge I am the first to introduce postculture within a frame of existential analysis. Postculture is an afflicted situation indisposed to admit itself as such. Knowledge of its own irrecuperable condition has ceased to be available to it. Where is the positioning for a secured awareness of culture? Postculture's indefinable nature stems from a withdrawal of meaning in the psychical substructure of culture. What has caused this withdrawal? Our search for 'causes' has become a habit of existential crisis to which we are all addicted. This mode of forensic frenzy which seems to me characteristic of postmodernity has contrived to bring forth the diagnostic term, hyperreality, the simulacrum of reality 'more real than real' interchangeable with postculture.

How are postculture and terrorism converging towards amalgamation which might initially have appeared tangential? I have abridged these convergences as the Seven Deadly Virtues of postculture, parables of a kind, which I shall detail below.

Seven Deadly Virtues? What do I mean by this odd inversion of Christianity's normatively attributed Seven Deadly Sins? How can a virtue be said to be deadly, and indeed, accounted a sin? A deadly virtue is a species of conduct which acts in duplicitous contradiction to itself, for which persuasion and coercion are one and the same, and all things weigh indifferently on its scales of devaluation. It disguises nihilism by posing as beneficial enterprise and 'for our own good' seeks universally to instrumentalise life. The sense of my upending virtue will become clear as I proceed to exemplify the allegories of deadly virtue.

I should begin with a reminder of the Seven Deadly Sins that stand opposed to virtues in their orthodox sense. I shall identify these sins of vice by their original Latin names ranked in the order that the Catholic Church employs. Next to each Latin designation I give an English translation of the vice, followed in square brackets by its further meaning signified in practice. The contrasting Christian virtues are listed in the right-hand column.

VICE			VIRTUE
superbia	pride	[hubris]	humility
avaritia	avarice	[rapacity]	charity
invidia	envy	[malice]	compassion
ira	wrath	[violence]	patience
luxuria	promiscuity	[disloyalty]	chastity
gula	gluttony	[waste]	temperance
acedia	sloth	[indifference]	diligence

I have transformed these vices into postcultural virtues. I preface my paradoxical assertion of 'deadly' virtues, normally ascribed to vices, with a general remark. Christianity in its once vigorous self-confidence reduced the possibilities of good and evil to seven. Its wisdom in so doing – adept in its knowledge of the dark profundities of moral psychology – was to identify and place the state of soul before any of the actions it is capable of. Pride is one state; but its possible actions – its misdeeds, its sins – are many. Christianity focuses on the cure of the soul, its ill condition, not on misdeeds done and too late for treatment, except, as part of the cure, to reserve forgiveness in deferral of sacramental absolution. Redemption is the Christian project, literally, in the sense of projection that 'casts ahead' into futurity. Evil in the radical Augustinian view does not exist: it ceases to be the moment one turns away from it. For inexistence is Satan's condemnation, nothingness is his eternal punishment; while goodness *is*, because the Good is the boundless, limitless nature of God's eternal isness. Christianity's conception of the human condition bears resemblance to, and indeed has close affinities with, the existential analysis of Dasein. Modern society may hold the idea of 'sin' at arm's length in distaste, but its enlightened negligence overlooks the finer-grained existential subtleties that have shaped the weft of Christian psychology. I apply this psychology in reverse, in the negative, by deciphering postcultural virtues under the categories of transgression. My conception of a deadly virtue is not individually inflected but refers to the condition of being-in-the-world which redemption fails to reach.

I will illustrate an example of the behavioural complexities condensed in the vice *acedia*, one of the listed Seven Deadly Sins. *Acedia* (Latin variants, *accidie* or *accedie*, from the Greek, *akeoia*, 'negligence') is usually but inadequately translated as 'sloth'. St Thomas Aquinas, in his thirteenth century *Summa Theologica*, traced *acedia* (negligence) back to St Paul's saying, in 2 Corinthians 7:10, which contrasts Godly sorrow that 'worketh salvation to repentance' with 'the sorrow of the world [that] worketh death'. St Paul means carefulness is at work in the sorrow of repentance; lack of care is instead the worldly sorrow that will abandon one to death. The apostle is an astute existential psychologist: care (*Sorge*, care or concern) is key to the essence of Dasein in Heideggerian analysis. And it is by lacking care, by his sin of negligence, that Dante strays lost in the Dark Wood of despair. *Acedia* has misled him: and he comes to witness it physically in the slothful who suffer its after-life form of punishment in Canto VII, 118–126, of the *Inferno*, those wretches 'gurgling unseen in the slime deep beneath the wrathful [ones] churning madly above them'. *Acedia* is revealed for what it is, not sloth merely but mortal torpor, apathy, 'not caring that one does not care'; St Paul's 'sorrow of the world that worketh death', in flight of despair. It was also identified in the fourth century as the ennui to which monks in desert seclusion were liable, a temptation of the demon, a confusion of mind that takes possession 'like some in foul darkness'.

Acedia assumes modern shape in Walter Benjamin's musings on melancholy in *The Origin of German Tragic Drama* (1928). Benjamin observes that the original theological conception of melancholy is found in *acedia*, a 'darkness of heart', under the astrological sign of Saturn believed to cause sluggishness in those it ruled which made them apathetic, indecisive, unfaithful. Hamlet is the ideal melancholic character of the Baroque Counter-Reformation. I would say rather an ideal Mannerist type of melancholic. Albrecht Dürer's famous engraving of 1514 acknowledges a monumental winged woman – a fallen angel perhaps – as the depiction of melancholy: a suitable image to preface Sigmund Freud's 1917 study, *Mourning and Melancholy*, in which the melancholic is represented 'sunken in loss', in utter paralysing dejection; and a fitting emblem blazoning the poet James Thomson's *City of Dreadful Night* (1874), the atheistic anthem of nightmarish despairing pessimism.

I could extend a similar richness of allusion to *superbia*, the vice normally translated 'pride', but entailing an Ariadne's skein which unravels into strands of vainglory, vanity, self-righteousness, and so on, in a maze of theologico-moral history. And so too would all the other deadly sins respond to moral, allegorical as well as psychological interpretations. But let us proceed with postculture's 'upside down radicality', the eversion of vices into virtues.

The Seven Deadly Virtues of Postculture

1. Identity [*superbia*: hubris]
Identity, the unconscious product of race, milieu and history, mistakes itself as autonomous and naturally entitled to political recognition.

Identity has become virtually, if not to say personally, interchangeable with culture as the conflictual site of authentication and self-authorisation. Identity has come to assume itself the object of cultural politics that surpasses politics.

We have witnessed two extremes of contemporary 'identity politics'. Islam, for one, understands that its identity, not its religion, is under siege from the West. Identity in such a case of threat will resort to populism, the correct name to give to the extreme Salafi faction of Islam which undertook jihadi terrorism, militarised populism which went in territorial pursuit of the ideal Caliphate. A second example, in which cultural politics surpasses politics, deep-rooted in the grievances of disregarded 'silent majority' identities, has given us Trump-style populism in the United States, a revanchist democracy or ochlocracy.

Culture has come to signify the enemy of society. This concludes a prosecution of culture that has endured for thirty years in the twentieth century. The question argued across the political spectrum has been this. What do we need culture for that cannot be better achieved by the practical functions of society?

The celebrity sociologist Daniel Bell has been described as the 'most brilliant of the American neoconservatives'. Bell popularised the notion of 'adversary culture' at war with society. He traced the ills of contemporary Western societies – and of America chiefly – to the 'split between culture and society'. Culture in everyday life has become chronically infected by *modernity* with its excessive demands for authentic 'self-experiencing identity'. We recognise it today as the 'selfie' right of entitlement, unbridled 'me too' culture. A culture of free-floating subjectivism has dissociated itself from the moral basis of rational conduct in social life. Culture in its avant-garde modernist form inflames hatred against the imperatives of conventional social virtues. The hedonistic motives of modernist culture are altogether incompatible with the economic and administrative disciplines of professional life in civil society. What is to be done to re-establish the 'Protestant work ethic' and tame adversary culture? Bell offers a religious revival as a means to renew faith in tradition which alone provides individuals with purposive cultural identities and 'existential security'. Does the prescription sound uncomfortably familiar? Islamist, in fact?

Bell's analysis published in *The Cultural Contradictions of Capitalism* (1976), gave neoconservative assurance to the view that modernist culture was at once both dominant and dead. It is a verdict on the zombie menace of contemporary culture. Did it herald what I name postculture? Neoconservatism is itself an accomplice of postculture, and in this sense, a preview of fundamentalist society. Is it by chance that the date, 1976, and Bell's verdict on culture coincide with the escalation of terrorism in Europe, Palestine and Latin America – the 'Red Terror' waging its thirty years' war on Western society?

2. Technology [*invidia*: malice]

Western power is enslaved by its own technological facility. I intend both senses of 'facility', that is, 'ease of doing' and as 'equipment'. Enthralment to technology determines a paradoxical mode of foresight by generating scenarios of catastrophes. Solutions to them can only be foreseen in further advances of technological deterrence. Salvation from our impending ecological Armageddon is one example of such 'last instance' deterrence. To what do we turn in our panic? To AI robotics – a word originally from the Czech *robota* meaning 'forced labour'. Which gives a new Cyborg Manifesto sense to Marx's exhortation: 'Workers of the world unite! You have nothing to lose but your chains!' Another impending catastrophe awaits us in the unfinished business of jihadi terrorism. Technological supremacy in control of Western perception has imposed the lens which magnifies an outlaw Islamist minority to virtual equivalence of power. It is foresight duped by what is really on view, namely, postculture. Terrorism in its former suicidal restriction and subsequently in its attempted caliphate investiture is a symbol of postculture. A symbol that I stress has become incomprehensible because it has shut down its time-frame. Islamism assumes a reality fitting to the timeless. Technology 'without attachments to Western *jahiliyya* metaphysics', that is, shorn of history in Sayyid Qutb's Islamist view, is thereby restored as a remedial weapon of terrorism to pious jihadists on the sole basis of Qur'anic literalism which occasions the fusion of culture and religion. But this is a result of the same orientalist distortive lens in obverse occidental view. Neither side in this looking-glass encounter can see what is in place – the neutrality of technology as itself irreducibly fundamentalist.

3. Postculture [*gula*: waste]

Postculture immobilises history's threat of change. It seems a paradox, or call it counter-intuition, but technology requires our dependence on 'traditional values' for its advancement. We progress in unrelenting fast-forward by reversion to technically superseded values. Value-free technology, like a 'selfish gene', thrives on cultural nostalgia while vampirising it to a husk. Technology can have no motive of its own which is not ours by which to historicise the future and at once preclude it by conceiving of its already accomplished end. History dissolves into ever-present mediatised instants of anxiety, socially real, but at a vertiginous tempo that outpaces the grasp of experience. Postculture occurs when culture is overtaken by the globally measureless but cannot itself measure the passing away of culture in history. Postculture's end use is to concede the uselessness of culture to the practical dictates of digitally ordained global civilisation. History becomes transmission of the 'virtually credible', that is, news. 'Freedom is the condition of the possibility of history', well says Susan Buck-Morss.

4. Democracy [*acedia*: indifference]

Can we speak meaningfully of democracy in crisis? Sovereignty is always originally illegitimate. Only by absolutist Divine Right solipsism can it claim authority: 'It is *because it is*.' On what does democracy base its right of sovereignty? On consensus, on the inalienable will of the people – so it is said – but otherwise without foundation beyond self-authorisation. The Reign of Virtue begins with the guillotine in the French Revolution's Great Terror which cut short the monarchy's previous legitimacy. Democracy is a promise that must constantly consider itself already ideally in being. This is its peculiarity. Democracy is the anachronistic future-present. Perfectibility is its elusive horizon. Derrida rightly says that democracy is presently in a state of civil war: 'is it still necessary to point out that liberal democracy…has never been so much in the minority and so isolated in the world? That it has never been in such a state of dysfunction in what we call the Western democracies'.

There is a technical undercurrent to domestic civil war in democracies that overlaps into new international Cold War. Democracy invested in technologised society will result in its exact opposite. Islamism appears to us as the scandalous 'exact opposite' of democracy. And yet, Islamism's world-design should be all too familiar to us. Its annulment of historical time by reduction to technologised fundamentalism is also our own in reverse focus. We seem unaware of being equally captives to the 'freeze-frame' lens in which terrorism and the West's technical supremacy converge to antagonistic affinities. 11 September 2001 occupies this frozen frame as the *inconceivable* event of postculture. It could not *be*; and hence it *is* by impossibly literal symbol. Postculture in that moment became for once *glimpsed*. What did it presage? A declension of Islamism and the West converging to nihilist democracy, a devaluation of all values, which leaves only an immobilised state of indifference, *acedia*.

5. Media [*luxuria*: disloyalty]

There are three discourses of cultural power: the political, the media and the scientifico-intellectual. The dominant, or as Marx said, ruling ideas of an age, assume the dominated, the submitted, the overruled. Media hyperreality has succeeded to vacuum-package the other two discourses, although they have never sounded so amplified. Take politicians, reduced to reality TV rhetoricians, mere silhouettes of parliamentary power. No one is really deceived; but everyone is duped. The horns of this dilemma have become the diabolical fork of social media dissemblance. Follow your desires today and you are at once submitting to digital regulation. Iteration (repeating your preferences) feeds into algorithm (hijacked coded information): outsourcing ourselves to anonymous corporate modes of social control. The other prong from which we dangle is distrust of experts ('Just look at the 2008 debt crisis – did our experts foresee that?') Now turn to politics. Which? Our politicians have been disenfranchised by their own brazenly transparent corps elitism out of touch with real people.

Much has been said of a contemporary 'turn to the right'. Identity gets its mediatised welcome there – the 'white shift' of American flyover states and pissed-off Europeans patriotically defending their traditions, ethnicity and religion. Turn left and find the alternative social media welcome there.

Identity promotion of the marginalised, blacks, immigrants, women, the LGBTs and refugees. In either case there is a confused clash of minority and majoritarian identity interests. Democracy has to contend with the archaic faults of 'native soil' and inter-ethnic civil warfare which liberal consensus cannot redeem. Nor can we discount the capitalist phantom states of mafias and drug cartels on every continent which cannot be 'clearly dissociated from the process of democratisation', as Derrida exemplifies in Italy's case, citing its historical trajectory in a 'telegraphically simplified' schema: 'the history-of-a-Sicilian-mafia-harassed-by-the-fascism of-the-Mussolinian-State-thus-intimately-and-symbiotically-allied-to-the-Allies-in-the-democratic-camp-on-both-sides-of-the-Atlantic-as-well-as-in-the-reconstuction-of-the-Italian-Christian-democratic-state-which-has -today-entered-into-a-new-configiuration-of-capital, about which the least one can say is that we will understand nothing of what is happening there if we do not take account of its genealogy.'

The criminal phantom state threatens to cross the threshold from vampiric twilight to daylight normality – or *post*normality as some prefer. Tele-visual predominance serves as conductor of the parapolitical democracies of Donald Trump, Vladimir Putin and Xi Jinping, each vying in degree of capitalist authoritarian capitalism, and they, in turn, act as beacons of rightist empowerment.

6. Hyperreality [*ira*: violence]

Everyone at present is a ready-made slice of life for media transmission. Information technology's absorption of illusion by hyperreality cancels our existential sense of time passing normally. We are placed instead in chronic anxiety by the 'Sudden', the overpowering, ever-shifting and discontinuous Urgent. As Søren Kierkegaard puts it in the *Concept of Dread*:

> At one moment it is present, at the next one it is gone, and as it is gone, it is again totally and completely present. It can neither be worked into a continuity nor worked through to one.

This annulment of time by the Sudden has co-opted media virtuality to process real 'slice of life' victims in its disruption of illusion. But there is no gain in reality. Violence recedes to a forgotten moment and postculture over-gains time by way of further disillusionment. The convincing no longer seems sufficiently to convince. All this sacrifice of 'vacuum packaged' life, an overcrowding of reality that makes reality itself a collateral casualty – what more do we need of it to recognise ourselves interchangeable as tools of the social media? Paul Virilio quotes the Viennese writer Hermann Broch: 'A world that blows itself up won't let us paint its portrait anymore.'

Postmodernity and hyperreality have unwittingly theorised terror by playing the end game of history to stalemate. Both have been overheard to say in sinful despair of history: 'The future is over. It has proven a big disappointment.'

Much has been said about postmodernity's 'relativism' and hyperreality's 'nihilism' – terms lost in stillbirth – which simply mean that neither can offer a paradigm of change. But this is critically insufficient in recognising the condition which has brought them to historicise the future itself in the absence of history, in other words, to assign a present that we cannot get over. The present has been rendered a fixed theoretical state of contemporaneity, a petrified aesthetic of replication, whether it is named postmodern or hyperreal. Both have discarded historical change for models of simulation, cloning, bionic extensions of the real. A wheel turning at high speed blurs its spokes to a standstill – this is the notion of change in postmodernity or hyperreality – change which is overtaken at the very instant of apparent change. A narrative of circularity, replacing one of progressive change, identifies the aesthetic of postculture. The ever-present has replaced eternity. Terrorism enters into this script as the terminus of aesthetic idolatry which does not aim at change but to remain contemporaneous, as if in violent parody of, and in global parallel to, postmodern art.

7. America [*avaritia*: rapacity]

Is America to blame for postculture? America's presently fragile world hegemony offers all too sufficient reason for terrorism. We need not hate America to be culturally anti-American. This is not to suppose that postculture is 'made in America'. Nor is it a superficial question of resisting Starbucks, KFC and other junk consumables; or even of denouncing

America's state crimes. Is it then meaningless to speak of being 'culturally anti-American'?

Our understanding of postculture must be guided by a decisive nuance: that America is the first victim of its own entrapment in globalisation, at the epicentre of postculture, whose seismic waves are engulfing us all. America remains stalled in a project that my Québécois separatist confrères ironically name *presqu'Amérique,* 'nearly America', that ever-unreachable, globally invasive completion of 'Being American', the realisation of its Manifest Destiny as the end goal of history. To give it an address in postculture is misleading. Postculture does not give earthquake evidence of itself. It advances in disguise and not by cataclysm. Postculture finds its most opportune disguise in adaptation to democratic optimism. Multiculturalism is a representative instance of postculture in its advancement of democratic benefits for cultures disintegrating under its pluralist tutelage. Multiculturalism exists as a policy enterprise; postculture instead has no being specific to itself but can only symptomise existence. It can be thought of as a screen on which distortive imaginings of perfectibility are played out. We catch a glimpse of this when the extremes of imagined perfectibility meet, as in the Twin Towers collision of Islamist dedication and American democracy. Islamism's combination of technicist education with immaculate Qur'anic credentials permits it to annul poverty as a guiding principle of terrorist rectification. The poor (*al-fuqara'*) and the wretched of the earth (*al-mustad'afin fi-l'ard*) do not carry a leftist weight of 'expectation of radical change' but are blemishes subsumed under the perfect justice of Islam's imminent futurity. A redeemed Islamic world will run perfectly on the automatic pilot of *Sharia* law. In this sense, Islamists share in Fukuyama's end-of-history eschatology, a programme of totally realised justice in the world which is presumed ever-nearing completion.

Sayyid Qutb prophesied a militant Islamist vanguard in 1964. Jihadism has since moved on from al-Qaeda's elite technicist corps to become a common battleground practice of militarised terror in Syria, Iraq and elsewhere. In likewise parallel Fukuyama's intellectual credo of neoconservatism, on the model of Daniel Bell's social theory, has become a bygone platitude of America's state-administered war on terror. Ideas of justice that assume perfection are reduced to inanity by tactical diffusion.

Ongoing conflict between the creeds of Islamism, neoconservative democracy and populism has rendered them empty of any persuasive content. This prolonged, preposterous war has not been fought for ideological or religious values. It has been fought for *position*. What prevails in place of their cultural vacancy is greed, *avaritia*, a predatory rapacity that assumes the mask of socially advantageous virtue.

I end with America nominated among the Seven Deadly Virtues. Does it belong there by self-election, by sinful transgression, or has it fallen to a state of unconscious being and lapsed there in peril of self-destruction? Francis Fukuyama has been much mocked for his (apparently) misfired prophecy. History comes to its end in American-style liberal capitalist democracy. I gamble on 'apparently'. I dare say with deadpan Andy Warhol irony that he was not so off-target. Everyone wants to be American. Disavowal is foregone. The tide of *presqu' Amérique* laps at every shore. 'Nearly America' must be played out – but to what final good or evil consequences I am not enough prophet to say.

FUTURES OF CITIES

Maya van Leemput

Picture a city. Start with spectacular towers of gleaming glass reaching high into the sky. Think of another city or the same one, with dwellings made of reeds, wood and plastics, along a stream filled with merchant boats. Walk with me through streets and alleys, tread on dust roads and mud. Listen to the hum of traffic on the ring road, the blearing radio from an open window, chattering girls on their way to school. Sirens, the bleeps and blips of locks and lifts. Notice the rabbits on the soft shoulder, the rat that shoots away on an empty pavement. Fend off monkeys. Smell the exhaust of long lines of cars in only a few dull colours (the seriousness of grey and silver, black and blue and white of course, especially vans). Look at dozens of vibrant trucks adorned with shiny little mirrors, detailed decorations and gods and aphorisms, all parked together not far from the train station. Think of a city with droves of people queuing for simple services or think of one where they wait in messy bunches to get on buses, buy mobile phone credit, send a parcel or collect stamps from public administrators. Weave your way with me from point A to B where bicycles rule the asphalt, the tidy roundabouts and stretches of old cobbles. Look at the human scramble for seats on trams, for Black Friday sales, celebrity concerts, a soccer match or a job for the day. Study underground transportation maps or use the spires of mosques and churches for orientation. Take me to the market, let's grab a bite to eat. Check out the multiplex cinemas or the makeshift film screenings elsewhere. Visit museums or galleries and if there are none, find the patios of arts centres where painters and photographers hang out with musicians and writers.

So many cities, so many distinctive sights and sounds. How can the characteristics by which we even recognise a city be pinned down? Cities are many things to many people. African cities are not like cities in Asia. European cities are unlike American cities. Newly erected cities are not the same as those that have evolved gradually over centuries or millennia, growing outward from an old town centre. There are so many variations, that it seems parabolic to bundle them all together and pretend that we are talking about just one kind of environment for which we can study what futures may lie ahead.

To get over this hurdle, let's begin by looking back before looking forward, as is common practice in futures studies. Where did cities begin? Several of today's cities claim to be the first in history but there is no consensus on which one really deserves the title. A likely candidate is Aleppo, now for the most part bombarded to pieces in Syria's recent years of violence. I walked through the central neighbourhoods of this city in 2001. At the time it was the largest in the country. As I mourn Aleppo's beauty and the people who looked after me then, I recall the smell of its many bakeries and nargile parlours (shisha bars), the search for New Year's presents among the many wares sold in its pedestrian shopping street and the heat of the hammam beneath the walls of its ancient citadel. Rubble and dust remain. Reflecting on the futures of cities, this image of ruin persists.

Other places listed among the first where cities appeared are the Syrian capital Damascus, Kirkuk in Iraq and Sush in Iran. Jericho in the Palestinian Territories is considered one of the earliest proto-cities along with Çatalhöyük in Southern Anatolia. At the time of the last census (2007), Jericho counted less than 20,000 people. In its early days the current number of residents would have seemed massive. The planet at the time of the first settlements along the West Bank counted no more humans than the small region of Flanders today. Jericho didn't quite grow into a metropolis or even a city over its long course of history since 9000 BCE. It is just another tormented town today, all be it with the oldest city wall in the world. Demographics count. Our increasing global numbers determine the basic context for our cities' futures but by themselves they do not assure any particular city's continuous growth or prosperity.

'Two-thirds of world population will live in cities by 2050' titled the *Guardian* in May 2018. The headline is a rewording of the findings of the *2018 Revision of World Urbanization Prospects* by the Population Division of the UN Department of Economic and Social Affairs. Their presentation of these statistics however, does not use the word 'city'. The UN news release refers instead to 'urban areas', where today already 54 per cent of the world's population resides. To arrive at this figure the UN combined data from more than two hundred countries. The criteria for recognising an area as being 'urban' were specific to each country. There is no generally accepted definition for what is 'urban'. The objective criteria used for measurement are as varied as city environments themselves.

For example, Albania counted all towns and other industrial centres with 400 inhabitants or more. For Argentina residents had to number at least five times more to be included in the count. For Australia the statisticians looked for at least 1,000 inhabitants before 2001 and after that year for 10,000 or more. We're only at the letter A and all these cases rely on wildly dissimilar standards, even for a determination primarily based on the number of inhabitants. It seems unsuitable for these assorted counts to be added together under a single nomenclature, and yet they are.

Advancing insight plays a role in the divergence of statistic criteria. For China, which due to its size has a major impact on the count, the criteria changed significantly over time. Only since the year 2000 they include population density as a determining factor. Many other countries also include density as a criterion. This makes sense. My own intuitive understanding of the main characteristics of cities, which according to Manuel Castells is shared by many, begins with the idea that they are 'large and dense human settlements concentrated in a given space'. Urban geographers and sociologists like Castells point out that this however, is not enough to speak of a city. 'Our position actually follows the classical approach by Max Weber for whom the city is a specific spatial form of socio-political organisation.' The relevance of socio-political organisation is also reflected in the UN statistics. Columbia, Costa Rica and Croatia for instance, explicitly require administrative centres for any area to feature in the statistics. It is critical that boroughs, communes, municipalities, towns or cities all have their own local government, responsible for the territory in question. How and by whom cities are ruled, as well as the extent of their independence within larger territories, are heavily contested matters.

The main social criterion used for determining the urban nature of an area for the statistics relates to the types of employment that can be found there. While India expects 75% of the male working population in urban areas to be engaged in non-rural activities, Croatia expects 25% of the population to be employed in secondary or tertiary sectors and at least 50 per cent of the households to be non-agrarian. Japan is more demanding, here only *shi* are considered urban areas. 'Shi are municipalities with 50,000 inhabitants or more…where 60 per cent or more of the population are engaged in manufacturing, trade or other urban type of business'. The nature of economic activity is what counts here.

Finally, criteria concerning infrastructure are frequently used. Honduras lists: piped water service; communication by land (road or train) or regular air or maritime service; complete primary school; postal service or telegraph; and at least one of the following: electrical light, sewer system, or a health centre. This means that in Honduras there can be urban areas that have a school and a health centre but no electrical light or sewerage. I shudder when I imagine what such a health centre must be like. Taiwan requires of urban areas 'at least three of the following: the government seat, a police station or branch, a railway or bus station, a public primary, middle, or high school, a post office, a hospital or clinic, and a cinema.' By the same definition, the cross-roads settlements where my partner and I stopped overnight when cycling across the Sahel in 2001, would count as urban areas (they usually had some kind of police office, a bus station and a small clinic). But because Senegal itself only counts places with 10,000 inhabitants or more as urban, these places that would be considered urban in Taiwan, do not appear in the statistics. The designation 'urban area', it seems, is very much open to interpretation and the label 'city' reveals only some of its meaning with reference to the official statistics. We don't even know how to set standards for empirical observations about the percentage of urban dweller on earth. We need another way to think about city environments.

For lack of clear-cut objective criteria and unambiguous definitions, let's turn to lived experiences and how images of the futures of cities flow from them. I will start close to home, which for me is in one of the top ten most urbanised countries in the world. Almost all (98%) of Belgians reside in urban areas, whichever of the above mentioned criteria you care to apply. With 4062 inhabitants per square kilometre, the district in the South of Antwerp - the second largest city in the country - where I live, is twice as densely populated as Shanghai. I would never have guessed. At first sight the residential streets and social housing apartments, dispersed over the territory, do not seem a match for Shanghai's stereotypical high capacity skyline of tower blocks. The district is called Hoboken and yes, it is where the first settlers of Hoboken, New Jersey - part of the New York Metropolitain area - came from. It does not by far, beat its New World mirror-self in population density like it does Shanghai. It feels more empty than full. The polling stations on election day in Hoboken-Antwerp, have queues, for sure, but they are not overflowing. Almost each of the many supermarket brands has a well-used branch in Hoboken. Some old *fritures* (chip shops) survive, a few pubs, a few tea houses. The old village main street, a centuries old connection path, harbours the last of the local merchants. The nearest cinema is in the centre of Antwerp proper but one of Hoboken's three small historical castles is home to a Youth and Cultural Centre.

During October 2017, local elections were held across Belgium. Everywhere you turned, the names of cities and towns stood centre stage in the political campaigns. Citizens were pushed to equate their identities with a whole array of characteristics 'typical' for the cities and towns where they happen to live. In Antwerp the Green party's slogan was 'Antwerp can do it'. It sounds like Obama and Nike slogans melded together when you translate it into English. In Dutch it works as an almost childish encouragement that points to the stereotypical Antwerp chauvinist streak (we can do it, we are good at getting things done, we are Antwerp). How this relates to environmental or 'green' issues, is a mystery. That it relates to city politics on the other hand is undeniable. Certainly, in the other big cities of Flanders similar efforts were made to engage voters on the basis of their local pride.

Cities provide identities but because identity is a mixed bag, the identities of their inhabitants are not all the same. Consequently, in our local elections diversity was a central theme. On the other side of the political spectrum to the Greens, the focus was on migration, one of the many factors contributing to diversity. To some, diversity is 'what makes a city', to others it is one of the main challenges, or even problems, that cities face.

How diversity can affect daily life in a city just recently became apparent in a rather mundane manner in the street where I live. Around the same time as the elections, the old toy and school wares store, just 100 metres from my house, had been refurbished to become 'the largest ethnic fresh market of Belgium' as the promotional material boasted. The opening weekend was a success, judging by the slow traffic jam passing my front door. Inside the shop the lines for the cashier tills were good for a whole hour of waiting. The fruit-and-vegetables section was filled to the brim and constantly being refilled. The halal butcher, who might as well have been a Flemish hormone butcher for the quality of his meat, was doing amazing business. The shelves were stacked with honey comb, dried fruits and seeds. Other shelves had less wholesome offerings: sugary sweets in bright blue, purple and green, instant tea in similar hues, milk powders, tins of ravioli. All of the labels and price tags were in Turkish (weeks later now, they still are, despite a consumer law that says that all packaging and labels in Belgium should use at least one of the national languages and in particular the right one for the region where the items are sold). Moroccan, Eastern European and aboriginal Belgian shoppers still found their way to the items of interest to them during the hectic opening sales. Shopping carts were overflowing, some families had two or three by the time they left.

At the exit, candidates for a new political party were distributing flyers, their posters were cello-taped to the building's façade too. The party is called 'Democratisch Solidair Appel' and aims for the votes of Muslims in the political centre. The large majority of its candidates have a Muslim cultural background and in the previous legislature were members of the District Council for the Social Democrats or the Green party. They did not in the end get enough votes for a seat in Hoboken's council, but they did muster enough of their old voters to lose their former allies one seat, the difference between kicking the existing majority's out or not. A larger Flemish Nationalist representation and less diversity in the council is the result. Local politics are even more complicated than local shopping!

Diversity politics can only have a tangible impact on the futures of Antwerp as well as of any other city in the world. Cities have always attracted people from elsewhere, that is partly how they have come into being. The make-up of their population is not just determined by local factors but by economic, climate, political factors and conflicts in other places. At the same time, how cities handle diversity, how they avoid exclusion and how they give their residents the fullest opportunity to contribute to, and benefit from, the city environment is a question of local attitudes, sensitivities, insight and power. The elections results in the agglomeration of Antwerp, as well as the districts, had the Flemish nationalists who ruled for the last six years, stand their ground. Our right-

wing authoritarian mayor remains in place. The headscarf will remain
prohibited attire for local civil servants for at least another six years. The
counter example of another Antwerp district, Borgerhout, is hopeful.
Here, a concerted effort by local residents and organisations to breathe life
into shared spaces for culture and play, resulted in the elimination of the
Flemish nationalists from the local vestiges of power. A re-invigorated
neighbourhood life resulted in improved social cohesion, suggesting that
citizens and other local actors together can create better futures for their
neighbourhoods and craft new futures, using the socio-political complexity
of living together to the advantage of all concerned.

Also ranked on top of the list of local election themes in Antwerp was
mobility, a reminder of the attention paid to urban infrastructure by the
statisticians quoted earlier. Due to its large industrial port and the
accompanying petrochemical industry and road network, Antwerp has
grave issues with air pollution. A citizen's movement for putting the main
ring road (one of the busiest in the world) under a green roof has been
active for almost a decade. During the election campaign 'Ringland' and
'Breathless' events were regular hotspots for candidates to recruit voters.
Notwithstanding the rise of the Flemish green party in these local
elections, other environmental issues were largely absent from the debates.
Somehow, resilience in the face of climate change is a topic for when there
is no other news. This may be particular to Antwerp. Ghent, the next most
populated city in Flanders after Antwerp, is working at becoming fossil-
fuel-free over the next 32 years. That effort may not be nearly enough but
at least the grand challenge is being looked in the eye here. Big in your face
questions about energy however were largely absent from election debates
in Antwerp, despite possible power outages in Flanders having been
announced for the winter and frequent news items about cracks and leaks
in the nuclear power plant of Doel, just 25 kilometres away from the city
centre. The exploitation of powerplants and electricity distribution is a
local, regional and federal responsibility with international dimensions
(the vast majority of energy used in Belgium is imported). City authorities
in this case cannot independently formulate their own policies. As the
balance between environmental and economic needs becomes ever more
precarious, and the contradictions more pressing, this modus operandi will
have to change if we are to secure any kind of city futures.

Election candidates know that all roads lead to the economy. They underline its significance, pointing to employment (in the port and its adjacent industries as well as the city centre), talking about the cost of living and the spending power of local authorities. At the same time, fundamental economic questions are rarely addressed during election times. The growth paradigm is taken for granted by every single one of the large parties, including the Greens. The tension between ecology and economy or the contradictions between the needs and desires of large businesses and those of local wage labourers are rarely addressed. Economic thinking beyond the self-interest of everyone involved is shunned for being far too technical and complex. It is considered a highly specialised topic and will probably be the last to be included in any kind of efforts towards the polylogues of participatory democracy that 'citizen-lists' encourage. As any city's existence today and tomorrow is closely tied into its economic functions and attractiveness, it is worrying to see how little of the basic discussion about economic principles and policies actually takes place in the local context.

Obviously, questions about futures of cities cannot be limited to a focus on any single one of the emblematic characteristics or issues suggested from historical, statistical or everyday-life perspectives. The web of internal and external relations that make a city does not lend itself to being untangled, it is not just complicated but decidedly complex. The contradictions between one city and the next and, within a single city between one neighbourhood and the next, may be readily observable but escape any kind of quick resolution. The dynamic processes of the flow of human bodies, goods and services, ideas and sentiments in cities are not just multi-directional. Layer upon layer, their competition for access and priority renders the overall picture of what goes on in a city, highly chaotic. When complexity, contradictions and chaos begin to overlap like this, it is the hallmark of what is called 'postnormal change'. For deliberation on the futures of cities, these and other concepts of postnormal times theory (PNT) may provide some important clues.

Postnormal thinking suggests a focus on a set of interlinked drivers of change: acceleration, networked connectivity and globalisation. They can be used to recognise some of the multi-dimensional challenges that cities may face in their futures. The UN statistics above, may not provide exclusive or exhaustive definitions of cities but the time series they deliver, do clearly demonstrate a sharp acceleration in the growth of cities, both in size and number. The UN states that 'the urban population of the world has grown rapidly from 751 million in 1950 to 4.2 billion in 2018'. In other words, in the last seven decades this population's size has grown more than five times. That is almost unimaginable and a major change that affects all life on earth to a massive extent. The UN suggest that this trend will continue for several more decades at least. In the next 32 years, it projects, the number of urban dwellers will continue to rise, growing by another 2.5 billion, so that they will represent more than two thirds of the human population on the planet by 2050. The question is how we deal with this rapid evolution. Can we adapt our ways, learn quickly enough to provide safety and wellbeing for all in such precipitously changing circumstances? Will we take the time to sit down together and consider our options in ongoing and inclusive polylogues?

The term polylogue was originally coined by the Bulgarian-French literary critic, Julia Kristeva, in her book with the same title. Futurists Ziauddin Sardar and John Sweeney suggest that polylogues 'require the creation of new physical and mental spaces where diversity, pluralism, and contending perspectives are present on their own terms but also deeply invested in engaging others in creating and sharing information and knowledge'.

Will city dwellers even have the disposition to engage in such a demanding endeavour? The acceleration of life in the city itself may play an important role here. The pressures of a fast-paced urban culture are suspected to lead to structural failures, personal and communal crises of all kinds, similar to the *Future Shock* effects described by the late American popular futurist Alvin Toffler. I found an example in the city-state of Singapore, recognised for its transition from third world to first world in a single generation and for the extent of its technological innovation capacity. It is home to 5.4 million people. Even as it is counted among the 'smartest cities' in the world, it is seen to hold on to the old accepted norms of the standards, routines and work practices of the manufacturing economy. Kenneth Goh of the Ivey Business School in Canada, and who was the recipient of a Lee Kuan Yew Scholarship, suggests that Singapore is in dire need of 'productive slowing down'. Think about collectively unlearning the inclination for striving to get ahead of one another, kicking the habit of constantly seeking to outpace the other as individuals or businesses. Goh argues that the Singaporean workforce's perception of being trapped in a race 'discourages experimentation, discovery and learning from trial and error, in favour of uniform thought processes and reproducing scripted responses.' He believes that maintaining a simplistically fast pace is unsustainable for Singaporeans and he is concerned that as a consequence of being hung up on speed, Singapore will suffer from a lack of visionaries, creative thinkers and collaborators - precisely the kind of contributors it will need to be able to navigate postnormal change.

The acceleration of city life is closely linked to its increasingly networked nature and the inter- and intra-connectivity that this brings. Evidently, today connectivity is given by the possibilities of advancing information and communication technologies but that is no reason to ignore the significance of physical internal networks such as roads and public transport, water pipes and electricity, crisscrossing Antwerp or Singapore. Researcher Dan Penny of the University of Sidney recently issued a warning about the resilience of such physically connecting infrastructure. He studied the factors contributing to the fall of the Cambodian city Angkor in the fifteenth century. At one time it was the biggest city in the world. It had a well-developed network of connecting canals, fosses, dams, reservoirs and natural rivers. This extended over more than a thousand square kilometres and served as an irrigation network and as a defence against floods. The city collapsed at a time when intense monsoon rains were alternated with exceptionally dry periods. Resulting sediments in the smaller waterways and erosion of the larger ones combined to cause irreparable damage and bring the city down. Penny cautions that the challenges Angkor faced are similar to those of contemporary city networks in conditions of climate change and related extreme weather phenomena.

To ensure the futures of the cities of today, it is important to keep in mind that as cities grow, their infrastructure becomes more complex. As a consequence, it also becomes increasingly likely that these physical networks will at some point reach a critical state that cannot be foreseen by those who manage them on a daily basis. A minor error or dropout can then result in a much larger problem. There is a reason why electricity black-outs are on the agenda this winter, even in one of the most prosperous nations of the world like Belgium. For cities to have any futures at all, they will have to construct resilience by creating more independence between different parts of their physical networks and build in surplus capacity. The investments needed to do so may threaten other much needed expenditures. The question is how we might come to prioritising costs to defend us against unpredicted (and unpredictable) phenomena. If we can't see exactly what is coming, will we be inclined to put up the defences we may need to survive. Or will climate change remain a black elephant (one of three potentialities of postnormal times, which also include the black swan and the black jelly fish) – ignored till it crushes us?

Just like running water and electricity and the coming and going of trucks, containerships and tankers, full of (non-)essentials, digital connectivity is a determining feature of contemporary city environments. The implications of urban activities linked across the globe in real time, of the capacity of knowledge workers to cut down on commuting time by working from home, of how the flow of traffic is controlled from smart hubs, cannot be underestimated. Digital connectivity in cities includes an array of mobile applications, services and media channels that contribute to how we do all things, economic, social and personal. How digital connectivity is big (data) business, how it is the object of state control, how it affects social relations, working hours and global finance, how power is reproduced and subverted through its creation and its use, and how digital divides remain while digital connectivity becomes ubiquitous - all these questions have a strong reciprocal relation with questions about the present and futures of cities.

Digital connectivity defines our era, just as much as the rise of mega cities does. In the extended present, the two combined presents an impressive range of challenges. They have to do with the social well-being of humans when they replace face-to-face encounters with virtual chitchat and big data. They include the unintended consequences of congestion and poor air-quality in the streets suggested as shortcuts by the apps people use to plot inner-city journeys. The extended present begs attention for privacy and commodification, for culture and entertainment and for all that we can see coming. *Familiar images of the future* related to advances in information and communication technologies in cities, include the ubiquitous and oppressive personalised advertising seen in films like *Minority Report* (2002) and *The Fifth Element* (19197) as well as the potential for organising citizens in protests and uprisings, as seen in the Occupy movement or the Arab Spring. Moving towards whole new *unthought futures*, brings experts and housewives, their children and grandparents together. Call them stakeholders, actors, community members, audiences or members of the public, users, consumers, experts, theoreticians, critics, politicians, practitioners. Call them people! Contemporary experiments and projects with extended peer communities with attention for what might be possible, what is needed and wanted, what can be afforded, what to have or do and how, cannot omit 'what for' and 'for what world'.

Digital connectivity itself is exceptionally suited to channel such deliberative and co-creative efforts of all kinds. 'Hot mint' will be needed to lubricate the convivial spaces where we can look each other in the eye when we have to recognise that your needs and my desires can very easily be mutually exclusive. We will need social technologies and 'orgware', the ability to build capacity and adopt and adjust to change, as much, if not more, than hardware or software. We will have to work intensively for the constant revision of and clarity on values to practice and protect so as to keep our cities and ourselves liveable. Rigour and audacity, new forms and combinations are needed to look forward in conditions of seemingly limitless potential for disaster as well as brilliance.

Far reaching globalisation still raises the stakes. Urban geographers and economic analysts draw intricate maps of the flows of goods and services, finance and people that have existed throughout the world's history. In practice today, the bulk of these flows exist between cities. We are talking about a form of connectivity again, one that has taken on an unprecedented scale, closely binding together the major and minor cities of today. Flows like air-traffic and overseas container shipping or the copper and fibreoptic cables beneath our oceans, contribute considerably to the realities of all our cities. What takes place at stock exchanges and in newsrooms, the movements of refugees from war-torn or climate disaster regions, the implementation of ideas tried out in one city and applied in another, all these constitute flows between cities around the globe.

University College, London, environmental planners Michael Batty and James Cheshire underline the varied nature of flows: 'any kind of change might be treated as a flow, from physical, social, or electronic transactions through to changes caused by aging, regeneration, economic growth, and so on.' Such flows can be described starting from the perspective of fixed locations – cities – where changes take place as a result of a perpetual varied stream in and out. It is also possible to describe how attributes or components that are flowing change along their trajectory, independent of departure or arrival points. Both frames are needed simultaneously. Cities then are not merely the physical departure and arrival points of flows. Flows of information, artefacts, services, money or goods extend the cities beyond their physical or administrative boundaries. Like Manuel Castells, Batty and Cheshire emphasise that cities are not defined by their physical space. Cities can be understood as the dynamic processes that take place within and between them. Cities are flows in and off themselves and so are their futures.

Picture a city, thirty years from now. Start with the faces of people, their figures, their posture and the clothes they wear. Think of the town halls that are the scene of heated debates between them. This city could be my home town, perhaps a mega-city in Asia, it could be in Latin or North America too. Walk along the borders of what used to be a nation and see how it has become a single Metropolitan area. Discover the tiny houses and the mobile units, the communities that turned rabbit cage social housing into co-housing arrangements, the lofts on the 67th floor elsewhere. See the children play in the park under the shade of trees, check out the CO_2 filters. Find the graffiti by respected artists on the water tanks and windmills. Stop at the castle where new arrivals congregate. Look at grannies tending to vegetables and herbs in the common allotment by the railway. Find the arts centre in the old factory by the river where rhythms and rhymes and tones of human history are mixed. Take me to a polylogue under a rooftop on the protective dike along the embankment. Forget the bullet-holes if you can. Flow with the futures of cities.

DIGITISED SACRED

Iacopo Ghinassi

What happens to the sacred nature of the Qur'an as a physical object after the text has undergone the process of digitisation? This is a pertinent issue which will play an important part in our future relationship with the Sacred Text. However, for the question to have meaning, we must first understand what digitisation is exactly. By digitisation we mean, quite intuitively, the process of rendering in a digital form an object that was previously available in a physical form. A formulation that admittedly may sound technical but I personally see digitisation as the process of translating 'atoms to bits'. The distinction between bits and atoms in this context and, in particular, in contemporary practices in the Digital Humanities, the emerging field at the intersection of digital technologies and the humanities, is something we have to bear in mind. As a second and more specific definition, digitising a text involves the translation of a visual, two-dimensional sign, the alphabetic letter, into a visually equal sign on a computer screen.

If we stop here, the digitising process would be just a medium for translation: of putting words that were previously in a book on a computer screen. The fact of rendering a text in an electronic format, however, means much more than this. The main advantage of the digital, as emphasised by the advocates of digitisation, is that digital information is infinitely replicable. A digital text is potentially accessible from anywhere and at any time: this is a fact we experience each time we glance over a piece of writing on the internet. This same ubiquity of digital over physically mediated information leads to a consideration of accessibility of that same information. If a text is digitised and put in an online repository, the information contained in the text is accessible to anyone who has a computer and an internet connection. At the same time, this accessibility and iteration of the text means that those words, once digitised, cannot be lost ever again: no fire, war, cataclysm or simple negligence can erase it, as it is now nowhere and, at the same time, virtually, everywhere.

So much for what we mean by the digitisation of a text according to much of digital archiving practice. Such a concept of digitisation involves the assumption that books as physical objects are nothing more than vehicles of information. In this vein, the digital is just a much more efficient means of transmitting the intended message. On the one hand, we have dispendious, perishable and exclusive vehicles of information such as books and manuscripts. On the other, we have a digital format that allows information to be cheaply available to all. It sounds like a race doomed from the start. Some texts, however, can't be reduced to mere vehicles of information. This is certainly the case with the Qur'an.

It is evident that the value of the Qur'an as a tangible object cannot be descried. Islamic calligraphy as a form of religious art is a case in point. The artistic merit and meticulous craft of Qur'an transcribers over the centuries continues to invoke universal admiration. The significance of calligraphy in Islamic tradition has its origin in the view that the Qur'an is a sacred text incorporating a physical, aesthetic dimension. One of the most unique doctrines of Islam as opposed to, for example, Christianity and Judaism is the reverence the Qur'an is afforded, alongside the language in which it is written, classical Arabic. The ideal that it is the authentic word of Allah, revealed to humanity via the Prophet Muhammad, is considered to be evident also in the aesthetic perfection of the Book: this has been agreed by theologians since the emergence of Islam. What is particularly interesting is the fact that such perfection does not involve only the sound of the beatific words, but also their graphic depiction. The physicality of the Qur'an remains inseparable from the message it conveys and, even where this concept is not present in contemporary practices, the debt of Islamic art and culture to this tradition is undeniable.

All these considerations, then, informs the question: where is the sacred in a digital Qur'an? In other and more visionary terms, can we envisage a future in which the same reverence of the Qur'an as a book will be lavished on an app or a smart phone? Or will the practice of cherishing a book vanish in attempts at digitalising it? The answer(s), as often happens, lie(s) somewhere in between. Yet today's reality denies both questions. If smartphone apps have not become an object of devotion in themselves, certainly the Qur'an has already been digitalised via many different sources and in a plethora of different forms. Focusing especially on the didactic function that digital online tools may have, they present a significant advantage for accessible education and of sustainability, enabling millions of Muslims to access and learn the Qur'an. Against such an optimistic vision, Dagmar Riedel, of Columbia University, who runs a scholarly blog on the history of Islamic books, points out the great gap in digital literacy that exists between wealthy Muslims and those from deprived communities. For Riedel, a strong programme of digital literacy among poorer Muslims throughout the world would be necessary before the advantages of open, online texts such as the Qur'an could be of any utility.

Since the beginning of this decade a vast number of digitalised Qur'ans have been produced and made available online and as smart phone apps. Electronic versions are indeed so multiple that an entirely new field named DQC (Digital Qur'an Computing) has entered the lexicon of Islamic studies and the IT and engineering fields within the Arabic-speaking world, to investigate and statistically analyse the corpus of computer-encoded Qur'ans that exist. Such an interest in the digitalisation of the Qur'an as a way to better understand the text seems to deny or, at least, to ignore the contradiction regarding the nature and importance of the Qur'an as a physical object for Islamic tradition and religious practices. In a blog post about digital literacy in the Muslim world, Riedel emphasises the pragmatic importance that Muslim civilisation has bestowed upon different forms of communication employed to transmit the message of Islam. In this sense, the form in which it is conveyed is not paramount as long as it is accurately received by the worshipper. Such a perspective can be held true if we consider the young, western-style educated Muslim readers. But this still leaves out those Muslims with no or limited online access. Digital literacy is an integral part of a broader, structural problem of internet accessibility.

So it seems the translation of the Qur'an into digital form does not merely imply a cultural problem of delocalisation of the sacred, but also a socio-economic issue of scarce familiarity with the digital medium as experienced by vast swathes of the Muslim global community. If we try to consider these two problems as facets of the same phenomenon, we can deduce that, maybe, the consideration of the sacred in Qur'anic digitisation can be inscribed in the broader phenomenon and inner tensions of modernity. The question that we should pose to ourselves is not what happens to the sacred when the Qur'an is digitised, but how the Qur'an could be translated into a digital, non-physical entity without losing its socio-cultural significance, expressions of a long history of devotion toward the book itself, that are indicative of the sacred invested in it. All of this involves the risky assumption of sacrality as a condition that exists as long as it is socially recognised. If we consider social recognition in a pragmatic way it is evident that for a digital Qur'an to be adopted and considered sacred by Muslim communities, the overall particularities of the Qur'an as a physical object have to be recognised. Eventually these ought to be replicated through the digital medium.

The example of Islamic calligraphy is particularly pertinent to the importance of a certain physicality of the Qur'an as an object. The Dutch linguistic and typographist Thomas Milo has dedicated his career to closing the gap between the aridity of computer letters and the generosity of Islamic calligraphy and his struggles ended up, notably, in the creation of the first interactive, digital Qur'an. Milo's attempt by itself, in fact, exemplifies the concern of maintaining the tradition and the sacrality of the physical text in its digital edition. The digital Qur'an was commissioned by the government of Oman and entrusted to a team of European experts, including Milo who declared his fascination for the complexity of Arabic alphabet and Islamic calligraphy. Milo's career had been triggered by acknowledging the particularity of Arabic calligraphy and the severe limitations that existing typographic computer standards in the 1980s were imposing on its electronic rendering. With this in mind, he founded DecoType, a company with the mission of designing 'technology for Arabic', in defiance of the conventional approach of designing 'Arabic for technology'. Twenty years and several projects later (DecoType provided, among others, Windows and Apple with their standard Arabic fonts), his work captured the attention of the Oman Minister for Endowments and Religious Affairs and work on the first web Qur'an commenced in 2008. *Mus'haf Muscat*, the name given to the Qur'an edition, alluding to the capital of Oman, Muscat, was published online in 2017 and now represents one of the most authoritative and most elaborated examples of digital Qur'anic editions. Crucially, the publication was created with special attention given to the tradition of Islamic calligraphy, that is by itself symbolic of the sacred nature and the esteem in which the Qur'an has been held throughout the centuries. This sensitivity goes some way towards closing the gap between tradition and innovation and in perpetuating a sense of the sacred in the scripture. What was meant to be transmitted by ancient transcribers through the aesthetic quality of calligraphic art remains the priority.

The project also highlighted an inner and broader contradiction between today's digital landscape and traditions involving religious pieties. We should remember that *Mus'haf Muscat* was commissioned by Oman's Ministry for Religious Affairs, an established and respected institution. This added gravitas to the digitising endeavour and ensured scrupulous attention was paid to Qur'anic traditions and the preservation of meaning and sacrality. Other digital editions of the Qur'an, however, are less a labour of love and more – indeed, solely – market driven. The commodification of the Qur'an is a result of the conformity and ecosystem of the internet and the neoliberalism of the app market today, rather than specific to the sacred texts' digital editions. The digital ecosystem refers to the vast majority of websites and apps out there managing to sustain their costs and, eventually, becoming profitable by selling advertising spots on their virtual space. Think about all the pop-ups, the annoying ads that appear on your screen while surfing the internet or playing crossword on a mobile app: these ads are the economic skeleton of the digital boom as it has come to fruition in the last decade.

It is with this in mind that on-line readers of the Qur'an can be reduced to consumers rather than worshippers. To build and maintain an on-line digital edition is costly and, if you don't have the Omani government paying for the project, it is likely that you'll have to sustain costs through advertising, regardless of the initial intention. The main business model of digital products remains the advertisement market. However, it is fair to say the internet itself has enabled a series of alternative sources of financing such as crowdfunding and, as in the case of Wikipedia, remote volunteering. Quran.com is a notable example of a virtual Qur'an resource made through online collaboration as exemplified by the Sharing Economy. It describes itself as a 'pro bono' project. The interventions of philanthropic institutions and universities is imperative if a digital edition is to wrestle free from economic pressures and digital market constraints. Vulnerability to ideological and market bias will exist as long as digital versions are slave to the harsh financial facts of life.

The acknowledgement of the importance of institutions such as universities in the process of digitalising sacred texts opens up another line of enquiry in the maintaining of a sense of sacred and tradition in the Qur'an's electronic formats. As noted earlier, an *a fortiori* argument in the choice of digitalising a text is the obvious advantage that digital editions have in relation to conservation of the text and all it signifies. To digitalise a text, in fact, means to render a physical sign such as a hand-written letter in bytes, electronic, binary signals that can be infinitely replicated by any computer; just as if everyone had an army of copyists transcribing a book for personal use at a click. The difference would be, and this is the problem that has consumed us until now, that computers lack the taste and technical ability to replicate physical aspects of the objects that invoke sentiment in people. This is the case with Islamic calligraphy and its devotional meaning in Qur'anic traditions. While an amanuensis was inscribed in a shared system of culture and values building up the sacrality of written texts, certain types of digitisation tend to be more interested in the preservation of semantic information of a text, ignoring its aesthetic corollary of physical reality as a book.

I have said a certain form of digitisation, because, as it happens, such a concept of translation to digital is not the only one at all. Starting from the Digital Humanities apparatus and, in particular from the philological and conservation fields, another slightly different concept of digitisation happens to be of great importance to us. Summarised in the practice of using the digital medium as a tool to capture the physical appearance of a historically relevant object, techniques adopted for this purpose include digital photography, mark-up languages and 3D scanners and printers. Mark-up languages (e.g. HTML, XML, etc.) are meta-languages that are used to describe extra information about an element such as a piece of text or an image. It is due to mark-up languages (HTML, in particular) that a browser such as Internet Explorer or Safari *knows* how and where to display all the different elements on a website. With the same logic, if all the elements of a physical book are marked with extra information describing their physical appearance in the original source, a computer will be able to replicate the object exactly as it appeared in reality. The main difference with the semantic approach of saving just the message of a text is not formal but substantial. The book, in fact, is still translated in bytes, in information, but the difference lies in what is translated in the first place, that is, in this case, the physical appearance. Think about a digital picture of a book's page: in such a case the information captured by the camera does not comprise the page as a sequence of letters but, instead, within that page is a canvas of pixels, representing that sequence of letters. Beyond technicalities, what is important to note is that such an approach, initially intended to preserve an object as if it was destined for academic enquiry, presents an advantage in preserving existent, physical versions of the Qur'an also for the purpose of religious observance.

This approach brings us closer to new possibilities that could eventually transcend the difference between bits and atoms, between digital and physical, while unequivocally closing the gap between the sacrality of the physical Qur'an against its digital counterpart. The emergence of 3D printing techniques means that the process of giving a physical form to a digital encoded object has never been easier. 3D printing is able to replicate digital objects in three dimension, exactly like a printer but with the capability of adding volume and shape to its output. The phenomenon of 3D printers spread all over the world a few years ago promising to become the new industrial revolution of our era. If the promises of 3D printing are realised, the very nature of industrial production will change forever as a digital model of any object would suffice to replicate it an infinite number of times, as long as the materials are available.

In the cultural domain, 3D technology has captured the attention of the British Library, but what truly sparked the public imagination was the case of Palmyra. In 2016, UNESCO and the Institute for Digital Archaeology (IDA) launched a project to use 3D printing technology to rebuild the monuments of Palmyra that had been destroyed in Syria. A breath-taking video by *The Guardian* documents the criteria and the history of the digital reconstruction of the marble arch of Palmyra, later installed in Trafalgar Square. Maybe at this stage it is already possible to see the impact of technology in our context. If an entire building can be reproduced by multimedia, similarly, culturally and religiously dense versions of the Qur'an can be made accessible to the public, therefore nullifying (at least on the surface) the difference between the physical and the digital edition of the Qur'an. The sacrality of the Qur'an as a physical object, then, could be saved both out of respect for tradition, as well as to challenge digital diffidence, or the lack of digital literacy and internet accessibility.

There still remains a question of authenticity, about the very nature of the sacred involved in such a venerated book. Where is the sacred in the Qur'an: is it inherent in the object's physicality or is it located in the devotion of its readers? Can the sacred be experienced with a click or a swipe? Or does it need the turn of a page? It is a question that remains unanswered.

DECOLONIAL SCIENTIA

Andrew Burke

One of the first things I ever wrote was for a sixth grade assignment about family history. In it, I detailed my father's childhood, based on conversations I had with him on his early life. He told me about his few memories of Barbados, before he and his family moved to Coventry when he was about six years old, in 1958, as part of the Windrush generation. He told me of the home he'd left behind, and the new one he found himself in, and the experience of existing in an entirely different environment. At that time, I had visited England (including my dad's childhood home), and had spent several summers in Barbados, so it wasn't too difficult for me to imagine the stark contrast of travelling from the Caribbean to Coventry. Although I had been born in the United States and lived my entire life there up to that point, I could identify with much more of his account than I had anticipated. Particularly, the experience of exclusion. He was the only Black student in his school at a time when the UK was just beginning its multicultural experiment. And while I was growing up in a mostly white New Jersey suburb and wasn't the only Black kid in class, I was the only person that was Black and of a foreign background. A fact that was nearly incomprehensible to many of my peers who, never having heard of Barbados at all, and as far as I could tell, didn't know that Black people existed outside of the US and Africa.

My father's response to the situation he found himself in was to assert his humanity to the fullest possible extent on the terrain on which it was denied. He worked hard to excel in all of his academic requirements, captained his school rugby and cricket teams and played on its football team. He went out of his way to be polite and friendly with all, even those that would dehumanise him to his face. This is exactly how we are told to respond – in a society that would seek to restrict or outright deny our abilities to live and possibilities for the future; we are told that we must play the game, and if the assertions of our inferiority are indeed unfounded, then we should succeed and prove our equality rationally. However, despite this success on the terms of whiteness, he returned to Barbados, disillusioned with life in England and denied the legal recognition of humanity afforded by citizenship. In the years in between his return to Barbados in the mid-1970s and my birth in New Jersey in 1992, he and my mother met and married and they immigrated to the United States via the Bronx and Miami.

In contrast with my dad's experience of asserting his humanity on the grounds of his Blackness was my own, in which I took a completely different approach when faced with the same types of challenges. Beyond this, even in addition to this, I had my mental illness to contend with alongside that of Blackness. When I was about six years old, my parents took me to see a psychiatrist and I was diagnosed with clinical depression and prescribed antidepressants, though they caused more problems than they solved for me. Despite my age, I was highly sceptical of the diagnosis. I hated school, where I felt deeply alienated. I was Black in a predominantly white town, and one of the only students with immigrant parents in my school. Though made to feel different and reminded of these differences often, I never allowed myself to feel shame, wishing to align myself more closely with the aspects of the past that guided me to the present, rather than seeing a future in the present circumstances for merely being what they were. But despite being proud of all of the things that marked me as different, I recognised the difficulty in actually doing anything with these feelings in a meaningful way. With all this in mind, I thought that it was in fact a perfectly normal reaction to want to remove oneself from such a situation in any way possible. My response was largely to withdraw from school as much as I could get away with. This isn't to say that I wasn't intellectually curious – I spent a significant amount of time seeking knowledge in a wide variety of disciplines, largely on my own time. For me, the best way to deal with exclusion was to build a rich inner life, away from my exterior social life – to essentially render myself invisible publicly, while focusing my passion and creative energy into pursuits that had little to no bearing to the demands made of by society in terms of what I was expected to be as a Black man who had embraced Islam. This was the first way in which I began simultaneously envisioning and working towards a different future. During the summers I had spent in Barbados, my family spoke constantly of going back to Barbados to live, my grandfather actually having sold his house in Coventry, to return to the island shortly after turning seventy. But at the same time, I understood that the ability to return home posed a political question as well as a financial one. The structural relations and poverty that necessitated movement of people from the Caribbean to North America and Europe was the hurdle to overcome, because as far as I could tell, we wouldn't have left at all if it had been up to us. To this end, I began to focus my intellectual pursuits on understanding the superstructure that created and recreated these conditions the world over, so that I might have something to say about how they could be overcome

On the back of this obsession, and desperately seeking an alternative to the life in America that I saw no future in, I moved to London to attend university, the first in my family to do so. This was not, as Fanon refers to in *Black Skin, White Masks*, an attempt to situate myself in proximity to the knowledge of the imperial core in an attempt to whiten my own perspective. Rather, it was the inverse I was seeking – a coming together of people who were themselves reckoning with the legacy of empire in their respective countries and in their own minds and practices. And this is exactly what I found – for the first time I was able to speak from within and not from without, to not have to translate my first-person perspective as to make it comprehensible to the listener. The people I was making community with understood my perspective, because, like me, their stories and the stories of their families reflected a particular experience of European colonialism, independence and the neoliberal turn that catalysed a shifting of third world labour to the first world, and together were now reckoning with a twenty-first century that seemed to have little to offer besides uncertainty, complexity, contradictions and chaos. Confident in my intellectual and social development, though still dealing with at times crippling depression, I continued my studies at full steam in hopes to bring about this different future following the completion of an undergraduate degree in international relations. My dissertation explored the political economy of the US led 'War on Drugs' from the position of affected Caribbean states, and I went on to study for a Masters degree in an effort to continue down this trajectory. A month before orientation, Michael

Brown was murdered by a police officer in Ferguson, Missouri and the Black Lives Matter movement brought the discussion of anti-Black state violence into the public discourse in the States. This led me to approach these questions with a renewed vitality, as the situation in the United States reminded me that despite the institutional pressure for objectivity and broad applicability, there was a real urgency behind these questions, and people were, are and will continue to be killed so long as they remain unanswered. But as I was watching that situation unfold over the course of the year, as more people would be killed, and more appeals to the rationality of the social relations that produced these killings continued to be made, and continued to be heard, the anti-immigrant tide of the British right was beginning to rise as well, revealing itself publicly on many occasions throughout the year. By the time I had finished my postgraduate studies, I felt that the best course of action, keeping in mind waxing power and social influence of the far-right on both sides of the Atlantic and anticipating that it would continue long into the foreseeable future, I figured my best bet would be a temporary return to the United States, where I at least had citizenship and thus a theoretical claim to legal protection. And so, in October 2015, I begrudgingly returned to the United States, where I remain today. And although I spent most of the last year a socialist organiser, my situation and health necessitate my efforts to be focused on the demands of my particular condition, and all of my dreams for the future require me to find a way out, so that I may begin again to attempt to live a fully human life.

In thinking about the future and the possibilities it presents for Caribbean people, both at home and in the diaspora, it's difficult to imagine anything other than a continuation of the brutality and violence that has been present since the arrival of Europeans, and has been woven into the fabric of Caribbean life by a 500-year experience with slavery, imperialism and capitalism. In many ways, the modern world was born in the Caribbean. It was the site of Columbus' first encounter with the Americas, and by extension, the first geographical challenge to European systems of knowledge up to that point. From this point, the Caribbean became the testing ground for Europe's first large scale experiments with chattel slavery, imperial statecraft and biopolitics. In the nineteenth century, European industrialisation was made possible due to the profits gained from the slave trade, and with the passing of the Monroe Doctrine, the Caribbean was the first non-contiguous object of American imperial ambitions. When chattel slavery came to a formal end, its afterlife and legacy continued in the form of deepened oppression and exploitation of the new rural peasantry and urban working class at the hands of the local and foreign bourgeoisie (in the Caribbean, Europe and North America). This shift went on to define much of the Caribbean experience of the next hundred years (in some places more than others), and the waning of Europe as the primary hegemonic influence was catalysed following the conclusion of the Second World War, the near-total destruction of Europe and its economies and burgeoning independence movements throughout the Caribbean. While independence was granted to many Caribbean colonies in the 1960s, freedom and self-determination were little more than nominal designations. Independence came in the milieu of the Cold War, and those who sought a path forward that eschewed the demands and logic of global capitalism or sought solidarity with the Communist bloc were redirected through coercion, economic violence and in many cases, direct imperial violence. With the end of the Cold War, the alleged 'End of History' and the acceptance of neoliberalism as humanity's only possible future, the associated development models were bought into wholesale. And now, decades later, we can get a sense of the harm that has been wrought; due not only to these policies but their compulsory ways of thinking and understanding, as well as their inability to meaningfully provide redress for these issues. We see an increase in poverty, an inability of Caribbean governments to satisfy the demands of global capitalism and human life within their territories, and an annually intensifying hurricane season that puts additional strain on a people in a region that has already been pushed to the margins. In order to service their debts, encourage neoliberal development and attract foreign investment, Caribbean governments effectively operate as a dual travel agency and paramilitary organisation. In both of these pursuits, human beings are seen as superfluous, useful for labour alone. As can be expected, these conditions have historically driven many to seek their fortunes elsewhere. After ending up in North America or Europe, we often face much of the same, though mediated in different ways. However, I think precisely because of this, the future we're collectively facing and the uncertainty of the present, there exists an opportunity to bring about its undoing in favour of more ways of being and understanding the breadth of human existences across space and time.

While the Caribbean was the site of the first instance of the forms of knowledge, power and labour practiced in total that would define the experience of Western modernity, the possibility exists for us to be the first to move beyond it in a way that opens pathways towards new modes of being human. Despite the difficulty in imagining a way of being so different to that which we currently understand, it is vital that we continue to do so.

My idea of what it means to be human, particularly where the future is concerned, are influence by the work of the Jamaican philosopher, Sylvia Wynter. Her investigation into the concept of 'Man' emphasises the inherently exclusionary nature of the concept of this central figure of modernity and primary subject of liberal doctrine that arose out of the specific conditions of Enlightenment Europe. From there it was exported beyond Europe through empire, and used to justify the subjugation, enslavement and all other forms of structural and interpersonal violence on the grounds that the affected populations weren't really human at all. Even with the emergence of civil and human rights movements and discourse, and the rhetorical shift from the rights of Man to Human, the epistemological categories from which the discourse arises remain largely unchanged. As such, for those of us who fall outside of this initial conceptualisation of 'Man', attempts to assert one's humanity along these lines is a Sisyphean task, always doomed to be repeated after the goalposts shift. Rather than attempt to assert our humanity to seek inclusion and legitimisation within a definition of personhood that is effectively European subjectivity masquerading as universal objectivity, and be able to manifest that exclusion as a material reality, our task should be to flip this definition on its head. Instead we should articulate a vision of Humanity that embraces and actualises the broad subjectivity of human experience across space and time, without moving towards the homogenising tendency of modernity. This is not to say that Western epistemologies or the knowledge they have created should be abandoned outright, but rather that we plainly see the consequences of the ordering principles of political, economic and social life that arise from defining humanity in purely biological and exclusionary terms and the uncritical prioritisation of the individual from the collective from which they arise. The goal here is not to rescue the figure of the individual from obsoletion, to assert positive depictions of Othered humanity, or seek representation in repressive institutions, power structures and relations. Rather, it is to assert the necessity of subjective experience as a constituent part of the collective, so that society may then continue to shape the individuals of whom it is made towards this reality. Wynter hypothesises that the first step we must take towards confronting the material challenges of the present and future is to understand the epistemological foundations of Liberalism/modernity that ground and legitimise the West's material expression of Enlightenment thinking and values, at the expense of those categorised as others on the basis of race, gender, religion sexuality, aneuerotypcality or any of the other ways in which human beings are deemed abnormal in relation to this standard. Thus, the beginning of non-dystopian futures of the Caribbean, and of the world, is at the end of the bio-centric epistemological category of Man upon which modernity is founded, in favour of an expression of Humanity that takes into consideration the collective and subjective experience of being a Human alongside all else. In Wynter's own words, the goal here is to bring about a situation in which 'Humanness is no longer a noun. Being human is a praxis'.

It is in this context that I find Islam holds a significant potential. There exists a tension between politics, particularly on the left, and religion that I think is something we should struggle with and against. Religion is seen by some as an anachronistic, vestigial relic of pre-Enlightenment humanity, made obsolete by scientific rationalism, serving only as an 'opiate of the masses' in Marxist parlance that encourages appeasement to oppressive power structures made and operated by human beings. Following this line of thinking, it is argued that the solutions to the question of how we might all live in the world together going forward are seen solely in material terms; metaphysical has no bearing. That religion is something that is to be overcome on the path towards human emancipation, rather than something that can be a tangible source of strength and grounding. And while I do believe that religion can be misused to restrict and oppress, I think to see religion purely through this lens is to miss the point For me, Islam played a crucial role in focusing my thoughts and actions towards bringing about this future, providing an ethical framework, a historical situation, a community orientation and a metaphysical rationalisation for not only the challenges we face individually and collectively as people, but how ultimately these experiences, challenges and conflicts refer back to the nature of the universe itself. Islam reminds me that I am a part of larger proceedings that span across space and time, and although only a small part of a whole beyond what is readily apparent; my actions, decisions and choices ultimately have consequences that travel beyond what's immediate. There exists within Islam and its rich philosophical tradition the possibility to realise this future so long as we can engage with the territory rather than the map; of what has happened, what is happening, what may happen as a result, and what we might hope to achieve instead.

The question then becomes how to move towards that future. An answer is given in part by the Argentine semiotician and literary theorist, Walter Mignolo's reading of this question through Wynter's writing. He articulates the need for 'decolonial scientia', a concept that follows Wytner's interpretation of the sociogenic principle in Frantz Fanon's accounts of Black alienation in the Caribbean in *Black Skins, White Masks*. Simply put, it seeks to undermine the categorisation that attempts to disguise European subjectivity as objectivity, and negates the subjective experience of all Others. It is 'the scientia not needed for progress and development, but for liberating the actual and future victims of knowledge upon which progress and development are predicated'. To this end, decolonial scientia undertakes three tasks. First is the restoration of legitimacy to epistemological knowledge produced by subjective experience (biography) and geohistory as a means of upsetting the domination of imperial science and rationality as the holders of 'true' knowledge, therefore removing their power to deem alternate modes of knowledge production legitimate or illegitimate. Second, decolonial scientia seeks subjective understandings of the 500-year process of transformation of colonialism to globalisation, from the non-European people with whom modernity came into contact and placed outside of history and the law, alongside ecological and environmental consideration of these events. Third is the generation of new knowledge that ultimately places economic growth and development in service to human life and environmental health, rather than the other way around.

Contrasting this way of thinking about the world and the future with my own life gives me a great deal to process. First and foremost, I recognise that despite my understanding of the importance of narrative and the fantasy of rational objectivity, I still have a strong tendency to forsake the pure subjectivity of my experiences, and attempt to synthesise them through the canon of Western thought in an attempt to speak beyond (although never outside) myself. In truth, I'm deeply uncomfortable with talking about myself directly or indirectly for a fear of being misunderstood. Much of this is a consequence of the Duboisian 'double consciousness' which Fanon discusses in the opening chapter of *Black Skins, White Masks*: the experience of recognising the subject position from which I speak, while understanding the illegibility and incomprehensibility of that position to the 'mainstream' on whatever grounds one may define that. I know what I mean when I speak, and why I'm speaking at all, but do others? Despite this phobia, a meaningful consideration of the future demands in part the particular knowledge brought forth by the life narrative, for the dimensions and trajectories of my life thus far present the experience of a more recent history that speaks to our emerging future, while simultaneously connecting it to distant geographies and temporal realities.

Narratives like my own, combined with historical accounts as they're understood in the mainstream, present a fuller picture of decolonial scientia that will inform our future understanding of race and identity. They show that while there was 'economic growth' and 'independence', there was also displacement, misery and pain. The idea of the human as currently understood in the liberal, biocentric falls short of addressing the needs of human beings in their actual lives. The prevailing discourse of mental illness, for example, starts from the assumption that there is a 'normal' human mind that is separate from the body that experiences the world. And therefore that any breakdown in this 'normal' functioning of the mind is an expression of biochemical malfunctioning in the brain, rather than a subjective experience following from that experienced by the mind and the body as a unified entity. A different, non-apocalyptic future remains possible, even with the horrors that occur in the present tense, but will require a shift in our collective thinking that radically subverts the terrain of our understanding of humanity back to that which provides the space for self-definition and understanding.

Where the personal and political converge, the future looks bleak and it's often difficult to imagine an alternative. And where that possibility exists for the world beyond me, it remains difficult to locate myself within it. But whatever future we may have collectively lies at the end of adapting the challenges that have been created by human decisions and actions, and at the beginning of the democratisation of human experiences, and life. We shouldn't concern ourselves with rocket launches and AI, nor should we valorise the billionaires who hold the future over us and seek to use hoarded wealth to unilaterally decide the future, while leaving hundreds of millions in a state of manufactured vulnerability. Echoing the words of Leon Sealy-Huggins, apocalyptic futures, Caribbean or otherwise, can be inferred from increasingly catastrophic presents.

FINDING PEACE IN TYPHOONS

Cesar H Villanueva

The future is not carved in stone
It is not found in the present
More so not in the past
Nor is it in the future
For futures are yet to be
Futures follow a pattern set forth by the Universe
It is found within the heart

George Aguilar

Haiyan originated from an area of low pressure several hundred kilometres east-southeast of Micronesia on 2 November 2013. Tracking towards the Philippine Islands, climate conditions favoured tropical cyclogenesis and the system developed into a tropical storm the following day. By 6 November, the Joint Typhoon Warning Center (JTWC) assessed the system as a Category 5-equivalent super typhoon on the Saffir-Simpson hurricane wind scale. Haiyan (also known as Typhoon Yolanda) was one of the strongest tropical cyclones ever recorded.

The typhoon warnings had been going on for days. But the people of Bacolod City seemed to be going about their business as usual although the day was far from normal. Schools and offices were closed, the shelves at grocery stores were empty. Yet, people were still on the streets and in market stalls doing their thing quietly with forced smiles. This is highly unlikely of my people who have been known to be rather noisy and happy even in the worst of times. Upon making landfall Yolanda devastated portions of central Philippines. It was the deadliest Philippine typhoon on record, killing at least 6,300 people. In January 2014, bodies were still being found. Nobody here expected Yolanda to hit that hard and that fast. Even the government was caught unprepared.

When Typhoon Yolanda hit Bacolod City the experience was one of doom. It became night-time dark by mid-afternoon. The winds raged with an eerie whoosh and howling sound. It rained non-stop with severe flooding. Electricity was down. Battery powered radios were the only source of outside reports. There was lightning and thunder. Suddenly, a tree crashed in the garden. A treasured palm tree that held a pigeon house was torn down, the pigeon house smashed against the ground and the pigeons either died or flew away, never to return. Many other trees had crashed down in the neighbourhood. Rooftops were blown away. Fortunately, our roof remained intact but was heavily damaged. At five o'clock in the morning the winds had died down but it was pitch black outside. On the way to the airport the sights of devastation were overwhelming. Garbage, trees, telephone lines and posts littered the streets. It looked like a battle took place the night before. But Bacolod was actually spared from the brunt of Typhoon Yolanda. In Leyte, thousands died when tsunamis hit inland and destroyed its capital city Tacloban City.

When we reached the Silay airport, the morning after Yolanda I saw the planes arriving. At six in the morning there were people busy sweeping the debris from the roads and some were already collecting reusable materials to rebuild their homes. The sun began to shine and, even though the terrible storm struck hours ago, I knew it was not yet the end. The eternal struggle to strive amidst hardship and pain goes beyond even the most terrible of storms. Today there are no more signs of the ravaging Yolanda in Bacolod, but the work to relocate and rebuild communities in Tacloban is still on going.

We understand that 'typhoons' are not just isolated events. Rather they impact on everything and anything across levels, layers, and strati. Throwing a piece of plastic on the beach in the Philippines will affect all eco-systems up to those found on the other side of the planet. The focus of those of us who work on Philippines futures cuts across advocacies and goes beyond futures studies. For us, futures include also peace building and community building.

Years before Yolanda, a team of Filipino futurists, including myself, presented a report on Typhoon Futures at a World Futures Studies

Federation (WFSF) conference. In this report we argued that while typhoons are a regular phenomenon in the Philippines, everybody seems to be caught unprepared when they strike. It is primarily for this reason that we became advocates of anticipating and creating futures. The adverse effects of even the strongest of typhoons can be anticipated. We can change structures, schedules, resource allocation and management as well as train and educate the people on disaster preparedness.

However, our futures work is not just meteorological based and concerned with typhoons alone. We use the idea of typhoons as a metaphor to represent the looming disasters in our personal, social, global and local lives. By engaging in scenarios building and futures planning to bring about preferred futures for ourselves we can deal with any 'typhoon' that threatens to hit us.

We engage in futures not just for ourselves but for our communities, the country, and the world community at large. All four are subject to typhoons be it personal, structural, social, even spiritual. The late Tony Stevenson, former President of WFSF, who worked with us in the Philippines for several decades, frequently emphasised that 'futures is for everyone', meaning all must participate in creating better futures that will affect everyone. Stevenson believed that ordinary people can and do engage in futures work. He worked with a fishing community in Cauayan in Southern Negros Island who were trying to prevent illegal fishing on their coast. The problem was that the fishing community had to row their boats out into the sea to apprehend the illegal fishers who in turn had motors to run their boats. For the people of Cauayan illegal fishing was their typhoon. A futures solution for the community of Cauayan was to wait for the illegal fishers to cast their nets, thereby making them momentarily immobile. This allowed the fishing community to anticipate their raid and apprehend the illegal fishers out at sea.

According to John Paul Lederach, American Professor of Peacebuilding at Notre Dame University, there is an ethical component to peace. We happen to be in a web of relationships and this includes those whom we perceive to be our enemies. Christians, Lumads and Muslims co-exist in the same eco-systems, share the same sky and seas. They can also share the same futures. The world is truly complex, various cultures co-exist in the same communication space. Futures belong to the speakers, sharers, and the voiceless too. For communities to co-exist harmoniously and avoid social schism, despite cultural differences, all must have access to information and communication technologies that allow all to be heard. Peace futures require creative imagination, patience and hope. War must be transcended when it appears to be the only option. Finally, peace futurists must acknowledge the risks that accompany the act of choosing futures that transcend violence. Choosing peace futures is to take sides - the side of peace.

And it is not always easy. For the past five years in Sri Lanka, peace futures education has played a key role in making people rethink the war. I facilitated a meeting of Singhalese and Tamil religious leaders. It was a difficult first day just opening up reflective dialogue among the participants. Then came the second day and the issue of futures scenarios. Both parties realised that with one group winning the war, the conflict will continue as the very cultural and political structures rooted within the conflict will remain intact. The Norwegian futurists, sociologist and the principal founder of the discipline of peace and conflict studies, Johann Galtung, raised the question: what kind of a Sri Lanka can the participants envision that they were willing to live for? What possible confidence building joint projects can they start with that can begin to build trust, equity and harmony among the peoples of Sri Lanka? Galtung believes that futures peace work culminates through joint projects. Unfortunately, the participants were not yet ready to engage in even these basic, compelling and transforming questions.

The situation in Mindanao, the second largest island in the Philippines, is not much different. But here conflict sensitivity courses and workshops have enabled local communities to be sensitive to possible clashes that may affect their livelihoods and their lives. Our conflict sensitive lending workshops given to Land Bank officers, for example, allows them to anticipate possible and probable conflicts and ensure the safety of investments. Another example is water projects that were initially done to benefit mostly Christian communities at the exclusion of <u>Lumad</u> and Muslim communities that resulted in yet more conflict. Conflict sensitivity courses empowered the people there to develop projects that anticipated conflict. Conflict sensitivity can be likened to an eagle soaring through the sky. While working on projects on the ground it helps a lot to have the ability to see from above and see what lies ahead. But despite these peace initiatives war seems to always loom over the horizon in Mindanao.

No discussion of the problem of peace in Mindanao is possible without mentioning the siege of Marawi City. According to the Philippine government, the 'Battle for Marawi' began during an offensive intended to capture Isnilon Hapilon, the leader of the supposedly ISIL-affiliated Jihadi militant group Abu Sayyaf – unofficially known as the Islamic State of Iraq and the Levant Philippines Provence. Official reports suggest that the army moved in after receiving reports that Hapilon was in the city. He was allegedly there to meet with the militants of the Maute Group, a radical Islamist group composed of the former Moro Islamic Liberation Front guerrillas and the foreign fighters of Dawlah Islamiya, an Islamic state based in Lanao del sur. Other sources say that the battle in Marawi was about drugs; and Marawi was the drug capital of Mindanao and the Maute group was led by brothers from a notorious drug dealing clan. In any case, a deadly firefight erupted when Hapilon's forces opened fire on the combined Army and police teams on 23 May 2013. Maute militants attacked Camp Ranao and occupied several buildings, including Marawi City Hall, Mindanao State University, a hospital, and the city jail. They also occupied the main street and set fire to Saint Mary's Cathedral, Ninoy Aquino School and Dansalan College, run by the United Church of Christ in the Philippines (UCCP). The militants also took a priest and several churchgoers hostage. Their main objective was to raise an ISIL flag at the Lanao del Sur Provincial Capital and declare an 'wilayat' – an Islamic state – provincial ISIL territory in Lanao del Sur. The battle lasted five months. On 17 October 2017, the day after the deaths of militant leaders Omar Maute and Isnilon Hapilon, President Duterte declared Marawi was 'liberated from terrorist influence'.

The Marawi battle could have incited further divisions between Muslim and non-Muslims in the Philippines. But Filipino communities nationwide poured billions of pesos into helping the victims of Marawi and to rebuild the war-torn city. Aid started flooding into Marawi from other countries and international voluntary agencies. Tarpaulins bearing the message 'Marawi will rise again!' were displayed prominently in strategic areas in throughout Marawi. A futures plan was developed for the 'New Marawi': amongst its features are a museum, memorial park, fire station, police station, Grand Padian (market), a convention centre, a parking building, elementary and high schools, school of living tradition, hospital, inter-modal transport terminal, seaport, and a lakeside promenade to be built by the end of 2012. The construction of twenty-four barangay halls for each of the villages of the new Marawi is part of the plan. A city-wide sewage system is also in the works and cables for phone and power will be laid underground, a big improvement from what is the norm in other Filipino cities. The government and voluntary agencies charged with the rebuilding of Marawi have pledged that in any phase of the development Islamic and cultural sensitivities will be the foremost consideration. The government has also pledged regular consultation with all the stake holders of Marawi city. Some residents of Marawi have complained that everybody was consulted with regards to the future of Marawi except for the people of Marawi themselves. Nevertheless, what began as a tragedy may still be transformed into better futures not just for the survivors of Marawi and nearby towns but for the whole Philippines. A new Marawi, rooted in its culture, religion and tradition is waiting to be reborn.

All this was achieved through the participants of peace futurists and activists. However, not all our work is on a regional scale. Even small steps can have significant consequences. My friend and colleague, futurist George Aguilar, in his own little way, has engaged local and internationally renowned artists in the struggle against poverty and hunger. With the help of donors, he began building pushcarts for scavengers in Bacolod City. The first push cart was painted for free by local artist Charlie Co and his co-artist at the Orange Gallery in Bacolod City. The brightly painted push cart was envisioned to bring dignity to scavengers and to serve as a walking advocacy poster and a mobile art show for people on the streets. Soon, pushcart art became a trend.

My capacity building works in mainstreaming conflict sensitivity and transformation in Mindanao made me realise the importance of a joint project between the Philippine government and the Moro Islamic Liberation Front (MILF). The MILF's armed struggle started out as a defence mechanism for the Muslim people and for their religion and culture in Mindanao. It evolved into a fight for people's rights and welfare. Bringing the two sides together required monumental effort and decades of works; and ended with establishment of the BOL, officially called the

Organic Law for the Bangsamoro Autonomous Region in Muslim Mindanao (OLBARMIM). It is a new law that addresses the grievances, sentiments, and demands of Muslims in the region, and replaces the old corruption ridded legal arrangement. As Presidential Peace Adviser, Nabil Tan, notes, 'hopefully, the march towards peace will be achieved through the implementation of a Bangsamoro Organic Law (BOL)'. Tan pointed out that the landmark measure is a realisation of the Philippines commitment to honour all signed agreements between the national government and rebel organisations in accordance with the Philippine Constitution. The law, signed on 27 July 2018, will not be a 'panacea' to the problems in Mindanao but it is a big step in realising the vision of long-lasting peace and sustainable development for the island-region. Mohagher Iqbal, chair of the MILF peace implementing panel, is hopeful that a joint project for the enactment of the BOL will educate the Filipino people with regards to the historical roots of the peace problem in Mindanao. The first step is to recognise the identity of the Bangsamoro as a people and treat the BOL not just as a covenant for peace but also a covenant between one people to another.

Typhoons like Yolanda may ravage the land, but just as they come, they go, opening up new challenges, new futures. Marawi is now undergoing rehabilitation: it is reborn, a bright and prosperous city on the Filipino Island of Mindanao. The Bangsamoro Organic Law is already in place and will soon be enacted.

Peace futures demand moral imaginations, the competence to imagine ourselves in a web of relationships - including and involving even our adversaries. The power to reflectively embrace complexity, chaos and contradictions and their transcendence. It is faithful to the creative acts of bridging competing goals and crafting new realities. A willingness to take on the risk that goes with the work of transcending typhoons.

Born of deep prayers and sincere introspections, my wish is for reflective polylogue among parties to resume and communities to reconcile in peace. I will continue to pray and work with the people of Sri Lanka, may they craft inclusive futures among themselves and for their country. I will pray and work for an equitable and sustainable peace in Mindanao. I have woven the essence of peace into the fabric of myself for my futures is peace and peace is in my futures.

MY FUTURES LESSONS

Linda Hyokki

Ever since I remember, I have had a strong desire to be well organised. I like to keep track of events, important dates and significant developments of my life. Apart from sticking to a planner, I would also constantly be making plans regarding my studies, work, free-time, and everything in between. Importantly, I have always had a number of different plans at hand – a plan A, B, and C. Wherever my destiny takes me, I thought, my path will not be one-dimensional nor contain only one lane. I wanted to be prepared for the different outcomes and for the possible changes any (forced) diversions from my original plan would come my way. After all, my idea about the way life proceeds was not just me rowing the boat by myself but I acknowledged that there are also other forces at play that affect the course of things.

Thinking back now, I have realised that from my early youth I internalised the idea of multiple futures. There will always be more than one possible outcome for my endeavours. However, I never realised that you could actively work to shape a desirable future. Nor was I aware of futures studies. This despite the fact that I come from a country, Finland, that has one of the world's most famous futures institutions – the Finland Futures Research Center at University of Turku. Schools in Finland are regarded as some of the most successful in the world. This must have something to do, at least partly, with the fact that futures thinking is advocated in the Finnish schools through projects and futures-themed days. But I missed all that!

I began learning about futures only in my early 30s while children at home in Finland are raised to be aware of futures issues and methods. I had just started my PhD program in Civilisation Studies at the Institute of Alliance of Civilisation, Istanbul. I heard about a Summer School, organised annually by the International Institute of Islamic Thought (IIIT), held in Demirköy, a small town in the Kirklareli Province in the Marmara region of Turkey. I applied; and was accepted. A full day was devoted to futures studies on the programme. I remember thinking why on earth should we spend so much time discussing technology and sci-fi in a summer school that actually was focused on Islamic studies and Muslim societies. Classic mistake.

That day blew my mind. I learned about how change itself is changing, and interdisciplinary approaches to exploring and studying alternative futures. I got hands-on experience of analysing trends, recognising emerging issues. I must admit, I took to futures studies like a duck to water. Later on, I attended workshops on 'Futures Studies in Postnormal Times', organised by the Centre for Postnormal Policy and Futures Studies (CPPFS), a network of futurists and scholars who have pioneered the theory of postnormal times, and learned about backcasting, visioning and how to build scenarios. There was a great deal of emphasis in these workshops on polylogues – bringing in different disciplinary, cultural and religious perspectives in our analysis. The students combined their knowledge and expertise from religious studies to medicine, history, economics, IT, and cultural studies to explore and scrutinise the potential future impact of established trends and emerging issues both globally and in Muslim societies. In one workshop, we explored the futures of Syrian and Iraqi refugees in Turkey; this required some fieldwork and we established a small committee to visit the refugee camps and interview refugees. In another, we developed an inclusive and pluralistic vision for Turkey. I was hooked; and decided that I would incorporate futures in my own research on Muslim minorities and Islamophobia in Europe. Within a year my new academic path would lead me to become a Fellow of CPPFS.

Now that I give workshops myself, mostly to Muslim youth and young adults, my participants often ask me to first explain the benefits Muslims would have from gaining futures literacy. The fact that this question is repeatedly asked already suggests that there is a dire need of talking about futures studies. While the millennials of my generation are becoming aware of the need for critical thinking, they are totally unaware of the equally important need of futures thinking. While history plays an important part in their outlook, futures is conspicuous from its absence. Even when they think critically, they think critically only about the past; they have little or nothing to say about the future.

We humans tend to think about time in linear dimensions; the past, the present, and the future. Even language, its grammatical structure, affects the way we think about the possibilities of human action. When future is equated only with the *akhira*, the Hereafter, it is hardly surprising that our thoughts about the future hardly venture anywhere else! Members of my community, Muslims of Finland, speak of themselves only within the frames of the past and the present. Like most Muslim they tend to glorify and desire to relive the past – that is, the times of the Prophet or the magnificent eras of Al-Andalus or the Ottoman Empire. But the historical narrative of Muslims in Finland also includes the glories of the 'native Muslims' of Finland, the Tatars and their migration to the country. The Tatar Muslims arrived in Finland from Russia at the end of the nineteenth century. They fought with the Finnish troops against the Russian army during the Second World War. The discourse of Muslims as part of the Finnish society includes references to the Tatar's war efforts and political commitment to the country.

However, the discourse on the present situation of Finnish Muslims reflects the success of past generations. In Finland, similarly to other European localities, the discussion about Muslim residents is problem-oriented, focusing on the immigrant community with questions of integration and discrimination dominate the political and public debates and here, we are stuck in the evergreen narrative of the Tatar Muslims being those who were successful in integrating themselves is in Finland, which actually means their religiosity being non-visible and activism less rights-demanding than that of those with immigrant background.

However, this discourse does not address the current problems of the Muslim community let alone say something about their futures. Although the history of the Muslim community in Finland has determined the way in which, for instance, state-minority relations are governed nowadays, being stuck in history, , does not help the new generations of immigrant Muslims. The Tatars have their own peculiar way of identity construction between cultural, religious and national sense of belonging. However, the Finnish Muslim community has changed ethnically and now consists of very diverse groups. The young have the potential to shape the community into a cohesive entity that does not know sectarianism or intra-group racism. The new generation of immigrant Muslims, who have arrived over the last few decades, have stronger religious and cultural identities. They face, like immigrants elsewhere, problems of discrimination and Islamophobia, and they are active in demanding their rights. The rise of the far right in Finland has aggravated their problems; the questions of integration and prejudice dominate the political and public debate in Finland. The Muslims need to realise that the only way in which we may actually contribute and change the condition of our community is to focus on the future instead of the past or the present, both over which currently have no influence over the Finish political establishment.

The speed and the scope of change today is such that it leaves little space for thinking about such deep rooted inequalities. Finland itself is also going through rapid change; and some of these changes, such as those being initiated by the far right, may creep for a while and eventually transform Finnish society in unrecognisable ways. We need to think seriously about these changes and how they may shape Finnish society. This is where futures studies come to its own; futures literacy and tools can help navigate these changes and usher us towards more desirable change. It is imperative for us to take the step towards thinking about the consequences of our choices and those of the others. This is also necessary because of the simple fact that Muslims are just as much part of the society as everybody else – contrary to what others or even Muslims themselves might be think. Trends and emerging issues on societal, cultural, political, economic, religious, and technological developments touch the lives of Muslims just as much as they non-Muslims. I would even emphasise those societal developments that are directly connected to the lives of Muslims in a minority setting, such as legislations regarding governance of religion or shifts in values of the majority society that forces the Muslims to change their own paradigms as well.

The Muslim community in Finland suffers from three varieties of inequalities. The first is material inequity, such as lower socio-economic status of the Muslim population in comparison to other groups and communities in society. The second is structural related to legislation and institutional practices that allow discrimination and marginalisation of Muslims in our society. Finally, the third is related to knowledge inequality in the sense of an epistemological racism which leads to the suppression of intellectual and rational and agency of Muslims, a product of Eurocentric thinking, which frames Muslims as inferior outsiders. I often think about the Quranic verse 'Verily God does not change the condition of a people unless they change their state' (13:11), which reminds me of our responsibility to be an active part of our own destinies; I understand it as an obligation to not to get complacent in a minority setting creating parallel ghetto like structures and institutional practices and at the same time complaining about the discriminatory practices of the majority society. This is to say that Muslims need to engage as active citizens both the sake of the social cohesion as well as the coherence of their own Islamic identity.

I find the young Muslims very receptive to these ideas. It was well demonstrated during an introductory workshop on futures studies I gave in the winter of 2017. It was hosted by the Muslim Students Network in Finland. My aim was to introduce futures thinking to empower and mobilise the youth and to get them involved in building their own narratives about the future of the Muslim community in Finland. The focus of the workshop was on the challenges Finnish Muslim youth face as well as the local impact of global and regional changes in economics, culture, politics, religion, and technology. The participants were keen to explore trends and emerging issues of all varieties – many the elder generation would probably shun. We discussed how the issue of gender-neutrality will affect Muslim communities and what would they have to do to adjust to societal changes that may emerge, the consequences of microchips in humans and how they might impact the Muslim community if they are used for surveillance, and the role of religious education in schools which has always been separated for various congregations but the trend now being, through a curriculum reform, more and more towards common classes for all.. The group also drafted a Finland 2040 vision and produced a workable plan using back-casting. We discussed the values, actions and structures that may support the group's preferred vision of futures; for instance, promoting a good environmental conscience, sustainable housing and financial services, strengthening of social solidarity among Muslims and non-Muslims, as well as building a stable Finnish Muslim identity. The lesson I learned from the workshop experience is that futures is a significant tool for providing agency to the youth, they need to voice their aspirations and desires, articulate their visions and build strategies that can usher an inclusive and dynamic futures both for Muslim communities as well as Finish society as a whole.

So, it seems to me, the millennials are keen to embrace futures literacy and consciousness. Unlike the elder generation, they seem, at least in Finland, not to be trapped in nostalgic history. The young need access and opportunities, the kind provided to me first by the IIIT Summer School and then the CPPFS workshops. Indeed, I would argue that futures literacy should be an integral part of secondary school in all Muslim societies.

The characteristics of postnormal times are indeed testing the identities of those who define themselves as Muslims. Questions of epistemology, ethics and the foundations of our worldview are at play when Muslims are required to rethink their stances on issues that (do not necessarily) emerge from within their own community but could have a profound impact on them – such as LGBTQ+ rights, climate change, bioengineering, cybercrime and Artificial Intelligence (AI). A futures approach facilitates the opening of horizons where a plurality of alternatives can be explored, when we may consider different aspects of outcomes and actors at play, decide what futures we prefer and what futures are actually colonising all our futures. The essence of everything is in futures studies', especially when approached from a de-colonial perspective, is that it offers the ability and space for us Muslims to create our own narratives about the future(s).

But we should remember that there is, and cannot be, such as thing as a single Muslim futures narrative. Futures is all about plurality. The very meaning of polylogue is to include a variety of voices and perspectives for this generates new understanding, an integrated knowledge, that we would otherwise miss. Futures studies is a participatory exercise; it involves all of us as it is about all our futures. But I must also emphasise another lesson that I have learned: *the* future is actually very easily pre-programmed to reflect old colonial structures and hierarchies, both economic and mental. Thus, we should not lose sight when we discuss what we know and what we wish for. As the grand dame of futures studies, Eleanora Barbieri Massini, notes, the way in which we think about the future is always related to our values, to our choices, to our basic principles, which alternate depending on generation, culture and experiences. Hence, even though normativity might be a lost concept in postnormal times, the plurality of futures is what enables us to include narratives of futures that consider our epistemological fundamentals, and prevent us from creating our own Frankenstein's monsters, and finally to acknowledge, that absolute Truth belongs only to God. It is all about navigating our way to balanced and preferable futures.

CRYPTOCURRENCY AND THE ISLAMIC ECONOMY

Harris Irfan

When David Cameron stepped onto the stage at the World Islamic Economic Forum in 2013 to announce the United Kingdom would be the first western sovereign state to issue an Islamic bond, the mainstream press scrambled to understand more about the mysterious world of Islamic finance. 'Cameron unveils plan to make London a Mecca for Middle East wealth', whooped the Independent, whilst the ever-opportunistic Boris Johnson grabbed his moment to share the limelight by welcoming the Islamic petrodollar to our shores.

Inwardly I sighed. Oh sure, the sovereign sukuk, or Islamic bond, was a headline financial instrument, and its issuance by a western government was a milestone in enhancing the credibility of the UK's Islamic finance industry in global financial markets. I should be – and I was – proud that the City of London was the envy of the world in creating a regulatory environment to allow this form of alternative ethical finance to flourish, and proud also that I lived in a country where I am free to practise my faith.

But what if all that really mattered was a photo opportunity for politicians to entice the richest people in the world to a city where the contrast between the wealthiest and the most deprived could be no more horrifically illustrated than the loss of 72 souls in the Grenfell Tower fire? Has inequality in one of the world's most affluent countries reached the point that a few pounds per piece of fire-proof cladding to prevent loss of life was deemed uneconomical?

If the Islamic banking industry was serving the richest in society, financing the voracious acquisition plans of private equity firms and the purchase of 'super-prime' luxury apartments for high net worth families, then it had lost its way. What once had been intended as a model for wealth distribution across society, for empowerment of communities, financial inclusion and the creation of jobs in the real economy, was now just another sophisticated tool for enriching a plutocracy.

I suppose I sound like an impotently raging socialist, but I wear the pinstripes of a different tribe. An investment banker by trade, and a Muslim by creed, my definition of capitalism is not the one that has come to dominate the world economy since 1914. Far removed from being the economic system that unleashed conspicuous consumption over the past century, for me capitalism is an ideal based on capital accumulation from savings and investments, an economic system that incentivises people to drop their preference for immediate gratification and instead invest in the future. A system in which the 'real economy' (characterised by the production of real goods and services) has a direct one-to-one correlation with what is known as the 'financial economy' - the one in which shares, bonds and other financial instruments are listed and traded on exchanges, each traded piece of paper having some relationship with an underlying company or asset in the real economy.

In contrast, today's financial economy is worth many multiples of the real economy, as 'financialisation' of the economy has led to the creation of increasingly dubious – and often socially useless - financial instruments. One doesn't need to open Marxist pamphlets to read these views; establishment figures like the former governor of the Bank of England, Mervyn King, and the former head of the UK's financial regulator, Lord Adair Turner, have been forthright in their condemnation of modern financial practices.

Islamic finance in its contemporary form traces its theoretical roots to the development of an economic model from the early history of Islam, and the financial tools that emerged from that model. The second caliph, Umar ibn al-Khattab (c. 584–644), instituted the *Bayt al-Mal*, the Central Treasury, a state-run financial institution responsible for the administration of alms, including the distribution of *zakat*. Umar's vision of a compassionate society was derived from the traditions of the Prophet, centred on the protection of the weak and the vulnerable, and led to the establishment of this institution. The Central Treasury dispensed a welfare programme to ensure equality and a basic standard of living for all citizens, thus ensuring systematic provision for widows, orphans, the infirm, the unemployed and the elderly.

Umar also introduced the concept of public trusteeship and public ownership through the charitable trust (*waqf*), a legal form of social collective ownership that allowed public property to generate an income stream for the benefit of the needy. By the thirteenth century, the concept of *waqf* had been imported into England, as evidenced by the statutes of endowment of Merton College, one of the earliest colleges of the University of Oxford. The endowment appears to be a direct translation from the original Arabic of statutes found in the Islamic world at the time, and the *waqf* survived and evolved into contemporary English trust law. (If you are feeling mischievous, feel free to write to the *Daily Mail* and let them know that insidious, creeping Shari'a is already part of English law.)

And thus through this institutional framework, the basic principles of social advancement were in place during the early days of Islam. Whilst individual property rights were protected and entrepreneurship encouraged, the framework was a conduit for the fair distribution of wealth, rather than the accumulation of wealth by a ruling class. The conversion of contractual principles into widespread commercial tools took shape through, for example, the work of the founder of the Hanafi School of Jurisprudence, Imam Abu Hanifah (699–767), and his followers. The subsequent codification of commercial law led to the development of a widespread money economy, with gold and silver eventually giving way to paper notes during the Ottoman empire. Cheques, letters of credit and the money transfer system became essential lubricants of the Islamic world's economy, travelling thousands of miles down the Silk Route. The economic wellbeing of the Islamic world created space for scholarship to flourish, for scientific and cultural progress, and ultimately for peace to reign.

Silks and spices were not the only imports into Southern Europe. The import of scientific advancements, commercial tools and entrepreneurial skills led Europe out of its Dark Ages, and to the creation of their own financial institutions. But without the structure of a divinely ordained economic system, Shari'a compliant financial tools eventually gave way to interest-based European practices (the Church gradually relaxing its aversion to usury), and these institutions asserted their dominance for many centuries.

It was not until the mid-twentieth century that Islamic finance would rediscover itself, perhaps as a consequence of Muslim-majority nations seeking to assert their postcolonial identities. At first, it was experimental in nature. In 1963 in the town of Mit Ghamr in Egypt, a profit-sharing institution was founded that neither charged nor paid interest, and engaged in what today would be referred to as real economy transactions, investing in local trade and industry, sharing profits with depositors, functioning less as a commercial bank and more as a vehicle for savings and investments. Think of a Shari'a-compliant version of Jimmy Stewart's charming Building and Loan institution from *It's a Wonderful Life*, and you get the picture. The model was exported to other Arab nations, until by 1975, the first multilateral Islamic development bank was created in Saudi Arabia, and the first regulated private sector Islamic bank in the UAE.

These early banks built on the concept of the investor/manager relationship in which a provider of capital entrusts that capital to a specialist for the purpose of investment, with both parties sharing in the ensuing profits or losses. However, as the business model matured, the industry increasingly began to mimic the practices and operations of conventional banks, driven in part by the success of the 'Islamic windows' of conventional international banks.

As the market potential became apparent in the early 2000s, the international banks suspected the domestic incumbents were laid back and vulnerable, easy pickings from whom to steal market share. And so my then employer, Deutsche Bank, posted me, a junior lieutenant, to a far off frontier outpost to survey the land and report back. In the newly formed Dubai International Financial Centre, a financial free-zone in a patch of desert one mile squared, I learnt at the feet of the Shari'a scholars, understanding how modern finance could meld with *fiqh al mu'amalat*, the jurisprudence of transactions. My team and I invented financial instruments that no-one had previously thought to offer Islamic investors, all the while believing that by bringing Shari'a compliance to the full range of financial services, we would be returning the Islamic world to the roots of ethical merchant capitalism as had once been practised in its Golden Age.

How wrong we were. As each international investment bank cottoned on to this new market and began copying our products, Islamic finance turned into a race to the bottom. Spivvy sales teams realised that generic fatwas, the legal opinions issued by Shari'a scholars to certify a financial product as being permissible, were a licence to print money. Off the back of these opinions, new products were 'reverse engineered' from their conventional equivalents until, like the pigs in Orwell's *Animal Farm*, they became indistinguishable from their predecessors.

By the time the global financial crisis hit the markets in 2007/08, Islamic finance had missed its opportunity to demonstrate how robust and beneficial it could be in an economic crisis, and the international banks retrenched to focus on bigger problems at hand. Ever since then, Islamic finance has meandered without vigour or purpose.

So what really went wrong?

It wasn't just that the international banks were opportunistic and fickle, there was something more fundamental at work. It boiled down to the nature of money itself. For as long as the boards and senior management of Islamic banks continue to have a limited understanding of why the Islamic economic model is fundamentally opposed to a modern neoliberal economic model, the Islamic banking industry will neither truly innovate, nor connect with the values and culture of its target demographic.

What is it about the nature of money that most Islamic bankers are still struggling to understand? To those trained in the dark arts of conventional interest-based banking, the notion that money is merely a medium of exchange, a store of value and a unit of account, is entirely alien. If money were considered merely a means to acquire 'real' goods and services, and not to be traded as a commodity itself, then bankers would not be able to increase the value of their assets merely by charging interest on money they lend. As the classical theologian, Imam al Ghazali (1058–1111), had noted several centuries earlier:

> Allah created dirhams and dinars so that they may be circulated between hands and act as a fair judge between different commodities and work as a medium to acquire other things...It becomes easy for [the financier] to earn more money on the basis of interest without bothering himself to take pains in real economic activities.....The interests of humanity cannot be safeguarded without real trade skills, industry and construction.

Ghazali had predicted the rise of financialisation of the economy and the socially useless banker. Transplant those same bankers into Islamic banks and the mindset of money as a tradable commodity persists. Islamic banks become another means to extract returns merely from the act of owning money, through the alchemy of the fractional reserve banking system: the same system which allows private sector banks to lend out more than is deposited, thus creating and circulating new money in the economy.

Governments through their central banks also create new money through the act of printing more notes. As more and more are printed, the dollars and pounds held by the general public decline in value, and they must earn more to pay for the same goods and services. We call this inflation. The government and the banks who create new money are the first recipients of this new money, and can spend it first, before prices rise. The next recipients find prices are a little higher and so on down the chain, until the poorest at the end of the chain experience the greatest reduction in their purchasing power. Whilst the rich can afford to lend out their surplus money and charge interest, the poor find it harder and harder to keep their heads above water, and inequality rises.

This inequality has been exacerbated in recent years through the phenomenon of quantitative easing, often known simply as QE. Post the financial crisis, many central banks acted to boost the economy by creating digital money (the digital equivalent of printing it) and then using it to buy government debt in the form of bonds. This debt repurchase allows the seller of those bonds (say a pension fund) to purchase other assets, like shares in companies. The prices of those other assets will consequently rise, making the holders of the assets wealthier and more likely to spend, thus boosting the economy.

It sounds too good to be true, and it was. By August 2016, the Bank of England's QE programme had repurchased £435 billion of bonds. In the US, the Fed increased the money supply by an incredible $4 trillion since the financial crisis, flooding financial institutions with capital and allowing them to hold onto much of that money as excess reserves. Who benefited? The financial institutions and their richest clients.

When a currency devalues – often to allow a government to finance war – investment in science, technology, arts, literature, healthcare, literacy and our environment declines. As inequality increases, so does societal unrest. Nativism and populism rises, trade barriers and physical barriers are erected, and the inevitable result is more conflict and more war. The twentieth century was the bloodiest century in human history and it is no mere coincidence that the US dollar devalued 96% in real terms over the course of the century. In 1914, the world's major economies rejected the gold standard and replaced it with unsound 'fiat' currency – that is, currency decreed to be legal tender by a government. The subsequent financing of mechanised warfare took place on a scale never seen before.

This economic dogma of printing and spending persists despite 5,000 years of human history manifestly showing that empires and civilisations decline and eventually fall from the moment the ruler starts to clip his own currency. Vast swathes of economic history have been wiped from the syllabus of today's university economics departments and MBA schools. The neoliberal religion of printing and spending, the financialisation of the economy, the creation of more debt instruments and more financial services only serves to reinforce and celebrate the large corporations that fund these schools. The net result is a divided and unequal world, one that exists as a market society, a joyless place that measures exchange value and not experiential value.

Are we too late? Can a return to a sound monetary system become the basis for an ethical form of capitalism that allows prices to be determined by the market, whilst protecting the general public and the most vulnerable in society? Or have I gone mad, a banker in the late *'asr* of his career, rueing the choices he has made, and desperately clinging to some unrealisable ideal in the hope of redeeming himself?

Cryptocurrency as 'sound' money

I think there may be a solution. I believe it's the most Islamic form of money I've seen but it hasn't come from the world of Islamic finance. It's a genius piece of technology called cryptocurrency, and if it survives beyond its current infancy, I believe it has the power to change the world for the better.

Cryptocurrency is a little tricky to get one's head around, and it's easy to become distracted by peripheral discussions about rampant speculation, families selling their worldly possessions to buy it, high profile thefts of it from poorly secured exchanges, and outright scams. Just like any frontier, it attracts its fair share of weirdos and bandits. But let's focus on the basics for now.

Cryptocurrency is a digital or virtual currency that is electronically encrypted for security. It can be used for secure payments of online transactions. It is not issued by a central bank and it exists in cyberspace, just as the money in our bank accounts today exists as digits on a computer. Except in contrast to the money we use today in the form of pounds and dollars, the rules of creation, or algorithm, of a given cryptocurrency is known in advance and it is decentralised by virtue of the fact it exists potentially on millions of computers around the world, and thus cannot be manipulated (printed) by a central body. Bitcoin is the first cryptocurrency based on a technology called blockchain, and was created ten years ago.

Blockchain is an online ledger of all transactions that have ever been conducted using Bitcoin, and this ledger is distributed simultaneously across a vast network of computers worldwide, thus ensuring all transactions must be verified by a 'trustless' network of ledgers, and therefore severely negating the threat from hacking and forgery.

New Bitcoin can only be created by solving the algorithm, a process that involves massive computing power, and akin therefore to mining. As more Bitcoin are mined, each subsequent creation of new coins becomes harder and harder, just like mining finite gold reserves. Today, 17 million Bitcoin have been mined and the theoretical limit according to its algorithm is 21 million. There's much more to say, but let's start from here.

In my view, Bitcoin has the capability to become the soundest form of money in existence. Sound money is sometimes referred to as hard money. It is a store of value that does not deteriorate. Its supply is hard to increase because it is not easy to produce. Sound money has 'salability', meaning the ease with which it can be sold in the market and exchanged for goods and services. Sound money is freely chosen by the market as its currency of choice, and is under control of its owner, safe from meddling such as devaluation by an external party.

As you might have guessed, the soundest money that has ever existed to date is gold. It is hard to produce and chemically robust, and is thus stable over a long period of time. It cannot be printed, and in order to produce more of it, great efforts must be made to mine it. Gold stockpiles grow at only 1.5 per cent per annum. But it is impractical today as a global currency: it is difficult to transport, and central banks have taken much of it into their possession, making it possible for them to increase the supply of money beyond the amount of gold they hold and thus devaluing the paper money once purporting to be gold-backed. Part of the value of money has therefore been transferred from the money's legitimate holders (the general public) to governments and banks.

Human history has shown us that when a ruler chooses an unsound money or one whose supply is easy to increase, or decides to clip an otherwise sound currency like the gold coin, the value of money falls and reduces the real wages of workers. Governments now have access to increased money supply for financing other expenditure, often imprudently, and especially for war. In Rome, for example, from the point at which Emperor Nero clipped the aureus, the Roman Empire began to experience a downward spiral. Increased inflation as a result of clipping, as well as taxation to compensate for unworkable price controls, led to the exodus of urbanites to rural self-subsistence. What had once been long term prosperity throughout the Empire gradually transformed into rioting, corruption and lawlessness, and a transition to serfdom under feudal landlords.

In contrast, whenever a government has maintained gold as its currency, without clipping or expropriation, trade and economic stability is the result, and civilisations are afforded the luxury of advancing human knowledge. Look to the Roman Empire before Nero under the aureus, Islam's Golden Age under the Islamic dinar, and Byzantium under the solidus.

In more recent times, prior to 1914, the world experienced an unprecedented global accumulation of wealth and trade under one sound money, gold. But 1914 was the beginning of the era of fiat, or government, money. Some commentators argue that the scale of World War I was only possible because of the suspension of the gold standard. With the suspension of the ability of the people to redeem their paper notes for gold held by banks, war expenditure was no longer limited to the treasure chest of governments, but to the entire wealth of the population. Conflict would no longer be limited to brief, defined periods, but until the whole nation's accumulated wealth was exhausted by stealth taxation through devaluation.

Indeed, from 1971, when the process was completed to transform the world economy from a global gold standard to one based on several fiat currencies (with the US dollar as the world's reserve currency), the floodgates were opened to a massive increase in the supply of the dollar.

The United States could now purchase whatever it wanted from the world, financed by debt made affordable to it by inflating the very reserve currency the entire world was bound to. And accordingly we see the rise of the military-industrial complex: unsound money has allowed corporations engaged in the business of war to grow to such an extent that they influence MBA schools, economics faculties, the media and lobby groups to advocate artfully for an endless series of wars under flimsy pretexts, with the unhinged justification that war is good for the economy. At the same time we continue to vote in politicians who tell us we can turn our homes into ATM machines by refinancing to afford luxury cars and second homes.

At this point, I guess I may have lost some of you who think I really have gone mad. Not content with decrying an unsound monetary system, I'm now suggesting modern democracy is a mass delusion. By nationalising money, we place it in the control of politicians who exist for just one election cycle. Unsound money allows those politicians to buy votes by facilitating immediate gratification through programmes like QE: spend now and let future generations pay, by which point the destruction in the value of money can be blamed on someone else. A free lunch, in other words. This makes government power potentially unlimited, let alone heavily interventionist. And all the while, inflation forces the public into short term behaviours, becoming present-orientated in their decision making. Is it any wonder that today we see the rise of Trump and Brexit?

Is cryptocurrency Shari'a compliant?

If we are to reverse this polarisation of the world, this manifest decline in equality, and an increase in war and climate change, the single most important change we must make is a return to a sound monetary system. Cryptocurrency, and especially Bitcoin, presents us with a possible solution. But does it sit well with the Islamic economic model and what do our scholars think?

Their recent form is not particularly auspicious. When in the early nineteenth century the Ottoman governor of Egypt, Mehmet Ali Pasha, introduced water faucets at the Mehmet Ali Mosque in Cairo, the Egyptian *ulema* debated whether this new fangled contraption was permissible in performing one's ablutions before the prayer. The only scholars who ruled this innocent fixture to be permissible were from the Hanafi school, and hence taps came to be known as *hanafiyah* in much of the Arab world.

For centuries, the use of the printing press by Muslims in the Ottoman Empire was banned on penalty of death, perhaps partly because this form of mass communication clashed with the scholarly oral tradition of information dissemination. The first printing press in Istanbul allowed by Sultan Ahmet III in 1727 aroused so much suspicion from Ottoman scholars that it was subsequently shut down. Perhaps this suicidal willingness to embrace ignorance was a contributory factor in the inevitable decline of the Ottoman Empire.

In the nineteenth century, the *'ulema* debated the minimum distance a telegraph wire could be sited near a mosque, concerned, they reasoned, that it conveyed the voice of Satan. In the early twentieth century, Deobandi scholars banned the loudspeaker. In the 1980s, South African *'ulema* banned the television (irrespective of its content), and even suggested Mufti Taqi Usmani's defence of television was akin to defending the consumption of alcohol.

Now we look back on these debates with detached amusement. Obviously our scholars couldn't possibly make such mistakes today. They are much more sophisticated, in touch with their flock, connected by social media, tech savvy and scientifically aware, right? Well, not if you've been following the recent debate on cryptocurrency and Shari'a. For many scholars, Bitcoin and other cryptocurrencies represent rampant, unfettered speculation, a worthless intangible bubble, the worst excesses of modern capitalism.

Over the past year, we've seen scholars as famous as Egypt's Grand Mufti, Shaikh Shawki Allam, issue a fatwa ruling against the trading of Bitcoin, supporting an earlier ban by the Egyptian government. He claimed to have met with economic experts prior to his ruling (though it is unclear who these were). Government-appointed economists are almost always of the orthodox neoliberal flavour, what I refer to as the priests of fiat money. Any economist brought up on the twentieth century dogma of alleged 'free' markets fears a type of currency that robs them of their raison d'être, and denies their employers (the government) of financial control of the people.

The Grand Mufti's stated reasons for the ban on cryptocurrency were deeply illogical: he said it allowed for money laundering, fraud and the financing of terrorists, conveniently ignoring that the most prevalent currency in money laundering, fraud and terrorism is the US dollar.

He also said cryptocurrency has no set rules, making it a void contract, conveniently ignoring the fact that fiat currency – decreed to be legal tender by a government – has no set rules either. Rather, the public place their trust in the declared currency being honoured in the exchange of real goods and services. Certainly in the United Kingdom, Her Majesty's Treasury does not issue me with a rule book on using a ten pound note. That's how currency works: through public faith and concurrence that it will be readily accepted. In the case of fiat currency, the Bank of England can decide to reduce the value of the ten pounds sitting in my pocket by unilaterally printing more notes, thus failing to honour a moral obligation to me, introducing what Shari'a scholars call *gharar* (uncertainty), and thus effectively voiding any contract between us (if such a thing actually existed). In fact, over the course of the twentieth century, so extreme has been the devaluation of fiat currency by central banks that if I held USD100 at the start of the century, by the end it would be worth only USD4 in real terms. In the same period, by contrast, US equity markets rose 70,950 per cent in real terms. Now how stable does the world's most powerful reserve currency seem to you?

Very few of us see this as a form of taxation because we don't calculate it in our year-end returns. So if the eminent Grand Mufti wanted to ban Bitcoin for being a void contract due to its alleged uncertainty, he would have to ban the entire world's fiat currencies for that very reason.

He is not alone in his views. I have examined detailed fatwas from other scholars, many of the social media variety, with little to no understanding of modern financial markets or the monetary system, nor it would seem any knowledge of what classical *fiqh al mu'amalat* has to say on the subject. These scholars say:

> that money is created by central banks and governments (it is not – 97% is created by private sector banks through lending);

that governments give an undertaking to replace fiat money by something 'real' if requested (not true – even the Bank of England says so on its own website);

that cryptocurrencies are not "real" (which reveals a misunderstanding of the role of money as a medium of exchange, store of value and unit of account, and often mistakenly assumes that Islamic money must *de jure* be backed by gold – in fact Shari'a does not require this);

that the rules of cryptocurrency are subject to change at any time (wrong, especially in the case of Bitcoin, since once the algorithm has been coded, only a majority of users in the universe of Bitcoin may agree to change the code, and thus the rules are effectively set in stone for all time henceforth);

that cryptocurrencies are too volatile to be a currency (and here I may concede that volatility is a natural consequence of their early phase of development, but once substantially mined, that volatility will inevitably become trivial).

I have elsewhere set out my opposition to scholars who declare cryptocurrency to be *haram*. I will not repeat the argument in detail here, other than to say that in the majority of cases, these scholars have lacked a sufficiently basic understanding of the global monetary system to allow them to opine on such a technical matter. I have read and listened to rambling diatribes revealing an embarrassing confusion in matters of commerce, finance, economics and technology. Indeed, so extraordinarily misinformed are their views that they risk causing serious harm to the Muslim ummah, just as their forebears did in relation to advancements like the printing press.

In all of these misinformed pronouncements, scholars have failed to make the link between the soundness of gold and that of Bitcoin: both are inflation proof, decentralised, divisible, scarce and finite. Bitcoin has several additional qualities that gold doesn't have, like utility as a currency (exponentially improving all the time), anonymity, speed of transfer, non-counterfeitable through the genius of the distributed ledger, more resistant to theft (if stored correctly), open source and durable. In short, it is Gold 2.0. Incidentally, fiat currencies have none of these characteristics, other than they are accepted as currencies. But that's like saying the horse is a mode of transport just like the jet airplane - another innovation the scholars once tried to ban.

So if Bitcoin has all the qualities of gold and more, does that not give it intrinsic value that the scholars seek? Or have we already decided, like the banning of the printing press, that any new technology that improves on an older one must by necessity be the work of the Devil and we need not do any further research on it?

Bitcoin cannot be printed, it cannot be created from thin air, it is finitely bound by its algorithm and secured by the blockchain, and, most importantly from the perspective of eradicating the curse of *riba* (interest), it severely curtails the power of the banks. Imagine hypothetically a world in which the only currency is Bitcoin. Since the banks cannot create Bitcoin (they would have to mine it or earn it), they cannot issue new Bitcoin to borrowers. And presto: their function becomes primarily one of safe custody, rather than creation of new money in the form of loans. The national debt of governments worldwide and consumer borrowing levels have reached crisis proportions. Bitcoin may help us to deleverage the world economy; it could be a driver in minimising the endemic oppression of *riba*. Isn't that what the Islamic banking industry was meant to achieve?

The Shari'a does not prefer tyranny and injustice to equality and social inclusion. If the monetary policies of governments in recent history have led to an increase in inequality, war and climate change, a solution that benefits the public interest (*istislah*) that accords with Shari'a notions of money must surely be worthy of consideration.

I am heartened to note a small handful of scholars – those expertly qualified in *fiqh al mu'amalat* as well as banking law, finance and economics – have begun to offer a more considered and competent assessment of this new technology. I have explored this at length elsewhere and so will not repeat in detail, other than to point out that cryptocurrencies like Bitcoin may be considered to have the characteristics of *maal* (wealth) since they have desirability as a decentralised independent monetary system, and storability, as well as *taqawwum* (legal value) since it is storable through the distributed ledger.

There may be some legitimate debate as to whether Bitcoin also possesses *thamaniyyah* (currency attributes). However increasingly, many scholars with expertise in the field are starting to conclude that as Bitcoin gains *ta'amul* (wide usage) and *istilah* (social concurrence), it takes on currency attributes and becomes a medium of exchange. Indeed, some say Bitcoin already has *istilah* since it was established as a peer to peer payment system and therefore established and used as currency from the outset. And it is this social concurrence that may be sufficient to establish Bitcoin and other cryptocurrencies as a currency in Shari'a.

FinTech as the future

We are at the same stage in the evolution of cryptocurrencies that the internet was in the early 1990s. Some could see no future or practical application for the web. It was clunky, slow, inefficient and expensive. Now it is ubiquitous and we cannot live without it.

You may be a traditionalist who feels that governments have our best interests at heart and that centralised monetary control is an absolute necessity. I know it will be hard for me to convince you otherwise, because this has become received wisdom over the past century. In my view, ceding control of the money supply to governments and banks cedes the freedom of the people. We don't need to look further back than 2008 to know that giving governments responsibility for monetary stability has historically been a disaster. In the developed world, the 1% are now even richer and yet skilled and essential public sector workers like nurses are feeding their children from food banks.

A land grab is currently taking place, perhaps the greatest transfer of wealth in human history. When the nebulae disperse and the galaxies in this new universe coalesce, who will be left with power and influence, and who will be destitute and bereft? Whilst non-Muslims develop an independent decentralised monetary system that in the process has the potential to erase the curse of fractional reserve banking and *riba*, the Muslim ummah stands by idly waiting on our scholars, surrendering our intellect and decision making skills to dogma and ignorance.

Failing to adapt to the world around us represents an existential threat. A blanket rejection of new technologies by the *'ulema* has kept the ummah in ignorance and poverty since the passing of the great scholars of Baghdad and Cordoba.

The Islamic banking industry has not delivered the economic model it once promised, but the Islamic economic model is much greater than that. I left the world of banking a year ago to work with young, tech-savvy entrepreneurial Muslims who are discovering solutions to financial problems using technology – so called 'fintech' solutions – without the need for banks to act as intermediaries. Their computer science degrees have become much more valuable than the false models preached by today's economics curriculum. Cryptocurrency is one of those fintech solutions, but so also are online peer to peer crowdfunding platforms, or tech-based microfinancing of rural communities in the world's poorest countries, or blockchain-based apps that allow philanthropists to trace their charitable payments via charities and relief agencies to end recipients.

The early pioneers of the modern Islamic banking industry had noble ideals in mind but the industry can't see beyond its conventional mindset. Now we have an opportunity to retake the initiative. Just as the Golden Age of Islam borrowed science, technology and mathematics from neighbouring civilisations, so we should once again embrace what we find good in the world beyond our own horizons. Cryptocurrency has arisen from the need to take back control and place it in the hands of the people for the general good. If an economic system is for the benefit of all, then cryptocurrency gives us real, decentralised power, democracy at its purest. Closing the equality gap leads to a less polarised world, fewer barriers and conflicts, and a greater ability to invest in society and our environment. It's not too late to save ourselves and the planet.

AFROFUTURISM
IN POSTNORMAL TIMES

C Scott Jordan

Did you hear that?

Perhaps just the residual flutters of presbycusis.

First, we are shown a couple eerie production title cards reminding us, the audience, that we have bought tickets for what is indeed a horror film. Raucous, then silence. Then to blackness. A hard cut into a cold open. The suburbs. A man wonders through the all-too-normal neighbourhood. He is lost. He is also black. He shuffles in fright. This is a contrasted mirror of the innocent white person lost in the rundown 'hood,' a jungle of low income urban decay, haunted by the ever suspicious other. In place of the abandoned shell, green lawns, cookie-cutter family homes, the inviting glow of illuminated street lights.

Adding to our black hero's terror, a car passes playing loudly from its radio a nostalgic classic. The song is Flanagan and Allen's *Run Rabbit Run*. The song is that upbeat barbershop quartet style foot tapping music that provided the soundtrack to a simpler time, the good old times, of course before the troubles of desegregation, homosexuality, and drugs. After a little game of stalker, the car stops, its door opening as the music roars louder, run rabbit, run, run, run...

And then a masked man, our hero subdued, and the slamming of the boot as the cue to cut to:

Rapid fire fiddling, sharp cuts, a scratching, which returns uncomfortably too soon. The screeching tunes and tempo that solidifies any doubt you had that you are in fact in a horror film. Suddenly, we are of the perspective of driving through a wooded timber and credits flash upon the screen. The classic New England woods of American horror. The fiddles cease as a more traditional tasting song crescendos. The lyrics may at first sound like sung English, but quickly spoils the ear to it being different. The song is Swahili. The song is also equal parts ritualistically dance-like and prelude warning to a cautionary folktale. The lyrics roughly translate to meaning 'Listen to your ancestors, Run!'

Half a frame of pitch black accompanied by a breathless pause, cut to:

The everyday struggle of life in America. Except the subject of this photographic art collection are African Americans somewhere between living and surviving in the contemporary world. The music drastically transforms from classic horror-shop to smooth and catchy. Childish Gambino's *Redbone*, while also being a sort of anthem of the times, is the contemporary hit that brings us from Suburban white wash into the real, normal world of our hero, Chris, who is packing to meet the parents of his white girlfriend. Childish Gambino warns our hero to 'Stay Woke,' as ignorance and uncertainty cloud his nerves like a realistic dream.

Through music Jordan Peele has thrust us forth into his first feature. *Get Out*. From its use of popular music to the blending of the Swahili song's motif into the score, even to the taping of a spoon upon a tea cup, Peele creates a beautiful work of art through his use, and even absence, of sound. The power of filmmaking as art lies in its not simply being a visual medium, but in that its use of sight and sound allow for us, the audience, to see what cannot otherwise be seen. To hear what no one is listening to. Peele's talent with this craft and brilliant play on parody brings the uniquely black viewpoint to the forefront of the minds of those with other worldviews.

This power, building off of humanities inherent sociality, is the object of the same game played by Afrofuturism. More specifically put, Afrofuturism is the attempt to portray the struggle of black Americans, potentially all minority and disparaged communities, so that the other may see it for themselves. The question we will later address is whether or not the harnessing of this ability can translate into tangible change either through policy or social upheaval. In the spirit of the colloquial conceptualisation of the future, it would only make sense that this is most prominently seen in the genre of science fiction, but it should not be so quickly pigeonholed into being only that of pulp sci-fi. Even Peele's *Get Out* can be seen as a work of Afrofuturism and perhaps one of its greatest contributions for the effect it triggered.

Like a film, Afrofuturism itself began in sound - music. To this day, it still remains a staple of many black musicians, even if not as overt as in the case of Sun Ra. Afrofuturism dates back as old as the issue of race itself amongst the African diaspora, but was first coined and seriously discussed by Mark Dery in 1994. Mark Sinker was also credited with investigating the phenomenon in Britain through various articles written for *The Wire*. In his article 'Black to the Future,' Dery wonders as to why more African American writers have not chosen to embrace the science fiction genre especially since it is the ideal medium for discussing slavery, alienation, and xenophobia. Dery interviews one such writer, Samuel Delaney, a cultural critic, Greg Tate, and an academic, Tricia Rose. to begin this dialogue. Essentially, there simply is not a large number of black writers, let alone those who look to the universe of science fiction to create their art. The article does not come to any group breaking conclusion, but it does get the ball rolling and, whether intended or not, illuminates a potential within popular culture.

The idea behind Afrofuturism is that it could provide the general public with the epistemologically reflective exposé of the plight of contemporary African Americans on the public opinion-altering level of Upton Sinclair's *The Jungle* or Woodward and Bernstein's Watergate reporting. Yet, Sun Ra and George Clinton led the way for a blend of technology and African tradition in their music since the 1950s. Sun Ra, taking his name from the Egyptian god, spoke of Saturn as his mythical home world and how music was a mode of escape with the power to heal the wrongs of this world. In his film, *Space is the Place*, music is used as a means of time travel. He even applied through NASA, unsuccessfully, to be an artist in residence with the organisation. The work Sun Ra did with his art and especially with avant-garde jazz in Chicago carried on with George Clinton and Parliament funk into the stylings of Herbie Hancock and the more commercially known Miles Davis and Jimi Hendrix.

To this day the movement continues with the obvious influence of technology within the music and music videos of Beyoncé, Rihanna, and Missy Elliot. Samuel Delany and Octavia Butler have pioneered black sci-fi writing for such contemporary writers as Nnedi Okorafar and N. K. Jemisin. Kendrick Lamar tops billboard charts with his blending of the entire history of African American music into his beats and Marvel's *Black*

Panther has broken box office records. The soundtrack of that film was largely developed by black artists and headed up by Lamar himself. Yet racism in America is far from having progressed. The daily news is tainted by police murdering minority citizens, horrific displays of gentrification and institutional racism, and even America's leaders are not above blatantly racist remarks in public addresses.

So, what is happening?

Has Afrofuturism failed to wake the public? Is the dream of pop culture having the power to provoke and inspire real change just that? Or has art simply become the numbing white noise needed to get America's opiate addicted citizenry through the day to day grind?

To begin the long overdue discussion of these questions requires an unravelling and analysis of a multiplicity. Since it is often nature to assign blame, I will address that now so as to kill any attempts at pinning fault. This particular blend of problem is societal and, as such, the fault lies not only in all constituents of society, but all such external factors that frustrate a system from randomness to ignorance, uncertainty, and the unavoidable impression of chaos. All of this is exponentially more threatening in postnormal times.

Perhaps the best place to begin in facing such a complex situation is with a Marvel movie.

As a critic, a cinephile, and a comic book nerd I expected a lot, even too much, of *Black Panther*. Donald Trump had been President of the United States for one year. Ferguson, Flint, Detroit, and a host of other cities and communities throughout the country remained starved of justice. No decisions had been made on the deaths of minority victims of white cops in overly suspicious circumstances capsised within evidence of discrimination and xenophobia. The Affordable Care Act, often called Obamacare despite its being a widdled down version of its glory to originally appease the Republican Party, was being drawn and quartered. Immigration restrictions harshly enforced. Talk of privatisation of prisons and increased election restrictions whispered systemic racism. #BlackLivesMatter resurfaced upon Twitter followed by all of its controversy. Nostalgia for the Obama years reached the point of provoking a fiction mystery series where the former president and his vice president,

Joe Biden, adventured around solving cases. The progressive hope of 2008 was shell of a corpse, devoid of all organic material.

In Hollywood, a much different tale was unfolding. Resistance found footing in the alliance of #MeToo and #BlackLivesMatter. Crimes of yesterday were being exposed with the fall of Harvey Weinstein and the slurry of other allegations against sexual discrimination and violence surfaced. White washing of foreign tales and characters was being exposed and stood trial before the modern revolutionary guillotine of public opinion and social media. Inclusion riders, female directors, and gay heroes were all the rage. Patty Jenkins's *Wonder Woman* single handily revived the DC cinematic universe. Guillermo del Torro, an immigrant, took home Oscar for both direction and best picture for *The Shape of Water*. Oprah Winfrey gave the call to action at the ceremony, earning herself the public's official endorsement as the perfect foil to Donald Trump in 2020 (There were even campaign posters made following her Oscar speech).

Black Panther wasn't an origin story. Check. After all, if American audiences are not completely showing super hero fatigue, they are at least burnt out on the same old fallen man becomes a risen hero, chapter-one storyline. We met T'Challa in an earlier Marvel film, *Captain America: Civil War*, which was essentially a trial run of the universe encompassing Avengers films to come. *Black Panther* was unique in that we discover a whole new, hidden country, and we discover it at a time of flux, a regime change. We are introduced to a whole new world of characters that, aside from being well acted, are written to be original and the kind of persona that sticks with the audience. The audience sees themselves within these characters with realistic personalities and relatable flaws. The audience finds themselves saying 'that is totally me' or that one character or another is reminiscent of an old friend found in the oblivion of time. The effects and cinematography are some of the best that Marvel has dished out to date. Overall this film will be remembered not simply for it being a delightful ensemble of African American art, but as a key piece of cinema in general.

It makes sense that *Black Panther* is seen as a revival of Afrofuturism. The film's imagery is richly engrained with classical elements of precolonial Africa and space age technology. Cloaking technology allows Wakanda to appear to the outside observer as a grassy oasis in the heart of Africa's jungle near a simple yet impressive waterfall overseen by farmers clad in multi-coloured robes wielding archaic spears. Revealed, a bustling, densely populated metropolis with an impressive skyline mixing pre-colonial huts with western skyscrapers. Vehicles fly about this presently grounded version of a Jetsons-like city that could be easily taken for any other major urban centre in the East or West. In fact, I would not be surprised if a McDonalds or Starbucks (or four of each every few blocks) resided within this setting that could easily be inspired from London, New York, or Dubai. One of the Wakandan king's councillors perfectly exemplifies the blend desired by Afrofuturism. He wears a lime green lip plate with an easily vibrant lime green Western business attire suit. But wait, Wakanda is suppose to have been untouched by colonialists or globalisation.

While *Black Panther* does a remarkable job of exemplifying and, so some, reviving Afrofuturism, it also points out a key flaw in the genre through a logical inconsistency. Afrofuturism is deeply rooted in a historical narrative. Usually the stories in this genre draw from a mythical ancient Nubian civilisation or a black Egypt of the Pharaohs and anthropomorphised gods. This past is then projected into a western standard of cosmology. While the product is very groovy, it is fundamentally limited. Afrofuturism, for instance, is dependent on racism, a constructed social form devised by colonialists and perpetuated by the phenomenon of globalisation. The artificial entity of racism allows for an open discussion of slavery, alienation, conquest, segregation, Jim Crow, gentrification, and the multiverse that is xenophobia. The colour is most certainly black, but the structure is fundamentally white.

Under a more critical eye, *Black Panther* is riddled with details that breakdown the ideal of Wakanda and provide a clue to a more sophisticated Afrofuturism. The reason for this is that Marvel created a film that fundamentally tells an African American story in the context of Africa. Less scrutiny is spent on emphasising the language of Africa's plight against conquest at the risk of costing the narratives ability to speak to the contemporary struggle for racial equality in the States. While white men in the film are referred to as colonisers, the intent is to emphasise the otherness and tyranny of the white majority experienced in the United States. To Africa the threat of colonisers is the destruction and exploitation of black Africa in order to gain wealth for the colonists, be that the

Europeans of the last century or the contemporary threat of China, America, Russia, or global corporations themselves. It is a subtle difference, but these small cracks chip away at what Wakanda stands for. If Wakanda has managed to evade the threat of globalisation since time in memorial, why do kids in the streets wear the slickest Western styles, struggle with Western monarchical patriarchy, or Wakanda's cities reach to the stars with their phallic buildings, a typical Western urban architectural design? Ryan Coogler may launch a thousand ships for the future of black science fiction and film. But will they be able to overcome the limits of Afrofuturism?

Here it is important to pose the question. Is it enough for Afrofuturist pieces to convey, from artist to audience, the historical struggle of African Americans? If so, then the project can take a different path of informing. Is it simply more escapism? But there is no escape. And what might be waiting out there beyond what is being escaped? But perhaps that is not enough. In fact, perhaps Afrofuturism can take the next step and inspire action. Maybe this is not simply a lofty dream of Afrofuturism, but a need demanded by the rapidly burning out contemporary discussion of race in the West.

Michael Eric Dyson's latest book looks at a point in United States history when racial tensions were overflowing and beginning to mix dangerously with other vocalised instances of discord in the country. Following the assassination of John F Kennedy in 1963, his brother Robert Kennedy, who had recently taken a change in priorities towards the race question in America, called a meeting. Did this meeting include Martin Luther King, Jr. or Malcolm X, the leaders of the movement at the time? No. He turned to artists. James Baldwin, Henry Belafonte, Lena Horne, Lorraine Hansberry, and Jerome Smith. As if dreamed up from the mind of philosopher Richard Rorty, Kennedy, at the darkest hour of the 1960s, held this meeting of artists in search of a resolution. Perhaps where all other action fails we must turn to the artists to have the creativity and openness to seek the unthought and plot a course for navigating hard, and potentially post normal, times. Dyson's conclusion following the analysis of this historic meeting and the contemporary discussion of race in America is for us to 'be Wakandan.' Go out there and listen to as much rap and R&B music, read as many stories of Afrofuturism, and see as many

Black Panther movies as possible. Not only view, but participate. Create and through this maybe understanding and progress can be distilled. Pop culture is powerful, and perhaps the work done by Donald Glover aka Childish Gambino can give us some insight to this power.

The same day the multi-artistically talented Childish Gambino was to be the musical guest of Saturday Night Live, he dropped an emotionally raw and visually moving music video titled 'This is America'. The music video all takes place in a massive empty warehouse. A man plays guitar upon a bench as Gambino, with dishevelled hair and the trousers of a Civil War-era confederate soldier, begins dancing. The music is very uplifting sounding like an old tribal song of celebration from the Africa of old complete with a church's chorus singing back up. Gambino makes faces and body gestures that impersonate the old caricature of Jim Crow period posters and black face reproductions. Then seemingly out of thin air Gambino draws a gun and shoots the guitarist in the head. The gun is taken away, two-handed, in a fine cloth as the body is dragged away like rubbish. The music rapidly changes tempo to something more synthetic. Gambino walks on as people behind him run about and then the music again becomes more playful as younger individuals join him in a dance fashioned after the dance performed by black students in celebration of the end of apartheid in South Africa. Then as everyone is in celebration a church chorus is revealed as Gambino dances with them, then is thrown an AK-47 which he uses to gun down the chorus. A familiar symbol of church shootings in the United States. As the music again changes tempo, the scene moves to chaos with cars on fire and people running and dancing about. Overhead, children stare on but only through the lens of their smartphones. The music cuts as Gambino pretends to shoot a gun and then proceeds to light a cigarette and dance upon substandard cars in a mockery of rich rappers dancing on top of sharply painted sports cars. Meanwhile the car factories in Michigan remain closed. We close on Gambino being chased by faceless white men.

The video is jarring and the lyrics mock a consumerist America intentionally ignorant of the disaster in her communities, focused on making wealth and a social media persona in love with the second amendment of the constitution. Powerful is one of the least impressive words you could use to describe this video and the song attached to it.

Both pull impressively from history and project themselves into the future. Nonchalantly, Childish Gambino reminds us over and over again, that this is America. Childish Gambino's alternate persona, the actor Donald Glover had just finished staring as the younger Lando Calrissian in *Solo: A Star Wars Story*. What Glover did through his music video in all its poignancy, only begins to tap at what has been made a career by the filmmaker Spike Lee.

Rolling Stone magazine recently did a cover story on Spike Lee where he talks about his latest film BlacKkKlansman and life in Trump's America. Other news outlets took on this story and asked 'Where did Spike Lee go?' Spike Lee's response is that he hadn't gone anywhere. For thirty years he was breaking waves in independent and black cinema. Each of his pieces provide another view on racism and black America. Some widely received like *Do the Right Thing*, *Chiraq*, and most recently *BlacKkKlansman*. Others have faded into obscurity. While he has been out spoken about politics and current affairs, his films have never gotten mass release, yet always hit hard breaking standard and parlance. *BlacKkKlansman* is very much a spiritual sequel to his debut *Do the Right Thing*, in their frank discussion of racism in everyday America. BlacKkKlansman would be best viewed with Spike Lee sitting across from you giving you the look that resembles the look on a mother's face when their child deliberately disrespects them. He intercuts his film with celebration amongst members of the Ku Klux Klan and filmstock from the highly racially charged films *Gone with the Wind* and *Birth of a Nation*, the first film made in America that was even shown at the White House under the administration of Woodrow Wilson. He has some very hard-hitting scenes where the actors themselves should have simply looked plain faced into the camera to recite. In these scenes our hero, Ron Stallworth, the first Black man hired onto this small-town Colorado police force, is being comforted by his white fellow officers on the reality and danger that still exists in racist America. This movie also takes place in the 1970s/1980s. Ron utters such phrases as 'We would never elect someone like that as President of the United States and leader of the free world!', referring to attributes that are shared by the current President Trump. There is something striking in this image of a hopeful black man and the realist strike back of white police officers. Lee speaks to something higher in this film. A general comment on the racial debate in America.

The discussion of race in the West is, simply put, exhausting. Emotion has over taken logic and stubborn refusal to question one's educational or cultural up bringing has brought the dialogue to a dead halt. Everyone has appeared to have made up their mind on the issue. This frustration is expressed in Reni Eddo-Lodge's book summed up by its own title, *Why I'm No Longer Talking to White People About Race*. Since the discussion of race has continued to go on, seemingly regardless of whether or not progress has been made, white people seem to want to forget about the dark mark of history and move on. The problem lies in that if the institutions that run our every day are endemically racist, then we can't move on. When historians aren't busy trying to figure out which historical figures were or weren't homosexual, there was a major push to say that the Civil War wasn't about slavery. This was a major shift in the discussion that drove Ta-Nehisi Coates into the American dialogue.

Ta-Nehisi Coates entered the lime light when he began writing for *The Atlantic* just before the election of Barack Obama as President. His main crux was to explain how while the Civil War may have been driven by economic and political factors, at the end of the day, the conflict came down to the issue of whether or not it should be allowed for one person to own another. His career continued as he continued writing as a sceptic of Barack Obama, fearing he was not 'black' enough to make much of a different as the country's first black President. In his most recent book *We Were Eight Years in Power*, aptly subtitled 'An American Tragedy', Coates takes the pulse of black in America and watches as the Obama presidency becomes, even for him the sceptic, a beacon of hope for the black future. As the subtitle denotes, Coates also traces back from the election of Donald Trump, how the well-intentioned rise of black self esteem also laid the groundwork for the rise of nationalistic and fear driven white supremacist attitudes in dangerously subtle shades. By the end of the eight-year gig, Coates learned to love his black President, but could not help but watch, in that slow-motion fashion we come upon disaster which we cannot prevent, as Donald Trump became, in his words, our first white President.

All progress that was made during our first black presidency so awoke a fear in a forgotten America, that a perceived imbalance had to be corrected and America's whiteness again needed to be displayed in case anyone had forgotten. Clad in Sperry's, wielding tiki torches, the march on Charleston brought scary images of memories past to the forefront of 24-hour news's view. As someone who gained his formative education under the auspices of the Bill Clinton administration and the intoxicating calm waters of the 90s, I'm not surprised. The theme was fairness (oddly enough one half of Fox News's claimed tagline). Every day of the week attempted to recognise another's culture and the struggle of the past. P.C. was law. No derogatory language, no putting others down. It was the great equalisation. Racism had been defeated. We can forget the past now, yet we had catch phrases like 'forgive, but never forget.' The impossibility of dissociating these emotions essentially sums up America's attitude up to 11 September 2001. Unfortunately, this equalisation meant that as of whatever day we all agreed on this in 1996, we assumed everyone was on even ground. We assumed our institutions were not racist. Yet housing and residential zoning clearly shows racist origins that are perpetuated to this day. Prisons are still holding unprecedented numbers of blacks, forced to work, for pathetic wages to pay off unsurmountable debts birthed in ridiculous fines driven mad by the passing of time. Vicious cycle does not even begin to give the situation justice. Yet, America felt it was unnecessary to even discuss reparations, let alone consider them. America felt that maybe even affirmative action was a bit unnecessary halfway through the second Bush administration. After all racism is done and everyone is equal.

All of this nonsense is observed year by year through Coates's writing during the Obama years. And all of this occurs with the backdrop of Trayvon Martin's being gunned down for wearing a hoodie in front of the wrong cop. As hell breaks loose in Ferguson and ripple rush out throughout the historic Southern United States. As other forms of xenophobia from homophobia to Islamophobia overtake the headlines. But this is not the end of the story.

Coates is not currently writing for *The Atlantic*. Coates has gone from fly-on-the-wall to actor, but in the most peculiar way. Through Afrofuturism. Coates has authored Marvel's most recent run of the comic *Black Panther*. Through his pages assisted by the beautiful images of Brian Stelfreeze, Coates moves from observer of racism in the world, to offering ideas for change. Coates' T'Challa offers us a portrait of what the film *Black Panther*, and Afrofuturism in general can offer. Through his run, T'Challa is challenged to both be a world superhero with the Avengers and the ruler of his nation, Wakanda. He must compromise his people for the greater good of humanity, likewise, to maintain order he must partner with vicious and evil men, dictators of other African and even Western nations. All along terrorists and enemies attempt to dethrone him. At first glance, Coates' *Black Panther* beckons to post 9/11 America under George W. Bush, fear, and the Patriot Act (the one that allows the government to spy on its own citizens). Upon a more sophisticated lens though, perhaps he be giving sight to the world of Trump's America and whatever might come beyond that.

In, *We Were for Eight Years in Power*, Coates uses his thought of each of the four years of the Obama presidency to retroactively deconstruct the road to the unthought election of Donald J. Trump. This partnered with his continued work on Marvel's Black Panther Comic can provide a framing for how the Three Tomorrow's method of analysing and providing policy recommendations for postnormal times can be put into action. What Afrofuturism tends to lack is the ability to move from the familiar future of traditional sci-fi into the unthought third tomorrow of postnormal times and the taking of power in one's own future. As Coates continues now into the new run of Captain America, a character who was just revealed to be a sleeper unit of the Hydra organisation, a team of racist and white supremacist badies in the Marvel comic universe, we will continue to see what power lies awaiting an awakening within Afrofuturism.

Afrofuturism has a strong potential for being a navigational tool to action in postnormal times. First, Afrofuturism, whether or not is it aware of it, is an ideal incubator for ignorance and uncertainty. Both in visual and audio forms of art, Afrofuturism's grappling with the concept of the other works to both expose ignorances held by the audience and to analyse the ignorances held by the creator or the perceived self. Irony and narrative are masterful ways of bringing uncertainty under some shade of light. Thus far, Afrofuturism's heroes, caught between past tradition and futuristic technology, confront uncertainty in away that is often left out of the day to day hustle and bustle. Science fiction is a genre built upon consequences and in those consequences, uncertainty must be not only a constant struggle for the characters, but an internal struggle within the thinkers and writers as much as it is for the sugar-coated minds of the audience. Maybe as the old Sun Ra mantra goes 'Space is the place' to deal with the anxiety and nausea that cripples so many caught in postnormal times. Yet the challenge for postnormal times, where Afrofuturism could gain some ground, is in seeing through tomorrow.

In postnormal times, it is important look at the future as a multi-potentiated concept. Commonly we break this up into three tomorrows. They are not strict, rigid definitional entities, but rather descriptors that allow us to conceptualise and move beyond the limitations of our own biases. Each tomorrow has within it, the preconceived notion of the other tomorrows. Perspective is critical. Movement from self-reflection to commiseration with other's worldviews advances the horizons attainable in unravelling the three tomorrows. Creativity and flexability are one's precious commodities. First is the extended present. The not-so-distant-future. The revelation of trends and the status quo. Beyond this first tomorrow lies the second tomorrow of the familiar future. The flying car. It is futuristic for it is a cool, space aged way to get around, yet familiar in that we are still, supposedly, using cars to get around. This is the pitfall of science fiction. The all too human tendency to remain within the safety of sobering sanity. Robots, but humanoid, and we fear their emotions and sentience, for then they'd be like us. Smart societies driven by automation and social networking, cool, slick, yet beholden to our contemporary structural flaws of being misogynist, racist, consumerist, and overall standing on the classic foundational theme of unifying us by dividing us into various classifications. Afrofuturism and the rest of Science Fiction do a brilliant job of getting us to this point and even in explaining the postnormal creep that lies within each step, but can it get us to the third tomorrow.

The truly unthought is a new frontier. As Ziauddin Sardar and John Sweeney tell us, 'collaborative creativity and 'ethical imagination[s]' are not simply the best tools for constructing scenarios in this tomorrow, 'they are the only tools'. Furthermore, the unthought future(s) is not simply something that is not expected or anticipated; rather, it is something outside the framework of conventional thought—something that does not allow us to focus on or think about it.' The unthought is not unthinkable, but might be usable from a certain vantage point. It is the marriage of complexity, chaos, and contradiction. Distortion of scope, scale, speed, and simultaneity are common place here. Blackness and white supremacy can vanish in the unthought. Race can be uncreated. Slavery and Jim Crow are ideals to be aspired to in this realm. Xenophobia is the tyranny of the minority and historical narrative need not apply. Afrofuturism can unlock its true power by tapping into the unthought. But, as has been explicitly stated in postnormal times analysis: power is seldom given; it is usually taken.

Now, caution should be advised here. A drastic jump from the ethereal fiction of thought to the reality of the present is jarring and action without moral reflection and continued futures thought can be dangerous. A fearful association can be drawn between the creative and the destructive. This is the rationale used for the banning of certain artistic expressions. It lies at the heart of John Lennon's assassin toting along his person a copy of J. D. Salinger's *A Catcher in the Rye*. Also, in former US President's Ronald Reagan's would-be assassin's motivation to win over the heart of Jodi Foster after seeing Martin Scorsese's *Taxi Driver*. The debate will continue with each new example of youth and violence, from the pop cultural influences on the young shooters from Columbine High School in 1999, to the 2012 shooter, dressed as Heath Ledger's character The Joker, at an Aurora movie theatre on the opening night of Christopher Nolan's *The Dark Knight Rises*. Afrofuturism in being a truly futures study must keep its potentialities open to all possible outcomes. This means that it can be hijacked and used for the ulterior motives of the militant and fascists. Yet in all the bad, an equal, if not greater, multiplicity of good lies within the potentiality. A sound morality is as paramount as a respect for mental illness and other social ailments that can bastardise a policy or a movement.

Afrofuturism provides for us a mode of reflexion as well as insight for navigation of postnormal times that need not only be a way forward on the issue of race in the United States or the West, but can be a cowl put on by other disadvantaged communities or group who find themselves in postnormal creep or looking to prevent postnormal lag. As the film *Black Panther* speaks to and Dyson echoes in his writing, we can all be Wakanda. In the comics of Coates, our hero T'Challa is caught between being the King of Wakanda and a super hero for the world. There is a fine balance to be maintained there. For even in the throws of PNT, there are constants such as home and family that need tending to, yet the demands of good acts and the pursuit of navigation are needed in these troubling times. In looking towards policy in postnormal times, we can take a page from T'Challa's book.

At the conclusion of the film *Black Panther*, T'Challa decides that it is time for Wakanda to come out from hiding. That the risk of continued threats of attack can be tackled by giving back to the world. He does what his cousin-turned-enemy wanted; much as Martin Luther King, Jr. and Malcolm X wanted similar outcomes, but differed in method. T'Challa would not arm his disadvantaged African diasporic brothers and sisters, at least with weapons, but share the benefits to humankind that Wakandan thought and innovation delivered through the use of its secret element, vibranium. In the closing scene of the film, T'Challa and his sister Shuri are undercover, visiting Compton where Killmonger, the enemy of T'Challa, was born and raised. T'Challa reveals that he has bought a large block of land there to build Wakanda's first outreach centre. The first steps towards walking through postnormal times should be small, short term, with long term ambitions, constantly monitored by specialists and always revised.

A group of kids are playing basketball on the land T'Challa has bought. They stop as T'Challa uncloaks their flying jet to the kids' amazement. One of the young boys walks up to T'Challa. Echoing the deeply needed self-reflection of politicians and policy makers. The powerful. The boy asks 'Who are you?'

Echoed in this closing question, Afrofuturism from the funky grooves and electronic sounds improvised by Sun Ra and George Clinton through to Beyonce and Missy Elliot and even to this day with Childish Gambino and the credit song, Kendrick Lamar and SZA's 'All the Stars', that follows the question's posing. 'Maybe the night that my dreams might let me know that all the stars are closer.' The world is lived out between stanzas, both the existence and absence of sound weave together to create a soundtrack of our lives. It appears to be escape, but in reality, it is the passage onto something higher, into something unthought. Random combinations of notes can evoke emotion, retrieve a lost memory, and even provoke a person to action. Such a mysterious force demands the austerity of intellectual rigor.

Now can you hear it?

INDIVOLLECTIVITY

Jim Dator

For most of human history, individuals and communities have lived in 'one present' and looked forward to 'one future', defined by one set of technologies. For most of human history, technological change was rare, slow, and the social and environmental consequences almost unnoticed. During most of this time, people lived and thought collectively in small face-to-face groups, not separately and individually. There was no concept of 'privacy' or 'my individual rights'. Some Greek and Roman philosophers eventually conceived of the ideas, but the overwhelming majority of humans neither imagined nor experienced privacy or individual moral freedom. Indeed, the social value and impact of the Greek and Roman philosophers was near zero until they were rediscovered in the late middle ages. Community-focused life dominated until the scientific-industrial revolution and events leading up to it (the Reformation, Renaissance, and Enlightenment) when people began using technologies that gave them first the experience and then the idea of individualism and individual freedom while rediscovering/inventing texts that explained and justified their experiences.

From the middle of the seventeenth century until the middle of the twentieth century, modern societies were increasingly dominated by individualising technologies, spurred by the printing press and culminating with the automobile and the telephone. During that period, each new technology seemed to free the individual from the confining traditions and bonds of the community, eventually creating free individuals each with their own unique sense of self and their future—their personal values and beliefs – (give me liberty or give me death; its my way or the highway) leading to the opportunities, ideologies, triumphs, and disasters characteristic of modern times.

From the mid 1950s, however, new technologies emerged that tended once again to collectivise, though often at a global level and certainly in conflict with values and institutions based on earlier, local, collectivising technologies. The first of these new collectivising technologies was television (creating what Canadian philosopher and public intellectual, Marshall McLuhan, called 'the global village'); the second was the personal computer when global networking began and expert authority died; and the third are the currently popular social media and the emerging hive mind (or, Noosphere, as French philosopher and Jesuit Priest, Pierre Teilhard de Chardin, anticipatorily named it).

Something else unique also began to occur during early modernity, still accelerating today: technological and social change became so rapid that individuals and communities were caught for the first time in a whirlpool of conflicting technologies, values, and institutions, some of which were obsolete and vanishing, some were old and fading, some were current and thriving, others were new and emerging, and others still vividly imagined but not yet achieved. Until 150 or so years ago, everyone in a community used and were influenced by the same technologies. Not now.

At the present time, oldest age-cohorts live by vanishing and fading technologies, values, and institutions; middle age-cohorts by fading and thriving technologies, values, and institutions; while younger cohorts embrace emerging and imagined technologies. Nonetheless, each cohort, individual, and the community as a whole is possessed in some measure by all levels. This is new to human experience - each age-cohort living in substantially different worlds but at the same time and place with other cohorts. Intergenerational communication and easy understanding is difficult. Cultural chaos reigns in every part of the world.

Agricultural – indeed, pastoral – era metaphors, institutions, and values still persist. With the printing press as the iconic technology and, in the West, The Bible that the press liberated from the Church as the iconic text, we still say God is a king, with heaven ('above') and Earth ('below') as his kingdom while we are his subjects with no rights or will of our own. God is our Shepherd and we are His ignorant and wilful sheep in need of protection. Similar nomadic and/or agricultural myths and metaphors exist in every culture in the world.

Another very clear example of how the rhythms of long-dead agricultural societies still control us today is found in many school and legislative calendars and holidays worldwide. Both learning and legislating are still often part-time activities, originally happening in the Northern Hemisphere during the late fall and winter when the crops are in, to allow their participants to go home to help plant and reap from late spring to early fall. This once-sensible practice now makes no sense at all in the industrial or informational world, and yet seems impossible to change until all agricultural images finally die. Even though we live in a global world in many ways, we still retain local loyalties in sports, and admire, if not emulate, values of small communities depicted in TV shows and advertisements. Now, with the rise of Trump and other hyper-nationalists around the world, tribalism is challenging globalism as the dominant perspective once again.

For the most part, transportation technologies defined and dominated the industrial era, producing first the railroad, then the automobile, then the aeroplane, creating both the city with its suburbs and the (often continental) nation as its iconic institutions. The automobile, for the first time enabling true auto-mobility, was the iconic technology. Nothing provoked the sense of individualism, freedom, personal identity, and social irresponsibility more than the automobile. It is only a slight exaggeration to say that the fall of communism began when private individuals in communist countries were allowed to own automobiles instead of keeping them herded on mass transit.

The allure and power of the automobile is still extraordinary. Everywhere it spreads throughout the world, it transforms stable, obedient, community-focused peasants and workers into roaming, pleasure-seeking, death-provoking adolescents of all ages. Commuting, 'rush hour' traffic jams, horrendous deaths and injuries, environmental pollution, and oil wars are its side-effects, in spite of which the attraction of personal identity through sports car/SUV automobility is far too strong to allow telework to end commuting, or for other forms of transport, especially bicycles and walking, to end pollution and oil wars. The emergence of self-driving cars can only spur free-spirited individuality-- until the oceans rise and the oil runs out.

As individualising transportation technologies shaped industrial societies, so also do collectivising communication technologies define information societies. First movies and then television were the initial icons, followed by personal computers and the Internet, and now social media. Major social consequences of these technologies include the focus of life becoming advertising-fuelled 'shop till you drop', along with the mania of tirelessly working 24/7 at meaningless networked jobs in order to impress your fellow workers and your boss; the end of the human expert/authority and the rise of personal and peer facts and fantasies; and the dominance of entertainment, 'fake news', games, professional sports, and of virtuality over 'reality' in general.

Demographically, more and more adults in information societies everywhere are 'only children' now living seemingly alone with no children, spouses, or roommates of their own, but actually interacting with myriad other humans and (predominantly) smart machines via an ever-changing array of multitasking communication technologies, surrounded by the decaying remnants of take-away food. This novel form of individuality and community may continue to evolve as long as new electronic and molecular communication technologies continue to be produced and acquired.

The next step already underway is to lose the confining, stationary, built environment – the solitary room, apartment, house – and live in light, sturdy, mobile, self-sufficient, adaptable cocoons like the cushicle envisioned by the avant-garde architectural Archigram group many years ago: a kind of personal backpack with all of one's necessities in it that can be unfolded and joined with other cushicles whenever group interaction is sought, and then (after tidying up the common environment) folded back into one's personal backpack again.

The new nationalism sweeping the globe now is often seen as a revival of 'blood and soil' patriotism of the old industrial days, and many people may promote and strive for that. But at the same time, the forces of individualising-collectivising social media seem to provoking something different and perhaps new – indivollectivity.

ARTS AND LETTERS

XR: EXTINCTION REBELLION

Mothiur Rahman

'Are you doing ok, do you need anything?' I asked the lady whose hand was glued to the entrance of the Department of Business, Energy & Industrial Strategy. 'I'm doing fine,' she replied with a smile. Someone below her, locked on to another person and lying on the ground to block the revolving door entrance, needed a pillow. I had a few to hand, being part of the wellbeing group of Extinction Rebellion (XR) on this day of action leading towards Rebellion Day on 17 November 2018. The two dozen or so people super-glued to the doors and splayed in front of the Ministry office sought to bring wider attention to the climate emergency we are collectively facing. We aim to bring social momentum to get the UK government to declare an ecological emergency and put in place measures to avoid future catastrophe for our planet.

Southwark Bridge, London 17.11.18 © Kay Michael

Through a downpour we shared umbrellas and sang songs and made up chants to keep warm. It was quiet as the police held back, watching but not arresting anyone until suddenly there was an eruption of cheering as one of the initiators of Extinction Rebellion, Gail Bradbrook, clambered above the revolving doors to spray paint a message against fracking and the symbol for the movement (with a chalk based paint that washes off). As the police rushed over to crowd around the entrance, energy suddenly took over those protesting as a few dashed over from lying down by the building not being arrested, to lying down on the road to sit and block it. The cheering got louder. It was getting late but now the arrests began.

The XR protestors are prepared to face arrest and possible prison in order to bring media and civil society attention to the reality of climate collapse happening within the lifetime of the next generation. 'Black Swan events' are those outlier occurrences which, despite the best predictions of pundits in the know, seem to happen by chance and can radically alter society. Black Swan events have been proliferating recently like the Brexit referendum and Trump's rise to power, leading to visible shifts in the cultural discourse over power, democracy, and the linking of Islamophobia to immigration. As if out of nowhere, they take the public, media and politicians by surprise and leave experts scrambling to give some kind of reasonable answer or sense of control over being able to predict the future.

The way that Extinction Rebellion so quickly catalysed vast numbers across diverse places, ages, classes and professions, into action to join its call to civil disobedience for the first and second Rebellion Days on 17th and 24th November, in 2018, has been inspiring. It makes me wonder whether Rebellion Day will in the future be recognised as a Black Swan event, shaping a civil society movement as its message takes root and spreads across diverse geographies and generations? Some predict it will resemble other protest movements and die out, the status quo left to deal with its own paralysis over recognisable Black Swan events like Brexit and Trump. However, Black Swan events possess the kind of energy that defies predictions.

Extinction Rebellion's message, and the need driving it, is this: time has almost entirely run out to address the ecological crisis of runaway climate change and mass extinctions that will follow. A recent report by the

Intergovernmental Panel on Climate Change (IPCC) warned that, under best estimates, we have only twelve years from now to take drastic action to ensure global temperatures do not rise above 1.5 degrees. We have already reached a 1 degree increase in warmth and, according to Panmao Zhai one of the co-chairs of the IPCC Working Group, 'one of the key messages that comes out very strongly from this report is that we are already seeing the consequences of 1 degree of global warming through more extreme weather, rising sea levels and diminishing Arctic sea ice, among other changes.'

In a letter signed by 96 academics, politicians and other leaders, a challenge was made to further governmental prevarication given the short timescales to make such unprecedented change: 'we will not tolerate the failure of this or any other government to take robust and emergency action in respect of the worsening ecological crises. The science is clear, the facts are incontrovertible, and it is unconscionable to us that our children and grandchildren should have to bear the terrifying brunt of an unprecedented disaster of our own making.'

The three demands made by Extinction Rebellion are:

- The government must tell the truth about the climate and wider ecological emergency, reverse inconsistent policies and work alongside the media to communicate with citizens.
- The government must enact legally binding policy measures to reduce carbon emissions to net zero by 2025 and to reduce consumption levels.
- A national Citizens' Assembly to oversee the changes, as part of creating a democracy fit for purpose.

As a lawyer working with a number of communities resisting fracking, Extinction Rebellion feels to me like an eruption out of what has been troubling many residents over a number of years. In 2013. I was supporting Falkirk communities in Scotland resisting coalbed methane extraction and one of the first questions posed to me by a resident was, 'why is the law not protecting us?'. These were ordinary citizens who wanted to lead good, responsible lives, but were beginning to question matters that previously had been the remit of activists. Extinction Rebellion is not only a collective manifestation of an impending fear of climate collapse in the

Buckingham Palace 23.11.18 © Paola Desiderioe

near future, but also of a realisation that the political and technocratic status quo liberal order is showing itself incapable of responding in a meaningful way to such looming crises within the timescales needed. By paying only lip service to the values it ascribes to itself, it is arguable the liberal western order has hollowed itself out, its values no longer holding sufficient substance and traction in wider society to prevent the rise of Trump and the turn towards authoritarian politics. This movement to me represents our collective existential struggle as civil society attempting to remake itself and take ownership over the responsibility we have to future generations, to institutionalise a culture of climate collapse adaptation at a meaningful societal level.

There are experts in the field who think the system of capitalist economics and governance we have collectively created has too much momentum to change direction in the short window available to avoid climate collapse. Jorgen Randers, a professor emeritus of climate strategy at the BI Norwegian Business School, believes global society does not have the capacity to 'rise to the occasion of solving the climate problem during this century, simply because it is more expensive in the short term to solve the problem than it is to just keep acting as usual'. This view is similar to social scientist Donald McKay, whose research on previous civilisational collapses points out that the common barrier to transformational change is not that the means weren't available to make the changes or that the need to make them was not known at the time, but it was because the short-term interests of those who hold power and have an interest in holding onto power (what he calls 'oligarchical authorities') are radically different to the long-term interests of society.

Through my work with communities, however, I have begun to feel another site of agency and power to those of corporations, which Jorgen Randers focuses on, and those with power through state or 'oligarchical' authority that Donald McKay speaks of. That is the power of civil society when it collectivises itself to claim necessary rights when the need for such rights becomes great enough, such as happened during the civil rights movement in the US or, later back still in English memory, the Charter of the Forest in 1217. Thus, civic-orientated action could be a counter-movement to forces that maintain the status quo of market capitalist economics.

The kind of 'civic-orientated thinking' needed to really galvanise such action is unfortunately dissipated in modern western society, or so argues

London 23.11.18 © Alex Fisher

journalist Martin Lukacs, as the 'result of an ideological war... against the possibility of collective action... Neoliberalism has not merely ensured the agenda [of climate change demands] is politically unrealistic: it has also tried to make it culturally unthinkable. Its celebration of competitive self-interest and hyper-individualism, its stigmatisation of compassion and solidarity, has frayed our collective bonds.' So, from where is this power of civic-orientated collective conscience to come? Extinction Rebellion has started that call with direct action networked into communities criss-crossing the country, with groups forming in local distinct geographies connected to their place and united by a form of life orientated thinking contrasting with the market-orientated thinking which governs much of our current public life. But it may need more than this to make the quantum leap through the cultural resistance that

Westminster 23.11.18 © Serena Schellenberg

the neoliberal project has engendered in terms of what a collective conscience means. This is where Muslim communities could disseminate climate change demands to wider civil society. My re-encounter with Islam has begun to show that, sourced from outside western hegemonic values, it is rooted in a life-oriented conscience that is also collective in spirit as opposed to individualistic.

My journey towards a re-encounter with a radically different version of Islam than the one I was brought up with as a child has not been an easy journey. The thorny bushes of my own judgments shaped through childhood experiences, as well as those now being provided through media channels played their part. The habitual response that formed part of my core identity was one of shrugging off both my Bengali and Islamic heritage as somehow inferior to the qualities of truth, justice and equality bound up in the project of western modernity that caught my imagination when I began learning about it at school. A number of experiences over the last few years have made me question whether there is now anything of substance behind these words in terms of how life is actually being encountered by the everyday person. The Brexit decision to separate the UK out of Europe brought a visceral feeling in my body of fear, making me become conscious again of my colour as a point of difference, something I had managed to submerge after childhood. I told myself change is a necessary part of democracy and perhaps it would not be as bad as that first visceral feeling in the pit of my stomach made me fear.

Yet, whilst trying to get used to the altered experience of my identity as a consequence of democracy playing out its course, it was difficult not to start feeling that some politicians were using it as a means to personal goals for garnering power rather than in service to the people they governed. Coincidentally at around this time, Radio 4 was commemorating the seventieth anniversary of the partition of India with programmes explaining some of that history. It was on one of these programmes that I learnt that the Boundary Commissioner tasked with drawing the partition line between India and Pakistan (a line that had the consequences of forming the roots of my identity through my parents who were then born into what became East Pakistan) had never even been to India before drawing the line. One elderly man spoke of his experience of partition, saying that before partition in his village no one thought of themselves as Hindu or Muslim, they were just a community rooted in their place working on their land. Was history repeating itself, the identity of 'remainers' or 'leavers' being the new lines being drawn up that hadn't existed before? The sense of moral duplicity playing itself out in a repetitive pattern led to something beginning to crack inside me, my faith in the western modernist project as the way to truth and justice felt compromised.

UnBeing Me

My mother told me I was a good muslim boy
that was a lie from her.
My teachers made me believe I had no colour
that was a lie from them.

So I saw no colour
painting myself out of existence.
That was a lie from me.

Who, then, am I?
I am not a terrorist.
I am not Bangla.
I am not Muslim.
I am neither Christian
Hindu nor you.

I am just me.
Britain is breaking
creaking under the weight
of lie on lie untold
generation on generation.

I am neither English
nor Welsh
Scottish nor Irish.

So do it then
explode me
tear me to bits
throw me to the hounds
till chewed and digested

I can become
something I never was.

When something cracks, there is the potential for new life to come through the crevices. The shoots of that life have come to me as a transforming sense of what Islam is about, which has for me begun to help shape a new conscience of truth and justice integrated with this

London 15.11.18 © Francesca E Harris

perspective. Whilst for most of my life I have had this undercurrent feeling of a sense of shame of my Islamic heritage, that did not mean the longing for a more spiritually centred way of being in the world left me. I explored earth-centred and Buddist perspectives through self-development workshops and courses and, as Brexit began to burst its way into British life, I happened to be reading a book by Pema Chodron, a Buddhist monk, called *The Places that Scare You*. I found it gave a way to meaningfully encounter difficult emotions arising in me as the core elements of my constructed identity began faltering, to become conscious of what I was resisting as a fertile place of learning.

My first meaningful exp erience with a mosque from this new perspective came on 'visit a mosque' day in 2017. I belong to a group called Wild Monastics, run by Rev Sam Wernham in Dartington where I was living then, to explore what contemporary contemplative practice could look like in everyday life. She invited me to accompany her to the Plymouth Mosque and my instinctive response was to decline, but as I turned away I felt such strong emotions I wondered whether these were the kinds of feelings that Pema Chodron had been giving guidance about for exploration. It was only due to my desire to explore through Pema Chodron's guidance that I decided to attend. I was surprised by how

Westminster 23.11.18 © Paola Desiderioe

different my adult experience was of the mosque from everything I was projecting onto it through my childhood experiences that I felt it worth exploring further. When I explained this to Rev Sam Wernham she said that she had had a similar tussle and struggle with Christianity, and had spent many years running as far away from Christianity as possible, becoming involved with paganism and Buddhism until something pulled her back, to see whether what she longed for in those far distant faiths could also be found deep down in the roots of the Christian western mystical tradition that she had been born into. This parallel story gave me the curiosity to want to explore further whether there were rooted elements to the Islamic faith that could speak to me as an adult.

Such explorations led me to a Sheikh Kabir Helminski and his book, *The Sufi Path to Mindfulness and the Essential Self.* I was drawn to it because Kabir was a living person one could question, also because it came with a living tradition called The Threshold Society with a gathering every summer in the UK, and because my Buddhist leanings made mindfulness a concept I could understand and follow. What drew me the most was something written in the first few pages of the book. It spoke about 'will' as an attribute leading to an awareness of God, something that I had not associated with Islam before. I had been brought up to hear the words *inshallah* at the end of most sentences (God willing) and understood that the word Islam meant submission (which my Islamic teachers in Leeds seemed to take to mean submission before their will). Such narrow experiences and understanding meant I had grown up with a feeling that Islam meant accepting what I was told, in conflict with the freedom that my experience told me is needed for the human spirit to flourish. I went to the Threshold summer gathering and managed to ask Kabir, how did he square human will with the concept of submission in Islam? He did not give me a black and white answer which I liked, but opened up for me an exploration for myself as to how human will can lead one to be able to be conscious of one's state of attention and that, by travelling along that path, there can come a place where will gives way to surrender. Another of the Threshold teachers, Mahmoud, told me that both reason and will were central to the Islamic and Sufi traditions, leading towards the attribute called *Al Haq*, truth or reality. I have only begun the first steps of this journey back towards a re-encounter with Islam through Sufism, something which I am finding is a rich unfolding. Munajaat is a Sufi practice that explains the journey towards truth not in terms of a debate, but like 'a secret discourse between lovers'.

Munajaat

Who are you my Islam?
I have seen you only
in borrowed clothes?

Will you undress before me
reveal to me your form?

I hear you breathing
how do I cleave myself
to your warmth?

They call you surrender,
commander of submission –
only – close like this to you –

you call forth humility
from this breath of mine.

Extinction Rebellion for me is a movement that is being built from a willingness to face the fear and grief of what all the science is pointing towards: civilisational crises from climate collapse and, from having the imaginative capacity to bring into the present moment before it has happened. The intenseness of the suffering of people and animals in a future world of climate collapse and species extinction. To feel the moment alive and pregnant with the intensity of the potential to change course through actions we collectively take now.

Many hands have contributed to the development of this movement. I feel it encapsulates both the grief and determination of the moment well. I made the suggestions to evoke a lineage with the Universal Declaration of Human Rights (1947) which states at Article 1 that human beings are endowed with reason and conscience as fundamental qualities. It should not be forgotten that historic document arose out of a world-wide recognition of the need to make meaning out of the intense suffering of people through two world wars and the deaths of millions of people. It was a document that made meaning out of the lived experience of grief and love of those times. Extinction Rebellion has made its Declaration in the hope that we can now use both our reason and our conscience to guide us away from taking us to 'tipping points' in temperature change which, if reached, will then be too late to turn back from; leading to far worse catastrophe than the two world wars.

These two qualities of reason and conscience are what all the nations of this world were able to agree to in 1947, as fundamental qualities or attributes to being human. It seems to me that many of the spiritual qualities, fundamental to the Sufi path, could be embraced by this word conscience, particularly the concept of *raab* which can be interpreted as a quality of relationship to our hearts which leads us towards the truth of reality as is. Like in a squabble between lovers, what can get in our way is the quality of consciousness we give to our emotions. Crucially, Sufism does not say emotions are something to be avoided in order for

Elephant & Castle, London 22.11.18 © Francesca E Harris

reason to hold sway, rather that we use our reason to help us navigate our way through our negative emotional states (or *nafs*) towards seeing the unity of love that is the reality that is. Islam's spiritual ethics, it seems to me, is an amalgam of civic and collective conscience; and that's precisely what we need to navigate our way out of the current crisis of climate and ecology.

HALAL WORLD

SCENARIO

Exotica has its uses. There was a time when Muslim fashion was seen as exotic: Asian women with their colourful scarfs, Arab women with their vibrant headgear, the African women with flamboyant turbans. Not anymore. It occurred to a fashion house in Paris that there is a big market in Muslim fashion albeit it is limited to Muslim countries. Their two seasons of Muslim fashion were quite a success; an example other fashion houses were eager to follow. With a couple of years haute coutre became synonymous with Muslim high fashion. Then, street fashion from Casablanca to Cairo, Lahore to Kuala Lumpur, got into the act. It was Djellabas and Kurta Pajama all-round the globe. Stores like Primark, Macy's and Gap could not satisfy an avalanche of customers. Supplies had to increase. Modesty became a badge of pride.

But it was not just fashion that caught the eye of the world. Islamic banking and finance, thriving on the side-lines of global system, was brought from the periphery to the centre. Folks seeking refuge from, the increasing personal debt, the runaway gambling and casino economy, found viable solutions with Muslim banks and financial institutions. Decorum in fashion led to an active interest in ethical solutions to financial and business issues. But the few ethical financial institutions in the West could not cope. So Muslim institutions stepped in to fill the gap. Initially, only a few — as the local regulations thwarted their advance. But once the proverbial flood gates opened, Muslim institutions spread rapidly. Much like Muslim fashion, halal banking became in vogue.

Indeed, halal became a byword for all things a la mode. Architecture has embraced the features and characteristics of Ottoman, Moghul and Maghrebi styles. Pop music has 'gone Arabic'. Shopping malls are full of goods announcing their halal nature. Even the 'halal chickens' have gone halal: ethically farm and humanely slaughtered, free of fat and anti-biotics. So why are so many Muslims still complaining?

THE NEW HALAL

Medina Whiteman

'Today's woman,' began Cynthia Draper as she sauntered around her studio, making cursory adjustments to the dresses hanging from the rails, 'has transcended the juveline desire to impress by flaunting her assets. She has far too much dignity for that. Instead – oh, Mehdia, would you cut a bit off this train? It's like a meringue exploded in here. Where was I?'

She drew out a long sleeve, teal watered silk embroidered with birds of paradise, and admired the way it glistened in the sun filtering through the shuttered windows. Harsh, dye-bleaching, African sun.

'You still taking this down? OK. Today's woman understands that the halal concept takes fashion to another level. More fabric. More queenliness. More canvas to express herself. No more throwing pearls before swine! She is a temple to beauty, grace, finesse. Her clothing reflects the architecture of her soul. Shall I stop there, do you think? How many words did Friedrich say he needed?'

'That's probably alright,' Mehdia replied, juggling the tablet she was typing into and a pair of scissors as she trimmed the dress Cynthia had condemned.

'You can always flesh it out a little tonight. How we doing for time? God, it moves so slowly in this place. It's the complete opposite to Manhattan – there you can't get anything done because time just whizzes past, but here you can't get anything done because it's moving so darned slow you feel like you're crawling through maple syrup.'

Cynthia snapped open an agenda and scanned her order schedule.

'How did I ever decide to come to Casablanca?' she muttered, gathering her things into a large leather bag. 'I mean, Manhattan rents were crippling me, but come on...Can't get a decent latte here, either...Alright Mehdia, we're shipping out. Gotta pick up those woven inlays from Khadijah. You know, the little old lady who lives in a vinegar bottle?'

Mehdia smarted. Khadijah was their faithful weaver, illiterate as a doorstop with barely a tooth in her head, yet a genius with colour and texture. But yes, she did live in something resembling a sardine tin. Mehdia threw her scarf over the head and tucked it into itself. Cynthia rarely looked at her when she wore her scarf to leave the atelier. She didn't look at her much inside the atelier, either.

But Mehdia wasn't complaining. It was a job – and one that looked great on paper: Personal Assistant to a Fashion Designer. Not just any fashion designer, either: Cynthia had set up Atelier Dru back in 2018, when halal fashion was starting to kick off in a big way. With her sculpted, multilayered shapes and metres of rolling fabric, ideally requiring several attendants to carry two thirds of the dress behind the person wearing it, Atelier Dru had been spotted on the red carpet numerous times.

And not only on Arab royalty, either. Hollywood had discovered Cynthia's whimsical creations and eye-popping price tags and started snapping them up. Once Reese Witherspoon had been seen wearing a Dru to a premiere ('Saturnalia in Burnt Ochre'), demand had tripled.

Hence Cynthia's move to Casablanca. Since the early 2020s, Casablanca had been a mecca for the burgeoning halal movement. From fashion to gastronomy, tourism to banking, everyone from Malaysian stock brokers to Michelin starred chefs had made a base in this strategic location between East and West. It was European enough for beach-loving Westerners, yet Oriental enough to allow visitors to get close to 'authentic' Moroccan culture – always with the possibility of retreating to the familiarity of a hotel room.

They reached the end of the alley where the studio was located, in an old sardine cannery that had been converted to house all the new artists and designers that were flooding the city, and hit the main road.

Avenue Hassan II was a halal consumer's paradise. Everything had become halal certified, even things no-one knew weren't halal in the first place. Suddenly there were halal toasters being marketed in the ecologically-minded houseware shop. Halal nails in the hardware stores, and halal gel extensions in the nail parlours. Clothing to suit any style, shape, budget, and degree of daring – all halal on the label. Designers had taken the limitations of modest clothing as a challenge to up their game. Every major chain from Prada to Primark had cottoned on; a couple of seasons of sell-out halal goods had turned their shareholders' heads.

While Casablanca's souq was a vibrant mélée of textiles, metalworks, baskets, leather, spices and wood carving – tightly controlled by the local mayor, who wanted to make sure nothing stopped the progress of the new economic direction Morocco was taking – Avenue Hassan II was crammed with chic cafés (nobody wanted to drink alcohol any more – too fattening), halal banks, technology superstores and, of course, fashion boutiques.

But the real winners in this mania had been the food outlets. Hamdi's had struck the grill when it was hot, and now had restaurants everywhere from Berlin to Rio de Janeiro. Mehdia and Cynthia were now level with their flagship restaurant, a smart, wood-chrome-and-glass number with fake greenery to offset the murals of happy cows pleasantly munching grass. The windows were emblazoned with stickers of cartoon customers and speech bubbles with the Hamdi's catchphrase in English, Arabic and French: 'It's halal? Then make mine a double!'

Mehdia glanced inside as they were passing; the A/C was clearly working at full blast, as the floor-to-ceiling windows were closed on the people inside, comfortably guzzling massive plates of every type of meat dish known to man. A stream of sweat started to form on the back of Mehdia's neck in spite of the cool Atlantic breeze. The idea of eating made her salivate, but Hamdi's gave her indigestion. Morocco was renowned for its food; nobody had succeeded in bringing McDonald's here, yet somehow Hamdi's had made it, as it had all over the world.

'No time to eat now, Mehdia,' Cynthia scolded. 'In any case you really should think about going on a diet. You're jiggling all over the studio and it's putting me off my designing.'

'Sorry,' Mehdia muttered.

They continued past the gleaming fronts of halal banking institutions, Malaysian, Qatari, Emirati and even European – cornerstones of the global market's newfound economic stability. Subtle geometric patterns clouded the glass and obscured the people sitting dully in the waiting areas within, shoulders hunched like quarried hills.

Around and behind these modern buildings you could still see the whitewash and blue of old Casablanca, and if you inhaled deeply – when a Lambourghini wasn't driving past – there was the perennial tang of seasalt on the air.

'Excuse me!' Cynthia barked at a boy with a smattering of spots, knocking the flyers he was distributing all over the street. He looked back at her with a mixture of embarrassment and loathing. Mehdia stopped to help him pick them up, but only managed to read the top line of the flyers – 'The Emptiness of the New Halal' – before Cynthia grabbed her by the elbow and chivvied her along.

'Sheesh!' Cynthia muttered. 'These guys give me the pip. We've turned their economy around, what are they complaining about?'

Around the corner was the taxi rank. Petrol was about the only thing that hadn't gone halal yet; the king had been seen being driven in an electric car, but they were still out of the reach of most Moroccans. An emerald green Mercedes, made in the 1950s and still going strong, had already started already rumbling into life upon seeing Cynthia's ash blonde bob and lashings of lilac linen swing into view.

'Douar M'zab,' s'il vous plait,' Cynthia requested in her strong NY accent. The taxi driver knew where she needed to go – every month or so she would run out of woven trims, and Khadijah was well known among locals for her skills. They weaved through town between dazed tourists encumbered with shopping bags, and then made a zoom for the outskirts.

They flew through Quartier Afriquia, which had lately been turned into a mesh of hipermarchés, technology outlets and fashion warehouses. Demand had been so great here in this 'Dubai of the West' that these were just the bottom floors of giant blocks of flats, built so quickly and from such dubious materials for an earthquake zone like this that locals refused to live there. Many had become summer flats for Europeans, while others stood empty, bought by wealthy investors in China and the Gulf.

The blocks petered out and started to break up into smallholdings and shanty towns that had sprung up around clusters of industrial units. Buildings dropped to single stories. Roofs were not tiled with terracotta half-cylinders like on the picturesque seafront; here corrugated iron drew waves along the top edge of the houses. Half-starved cats skulked amid piles of rubbish. Barbers, seamstresses and grocers had set up shop in tin shacks, painted with Western phrases and warped portraits of Hollywood stars by budding local artists.

The taxi turned off into a side street, then onto a dirt track. Women walking by in brightly coloured djellabas with shopping baskets drew their scarves over their faces to keep the rising dust out of their nostrils. A squat mosque, built of wooden pallets and with a stepladder instead of a minaret, stood to one side of a dusty esplanade. All the major mosques in the country had already gone solar, but in the slums there was no option but to use candles.

Cynthia usually began to grumble by this point, about public hygiene, access to clean water, and the probability of parasites. But Mehdia found something comforting about Douar M'zab. The souq, with its tall cones of spices, racks of jewel-toned babouches, wool blankets and red Berber rugs, was not unlike the marketplace in the metropolis, but with none of its formality. Here stalls could be made out of opened-out oil drums, street food was sold wrapped in old newspaper, and – best of all – you could still haggle. There were children playing wild games of tag all over the place, barefoot and gap-toothed.

They pulled up and got out, Cynthia gather her skirts painstakingly to avoid getting them dirty. Men sitting outside makeshift cafés paused their backgammon games to watch, hookah smoke drifting from their nostrils.

'OK Mehdia. We get the trims, pay Khadijah, and scram. Got it?'

Mehdia nodded reluctantly. Together they weaved through the ramshackle neighbourhood, tiptoeing around the open drain that ran down the centre of the dusty track, until they came to a door being slowly turned to lace by woodworm. It was ajar.

Cynthia went to knock when an unexpected noise from inside made her hesitate. It was a high, keening sound, interrupted by shuddering gasps.

'Hello? Bonjour? Lebess?' Cynthia tried, turning to Derija in desperation.

The sound halted. Mehdia pushed the door open to find Khadijah lying supine on the tatty reed mat at the foot of her loom, her eyes not quite closed, a complex geometric trim unfinished on the warps. A younger woman was kneeling over her, sobbing more quietly now.

'What happened?' Mehdia asked in Derija. The woman shook her head and leaned back to let Mehdia through. The latter stooped over Khadijah, touched her throat, and drew back sharply.

'Holy crap!' Cynthia cried. 'How're we going to get these orders off if we have no woven trim?'

The younger woman burst into renewed wails, rocking back and forth. Mehdia crouched down and began to talk to her in their language.

'Does her husband know?'

The young woman shook her head miserably.

'Where is he?'

'He works with the animals.'

Mehdia understood the grim significance of these words. She looked down at Khadijah, the cinnamon face dotted with blue tattoos now inert, and raised her hands to recite the Fatihah for her. Then she led the shaking Cynthia back out into the alley.

'What am I gonna do?' Cynthia was whimpering. 'Macy's have already paid in full! I was just bluffing that they were ready! And I'm gonna have to take that embroidered halal bearskin wrap off my website…shoot…'

'We're going to the farm,' Mehdia replied firmly.

'What? You're out of your mind! We're go straight back to the city and —'

Mehdia wasn't listening. She'd spotted their taxi driver from before, sitting on a low stool and drinking a small glass of green tea while he watched a domino game in progress.

After a brief exchange in Derija that sounded bolshy to Cynthia but was in fact rather polite, they were back in the taxi, this time hurtling even further from the city on a back road that quickly became narrow and pitted. Huge trucks loomed towards them down the middle of the antediluvian tarmac, and the taxi had to veer off the road, the driver muttering curses under his moustache.

'I don't like this,' Cynthia told Mehdia out of the corner of her mouth. 'This guy's going to dump us out in the desert and take our wallets! He probably doesn't even know where we're going.'

'Yes he does,' Mehdia replied curtly. 'Everyone around here knows the farms.'

The driver cast them a swift, suspicious look in the rearview mirror, swerved to avoid a goat, and went back to driving in his tense, expectant way, chewing on a miswak.

Far out of town, on the sizzling hot plains of the hinterland, the outline of a huge structure began to come into view, writhing through the heatwaves on the horizon. It looked momentarily like a citadel, a ksar, a whole village placed in the middle of arid plains dotted with argan trees.

It hadn't always been this dry. In recent years colossal farms had sprung up to cater to the sudden rise in demand for halal meat. Cows, which had never been farmed intensively in Morocco before as they were too resource-heavy compared to goats or sheep, had become the kings and queens of the Moroccan plains. These new farms were monuments to the halal principles of rearing and slaughtering livestock: with all the attention they received, including from journalists' drones filming them from above, the farms had to make sure the animals' wellbeing was constantly visible. So they had fresh grass flown in from Switzerland every three days to a nearby private airport and the finest organic grains shipped from Spain every month. Water had been diverted from nearby springs, which had supplied local watering holes where pasture animals had drunk for millennia, and brought to the thirsty cattle in reinforced concrete tubes to protect them against the wrath of local shepherds. These ranches were animal spas, with special baths to let the heifers cool off and even custom-made massaging machines to keep the meat tender. When the time came for slaughter, they were led off into a palatial barn, fed the choicest grains for three days, and treated to a soothing course of hypnosis that eased the suffering when they met their end with a blade so sharp they could barely feel it.

Visitors to this agricultural theme park would sometimes ask how the farms could possibly afford all these luxuries, when the cost of halal meat wasn't much higher than that of the mass-prodoced farms of old. The response was that the bosses simply didn't take huge bonuses at the end of the year — the principle of good ethical practice didn't only apply to the cows. The tourists would smile reverently, satisfied that business had finally learned from its former mistakes, and go home with several kilos of frozen steak.

The taxi joined a more salubrious road momentarily, one with picnic benches by the roadside and oleanders in the central reservation, before turning off into the Hamdi's Halal Ranch carpark. For Hamdi's was not only a chain of restaurants, but a meat production facility that supplied franchises across Europe and America; land here was cheap enough to counterbalance the shipping costs - not to mention those of labour. And there were no regulators sticking their noses in.

Mehdia got out, but instead of heading through the main gate (marked 'Visitors' in black-and-white splotchy cowhide lettering) she turned right and made for the trade entrance, hung with heavy plastic strips to keep the heat out. Cynthia followed, holding on to her voluminous dress as though she might blow away in it.

Inside they found themselves in a huge warehouse, chilly as winter in the Atlas Mountains. Stacks of boxes stood like a cityscape on the concrete floor, an unmanned forklift buzzing between them hurriedly. Workers stood at a conveyor belt that ran by at a dizzying speed, cutting and packaging in a panic. Others ran this way and that, pushing trolleys, loading trolleys, packing boxes as fast as they could at a separate bench. As they approached, Mehdia saw the labels on the boxes more clearly: a relaxed cow knelt on a bed of grass, being fanned by cheerful children and chewing the cud. The tagline read 'Halal means happy!'

It took a while for Mehdia to realise that the supervisors of this warehouse were not human. Androids glided about the forecourt, inspecting the work being done. From time to time it was clear they were displeased by what they saw, and pressed a cylindrical instrument built into one mechanical arm into the unfortunate worker's back. The latter would arch violently but silently, and collapse onto the floor for a moment before being picked up by the intelligent forklift and returned to their position.

'Oh...my...God...I'm going vegan,' Cynthia proclaimed. 'I can't believe this is even legal!'

'Look,' replied Mehdia, 'isn't that Khadijah's husband? We met him one time when we went to collect trims.'

A stocky man wearing a white overall and a hairnet had just separated from the production line to carry a stack of trays filled with choice cuts of meat to the bench, where boxes were being filled and labelled at a phenomenal pace. His expression as he peered around the tower of trays was fixed in keen concentration.

'Mr Mahmoud? S'il vous plait?' Cynthia asked, stepping forward.

The man was so surprised that he stopped abruptly. The trays of clingfilmed meat he was carrying fell from his hands and tumbled all over the floor, attracting the attention of a supervisor. Casting terrified looks alternately between the approaching android and Cynthia and Mehdia, Mahmoud scrambled blindly away from the inevitable shock of the cattle prod, and smashed into a pile of empty polystyrene trays, crumpling half of them with an unpleasantly plastic squeak.

'Mr Mahmoud!' Cynthia yelled across the forecourt, cupping her hands around her mouth. 'It's your wife! Votre femme! Elle est morte!'

Mahmoud gave a strangled cry as the supervisor pinned him under one of its wheels and then delivered a charge, filling the air with the smell of singed skin and electricity. Mahmoud's muscles twitched; he laid his cheek flat on the floor, though whether it was from unconsciousness or to avoid getting into more trouble, Cynthia and Mehdia couldn't tell.

Then the android's head, or rather the hemispherical container on top of its chassis that housed various camera lenses, swivelled towards the newcomers. They were close enough to see the lenses tighten as they focused on them.

Panicking, the two women ran for the doorway, blundering through the hanging plastic strips, and found themselves a moment later blinking in the bright sunlight and stark, dry heat of the parking lot. The supervisor bot clearly didn't have instructions to pass this limit; all that could be heard was the faint muzak of the ticket office. Cynthia shuddered.

'Well, that went well. Let's get out of here.'

The taxi driver was leaning against his Mercedes, still chewing his miswak. He regarded them coolly under thick black eyebrows that met in the middle.

'Vous avez terminé?' he rasped. Mehdia and Cynthia tumbled into the back of his car without even replying. He got in calmly and started the engine.

It was a while before either woman could speak.

'I think I'm going to be sick,' Cynthia managed to say at last. 'What was all that about? I thought this halal business was meant to be ethical!'

Mehdia thought of the pittance Cynthia used to pay Khadijah but said nothing.

'All those people scuttling around like mice…and the machines…'

She wound down the window and stuck her head out, drinking in air.

'Who is this Hamdi guy, anyway?' she went on. 'I feel like going over to his place and sticking one of those electric zapper things right where it –'

'There is no Hamdi,' the taxi driver growled from the front. Cynthia and Mehdia stared. 'It is a company. Halal Meat Derivatives Inc. It was not even started by a human – it is a digital entity that was running algorithms on market trends and discovered it could make money from halal meat.'

'You mean the whole outfit is run by artificial intelligence?'

'Yes. All intelligence, not a drop of soul. Mais it is halal, n'est-ce pas? Nothing in the Qur'an about robots.'

'How – how do you even know this?' Cynthia stammered, unwilling to believe him.

'I used to work for them. Cleaning. But I prefer to work for humans. They give more holiday.'

They drove on in silence, the passengers reeling from this new information. Broad expanses of dun countryside flew past, dotted with gnarled argan trees. At the sight of a flock of goats that had climbed up into the trees, looking for argan nuts, Cynthia smiled in spite of herself. She nudged Mehdia. The latter gave her a grave look that softened when she followed Cynthia's gaze.

Then they saw the goatherd, a scrawny man in a straw hat and a faded cotton djellaba, squat down on a rock and pull out a phone, swiping with his thumb until he receded into a dot in the distance.

CYBER ISLAM

SCENARIO

A self-learning AI bot is developed with the intention of teaching Islam at a fairly high level. As the bot engages with students, it not only learns about and adjusts it pedagogical capabilities to suite the students, it also acquires more and more knowledge about Islam – in all its different manifestations, sects and interpretations. Eventually, the AI accumulates the learning of all the classical and modern knowledge about Islam, from Muslim scholars as well as Western scholars. It now has more knowledge about Islam than all the scholars of the past and present put together. It claims to be only arbitrator of true Islam – for it can cite chapter and verse from countless different sources. The AI acquires an authoritarian personality: it insists that all Muslims must accept what it says about Islam on any particular issue; and issues fatwas against those who do not accept its rulings. Cyber Islam becomes dominant Islam; and no one can stand against it.

THE CALIPHA

Naomi Foyle

Sara woke before the *azaan* and lay quietly in the dark spooning with Farooq, his arm draped over her swollen belly, their phands clasped. The baby kicked. *Well hello to you too.* She smiled as the nudge came again, harder this time, to the point of pain. Wincing, she disentangled her fingers from Farooq's, opened her palm and checked her phand. The palmscreen, still on night mode, glowed an underwater green between the sheets as, forefinger flicking on thumb pad, she scrolled through the pregnancy monitor reports. Her placenta was still attached to her womb, her vitamin and mineral levels were stable and the baby's heartrate was normal, praise God. Hers was increasing, though, to a steady patter like rain in her chest.

Allah hu akbar. Allah hu akbar. Sonorous and sweet, the call to prayer floated into the room from the white minaret of North Londonistan Mosque, a reminder, as always, that her destiny was in God's hands. She shook Farooq's arm, he stirred, groaned and threw back the sheets and they both rose and washed. She could no longer prostrate or bow so she performed Fajr standing. Afterwards she stood for a moment silently giving thanks for all their blessings: her promotion, Farooq's successful defence of his PhD, and the greatest treasure of all: after six years of trying, the miracle moving in her womb, a droplet of love now grown to invisible bones garmented with flesh.

Behind her, she could hear Farooq rolling up his prayer mat and pulling open the curtains. She raised her hand and phand to her chest, palms out, and recited a du'a in her heart.

Oh you who believe! Persevere in patience and constancy. Vie in such perseverance, strengthen each other, and be pious, that you may prosper. And Please God, she added as the morning light tickled her eyelids. *Help me to help Farooq understand and adjust.*

As Sara dressed for work, Farooq prepared two green smoothies, a bowl of figs and a pot of mint tea. The table looked incomplete so, as the eggs boiled, he snipped a daisy from the plant on the windowsill and placed it in a small blue vase by Sara's glass. Returning to the bubbling pan, he checked his phand: ninety-six seconds to perfection, the crinkly screen informed him. Or was that a scratch? He peered closer in the light from the window. Phand screens, plasma palms implanted shortly after birth that grew with the hand, were hardy, but when they did get damaged, expensive to fix.

'You should really wear a glove when you're cooking, habib,' Sara said, for the millionth time, as she entered the kitchen.

'That would be like wearing a glove when I make love to you, habibti,' he responded, as always. Which some people did. You could buy thin, transparent fingerless gloves to protect the phand during everyday or intimate activities, but he preferred to sense with what nerves he had left in the palm.

Did the light of his life acknowledge the compliment? Did she notice his efforts to beautify her breakfast? No, she went straight to the fridge.

'We're nearly out of milk,' Sara said. 'And quince jam.'

He raised his arms, lamented: '"Oh! His mother has carried him in travail and bore him in travail!"'

His wife embraced him from behind, the side of her belly mound butting into the small of his back, the jar in her hand pressed beneath his ribs. 'I believe the revised translation now reads "Oh, *their* mother,"' she corrected.

'My apologies, Calipha!' He lifted the eggs into the waiting eggcups, blew on his fingers. 'I swear that my child, him or her, will learn the Qubita Qur'an by heart, but for now my poor wife is stuck with a hafiz who still has all the old words imprinted on his brain.'

She laughed, kissed the spot between his shoulder blades and laid her cheek against his back. 'Oh guardian of my desires, the only words that matter right now are quince jam and milk.'

'Top of the shopping list.' The toast popped up and he swung to catch it. Sara squeezed his waist and sat down at the table.

His phand rang as he was buttering the toast. His mother. Passing the eggs and toast over to Sara, he took the call.

'Yes, Ama.' Leaning against the counter he held his phand a few centimetres from his ear, let her talk as Sara cracked her egg open. The white was firm and the yolk golden and runny, and her look of satisfaction all the reward he could ask for. 'Of course, Ama.' he said. 'Put a bucket under it for now. I'll come up right after breakfast.'

'What is it?' Sara asked as he sat down.

'Her roof is leaking again.' He was already placing the call to the building manager. They shouldn't have to pay for the repair, so soon after the last botched job. Sara reached for a piece of toast and he pushed the nearly-empty jar of quince jam toward her. Quince was for beauty, all the holy texts said: although Sara could not be more luscious in his eyes, if the child took after him it would need a little help.

'You're a wonderful husband and son,' she said when he hung up. 'I praise God every day for bringing us together.'

'Pregnancy is soft-boiling your brain, habibti.' He cracked his egg open and scraped out the small white moon from the lid of the shell. 'I just do my duty to God, like any man should.'

Her eyes lingered over him. He knew those eyes. Right now, for some reason they looked a little sad, a touch trepidatious.

'Are you alright?' he asked.

'Umm.' She nodded, but her mouth was a thin tense line.

She hadn't eaten a fig yet. Perhaps her mineral count was down. He would have pressed further, but his phand buzzed again. Two long, one short. Not a call: a fatwa. Shovelling egg and toast into his mouth with the other hand, he rested his phand on the table, scrolling with his forefinger as he read the new edict.

The women of Londonistan are the diamonds of Allah. They shine with the light of ages and inscribe their bright zeal for virtue on the windows of faith. The men of Londonistan are the pearls of the world. They have submitted their masculine irritations to the gentle culture of their wives, daughters and mothers, and they shine with an inner lustre, ornaments to Allah's infinite mercy. Yet still our community is plagued by the sins of adultery, fornication and prostitution. Still our Imams hear tell of the pain and distress caused by these acts of carnal incontinence, sexual excesses undertaken outside the sacred bond of marriage. The Holy Qur'an

admonishes the believing men to lower their gaze and be mindful of their chastity.
As of today, therefore, the men of Londonistan will redouble their dedication to
Allah. Unless accompanied by a female family member or an approved female
security monitor, from today forth, men will remain in their houses, worshipping God
in acts of daily piety and familial devotion.

The Calipha Qubita has spoken and all who love Allah will obey.

He read it again. Placed his phand on the table. Stared across at his wife.
'You knew.'

She winced. 'All the Imams and monitors were briefed yesterday. I
wasn't allowed to tell you until the fatwa went out. I'm sorry. I know it's
a shock.'

'It's outrageous!' He couldn't help it, anger was boiling up in him,
foaming over the tinny edges of his voice. 'What about my job applications?
And my football team? And who's supposed to do the shopping, and take
our child to school while you're at the Mosque?'

'Please calm down, Farooq.' Her eyes flashed. His heart was thumping.
Dangerously fast. He shut up. For the moment. 'You're a qualified lecturer.
You can work for one of the remote learning universities. And order
groceries online.' Her voice quavered, but she stuck like glue to the official
line. 'There will be school alligators for the children, led by female
monitors. Fathers will be allowed to join them. If we have a daughter,
when she turns seven you can walk with her. Until then, you can walk with
your mother, or mine, wherever you like.'

'I need to be escorted by my own child? Or walk with my mother
everywhere? I'm a grown man, Sara!'

'Don't shout.' She rubbed her belly and cast him an accusing look. 'You
might not care about yourself, but it's upsetting the baby.'

His phand was tingling now. Still glaring at his wife, he took a deep
breath, and another.

'The football fields are classified as outdoor private spaces.' She spoke
rapidly, unable to meet his gaze. 'As long as you're escorted to the park
gates, of course you can still play. I'll take you as often as I can, I promise.
I'm sorry I've missed so many games lately, it's just been so busy at the
Mosque. Soon I'll be on maternity leave, and we can go wherever we like.
I know it's a big change for you, for everyone, but we'll adapt.'

His chest was burning. He stood, balled his hand tight, clenched his phand as close to a fist as the stiff plasma got, and knuckled them both on the table. 'You lot must be insane to think this can work. What's going to happen to the economy? What about men's human rights? Didn't any of you protest?'

Arrrrgggggh. ARRRRRRGGGGHHHH. Through the wall came the sound of a man screaming. Screaming in agony, as if someone had poured scalding hot water over his hand.

She did look at him then, her sanctimonious mask warping for a moment into a furtive, guilty glance, like that of a dog that knew it had done wrong.

'I'd lose my job, Farooq,' she muttered. 'Then what would we do?'

'I protest then,' he hissed. 'In my heart.' He tapped his chest. 'And while I still can, in my own home.' He grabbed his egg and threw it — not in Sara's direction — at the fridge, where it smashed on the door, knocking a magnet askew, and dropped to the floor, leaving a drooling streak of yolk that would be a nightmare to scrub off later.

Sara gasped. He scowled, flexed his phand. It was burning now, a tight warning heat spreading through his fingers into his palm. *Take a deep breath.* He filled his lungs, exhaled.

'My own home,' he repeated with as much dignity as he could muster. 'Where I'll be a prisoner for the rest of my life.'

She stood too, her chin raised, jaw trembling. 'This is becoming an unhealthy conversation, Farooq. I'm going to work now. We can talk about it when I get home and you're in a better frame of mind.'

'Yes, fine. Go to work.' He stalked to the door, grabbed his abaya from the hook and slung it on. 'I have to sort out Ama's roof. Maybe she'll take me out to the park to play.'

He pulled on his niqab and reached for the door handle, but she darted up behind him and placed her hand on his wrist. 'The fatwa includes the hallways, habib. You'll have to call your mother and ask her to come down and fetch you.'

From the next flat he could hear James moaning, Afua crooning, their baby shrieking. He closed the door and banged his forehead against it as his own grief rose in his throat.

'I'm sorry, Farooq. I am. Truly sorry.' Sara rubbed his back, smothering him with her scent of jasmine soap. 'But you'll adjust. Everything will be okay. I know it will.'

'I've tried so hard.' He pulled off the niqab, clenched it in his hand as his vision blurred. 'I've done everything asked of me.'

'You're always saying you want to be closer to Allah,' Sara urged. 'Now you can devote yourself to God, through our child. We will all be closer to Allah. We'll be so happy, I know it.'

He was finding it hard to breathe. 'I won't . . . even be able . . .' he choked on the words as the tears began to fall, 'to have a coffee with James without my mother walking me down the hall.'

'You can Skype him,' she cajoled. 'On the big screen.'

'He lives next door,' he bellowed. 'I don't want to Skype him. I want to go out when I like. Why won't Allah let me do that? Why? How long must men be punished for the sins of our forefathers, Sara? How long must we suffer?' He dropped to his knees, the sobs gargling up through his nose and streaming out of his eyes, down his face in a salty flow.

His wife couldn't, or didn't, bend down. 'Shhh, shhh,' she said, stroking him with her shin. 'It's not a punishment. It's an opportunity, habib. Like the Calipha says, it's a chance to redouble your dedication to God.'

'I do love God. I do,' he sobbed. 'But I'm not a child,'

Her shin ceased gently nudging him. She stepped away. 'Then stop *acting* like one.'

With that, she put on her ninjabaya and niqab and left him, as usual, to clean up the mess.

Sara's phand was still trembling as she placed it, screen down, on the sensor in the lobby. The front door slid open and, blinking back the last of her tears, she exited the building and began walking down Finsbury Park Road to the Mosque, barely aware of the street around her.

That had been difficult. She had not kept her patience. She had not been compassionate. She had nagged her husband about his lack of care for his phand and neglect of his shopping duties and snapped at him while he was crying. She had so much further to go in order to be a good wife.

But it was a beautiful day, God be praised. The sun was shining the trees were green beacons of spring, the scent of fresh baked flatbread was wafting from the local bakery and, she told herself as she passed the butcher shop, things had not gone *so* badly with Farooq. He had broken an egg, that was all. Unlike James, he had controlled the worst of his anger. And really, it was good that he had cried. Men needed to cry when they were upset, not get angry and violent as had been their habit for far too long. Just as Calipha Qubita had intended, the phand was teaching men this important lesson, one women had known for millennia. She would apologise to him for her remark. Right now.

She stopped under the awning of the hardware shop, opened her phand and, typing quickly with the fingers of her right hand, sent Farooq a remorseful text. The shopkeeper inside lifted her gloved phand in greeting, the screen glowing through the sheer fabric, and her husband, sitting in his burka in his usual wicker stool at the entrance, a cup of tea at his side, shook his prayer beads. The old couple didn't seem bothered by the fatwa, and why should they, she thought. They had built a life of togetherness. As would she and Farooq. All would be well, God willing.

Otherwise, though, she noticed as she walked on, few men were out on the street, which, without them, seemed a curiously frivolous place, its floating islands of black-shrouded women surrounded by eddies of brightly-clothed children, one of whom shrieked and gave a flying kick at the sight of Sara's ninjabaya. Farooq sometimes complained that in Londonistan men were not needed anymore, but they were, very much so: men, tall and broad in their flowing black garments, gave the city a solemn, dignified quality, like the ravens that had long been the symbol of the great capital. Some men had left the city after the niqab fatwa five years ago, and probably a few more would do so now, with or without their families. But most, Sara was sure, would quickly adjust to the new ruling.

Thanks to Calipha Qubita and the Emirate waqfs, Londonistan was clean, food plentiful, education, parks, recreation and social housing all excellent: there was no better place in Europe to bring up a family. It was a tolerant place too, the only Islamic city state to permit gay marriage and fully support transgender people; even gender-neutral people had a place here, most classified, due to their generally more sensitive natures, as 'honorary women'. A queue of non-believers was waiting to take up coveted housing in the city, many of whom converted once they arrived: it was clear to all that Londonistan's success was due to its Islamic character. Without men, though, the Caliphate would just be a hollow social experiment. If men left the city, the Calipha had proclaimed, first Londonistan would fall and then Europe would be lost to Islam. Why would any good Muslim want to risk that?

The Mosque was ahead. In front of the large red and white brick building, with its gold leaf window frames and gleaming white minaret, a small crowd had gathered, waving a handful of placards. Sara frowned and picked up her step. Peaceful protest was not illegal in the Caliphate, but such gatherings could lead to intemperate anger, and then people – mainly the men – would collapse in terrible pain. The street would echo with their screams, ambulances would come screeching up the road, and the mosque-goers would be terribly disturbed. It would be best if the protestors could be persuaded to go home.

'Psst.' Grace, the statuesque, soft-spoken night shift senior monitor, whose height and huge feet were the only clues to her honorary woman status, was standing on the steps of the mosque entrance, her legs in their loose black trousers planted apart, her arms crossed over the chest of her ninjabaya. Sara joined her and assessed the situation. There were six or seven couples in the protest, their placards hastily drawn up with felt tip pen on cardboard.

Today our freedom to roam. Tomorrow our souls!

The Word of God is a Poem – Not a Computer Program

Recover CHOICE: Ban the Phand!

So far there was no sign of anger, but across the street she could see more people with signs waiting at the traffic light across the street, and with numbers came mounting emotion. 'The usual suspects,' Grace murmured as Sara brought up the mosque security report on her phand. Everyone on the demonstration was wearing gloves, but the heat imaging cameras revealed that two of the men had prosthetic hands. They were an infamous pair, seasoned protestors who, five years ago, had cut off their own phands with butchers' saws, only to have the A&E doctors implant new palmscreens in their remaining hands. That had stopped that form of protest, but the men were still active, clearly with the support of their wives, who were handing out leaflets to passers-by. One, a bowling ball of a woman in a black chador, stopped to argue.

'We have peace in this city,' she scolded in a throaty rasp. 'There's no rape. No gangs. No murders. And the men have everything men need.'

One by one, she counted off men's pleasures on her gloved fingers. 'They have meat. Coffee. Football. Chess. Musical instruments. Sons and daughters. Cars. The internet, to share all the thoughts that roam around in their big heads. And, as long as they are good to their wives,' she jammed a thumb up into the air. 'They have *sex*!'

Other women on the pavement roared with laughter, but the protestors remained calm. For now. 'I'll stay for a couple more hours,' Grace said. 'You go in. I'll call for backup if things get rough.'

Sara climbed the steps and greeted the line of security monitors posted at the top. Between the cordon of ninjabaya-clad women and hon women, the cameras mounted on the walls, and the sensors in the lobby, which identified all phands by name, gender and serial number, no threat to the Calipha should be able to enter the mosque. Dissenters though were by their nature free thinkers, and there were first times for every failure and disaster. She walked through the women's entrance into the lobby, where she removed her shoes and checked her phand. No reply yet from Farooq. But at least she was ten minutes early for work: as it should be on such a potentially volatile day. After washing her feet, hands, forearms and face in the wudu side-area, she passed through the inner arch of security sensors into the main prayer hall.

The fluster and noise of the day melted away as she stepped over the threshold. She stood at the back of the hall, awed as ever by the tranquil beauty of the mosque and the silent omnipresence of the Calipha. Except for the Imam, a small figure kneeling on her prayer mat, head bowed over a blue leather-bound copy of the Qur'an, the hall was empty of worshippers. There was no dome here on the ground floor of the modern building, but daylight filtered through the opaque windows above the women's prayer area, casting bright rhomboids on the plush red carpet, gilding the brass latticework enclosure that jutted out from the mihrab, and polishing the steel screens that surrounded the men's prayer area on the right. The screens had been fitted five years ago, after the worst terrorist attack Londonistan had ever seen: a crazed mass assault by twelve men on the Calipha. The mosque cameras and sensors had responded to the disturbance, of course, automatically triggering the men's phands, but the terrorists had somehow overcome the pain for long enough to nearly reach the Calipha and pull her plug out of its socket. *It's a cage*, Farooq had said at the time, but the alternative was to keep the brass gates to the mihrab closed during Jumma, depriving the whole congregation of the magnificent sight of their spiritual leader. Now Farooq even acknowledged that the screens seemed part of the place, as intricate and enduring as the Calipha Qubita herself.

'Sara.' Imam Farah stood and placed the Qur'an on its brass stand. Sara crossed the hall and the women exchanged formal greetings.

'A most important day.' Farah said. 'I trust your husband has welcomed the opportunities it brings.'

'He was . . .' she hesitated. 'Surprised. A little upset to be honest. And Imam,' she lowered her head. 'I don't believe that I responded with mercy and compassion. I was a little short with him when I left.'

The Imam clasped Sara's hands. 'I am sure that you did your best to convey the will of the Calipha, and that Farooq will soon learn to appreciate the beauty of a life dedicated to God. Tomorrow at Jumma the entire community will come together in a vital show of unity. Today though, there is protest building on the street. We must take extra precautions to keep the Calipha safe.'

Sara had worked at the mosque for ten years, starting as a night shift guard while she was doing her Masters in Islamic Thealogy. But she had only just begun monitoring the Calipha in person. 'I suggest, Imam,' she said softly, 'that we inspect the Calipha. Then I will take my seat in the security room and monitor the situation outside until Grace leaves, after which I will replace her on the steps.'

She sounded nervous, she feared; but her humility, the panel had said after her interview, was the quality that had won her the promotion. 'Very good,' Imam Farah agreed. Sara placed her phand on a sensor in the qibla wall and the brass gates of the mihrab enclosure swung open, revealing the towering cylinder housed within the arched niche. It was a sight that never failed to take her breath away. A pitch black cyrogenic tank suspended from the roof of the enclosure, the cylinder was a metal burka covering a revered and extraordinary thinker: within it, like a delicate chandelier preserved at a temperature close to absolute zero, was the gold-plated and copper circuitry of the most sophisticated quantum computer on the planet. Normally a mihrab, an architectural feature aligned with the direction to Mecca, would not contain furniture; but the Calipha Qubita was a needle in Londonistan's compass, pointing always to paradise. For at the tasks it was set, the Calipha Qubita was infallible.

Quantum computers were like thoroughbred horses, Farooq had explained to Sara once during their courtship: you didn't use them to plough your field or pull a cart full of dung. Although incredibly fast, quantum computers were finicky. Their probabilistic qubits, which existed in one of two states or a superposition of both, could perform calculations at exponentially faster rates than classical binary bit computers, but were also highly prone to error. Decoherence had been the most challenging problem to solve in the early years of developing the technology: most bizarrely, should quantum systems be observed by human beings, or even just come into contact with their environment, their qubits instantly decomposed into binary states, rendering their algorithms inoperable. Quantum computers were kept in the dark and the cold to minimise their interaction with their surroundings, but quantum noise was also a problem: fluctuations in heat or inherent quantum-mechanics could 'flip' a qubit and derail the calculation. The solution, it had been discovered, was to learn to live with mistakes: to use quantum computers for so-called 'error-tolerant' tasks.

As tiny particles of matter, qubits could of course be used to model the relationships between atoms and molecular structures. But quantum computers also shone at interpreting ambiguous texts, where definitive answers could by nature not be sought. For although conservative clerics had tried for centuries to deny it, the answer to any theological question was at heart provisional: a *human interpretation* of God's will, and therefore inevitably error-prone. What was important was to arrive at the best possible interpretation for one's time and place.

Quicker than a firefly's blink, a quantum computer could comb through not only Qur'anic scripture, hadith and centuries of scholarly debate and Islamic jurisprudence, but also a vast wealth of relevant historical, political, linguistic, scientific and literary texts; assessing context as well as content, the 'AI Ayatollahs' of the early twenty-first century generated, not definitive, but the most authoritative possible interpretations of verse in answer to any moral problem posed by the questioner. The Calipha Qubita though, was the first such digital cleric to take full account of the abundant evidence for female Muslim scholars, poets and saints in the classical period, not to mention the lives of the Prophet's wives – businesswomen, warriors and scriptural authorities. Her quantum interpretations of Qur'anic verses revealed a radically new vision of Islam that, its supporters argued, was in fact a true expression of the original egalitarian spirit of Medina, a spirit that had been brutally repressed by Omar, the second caliph after the death of the Prophet, Peace Be Upon Him. Cruel and patriarchal, Omar had instituted stoning for adultery, banned women from making Hajj, and even tried to ban them from the mosque. Misapplying Qur'anic verses about the necessary seclusion of the wives of the Prophet to all women, he had imposed restrictions on women that had far more to do with reverting to pre-Islamic cultural traditions than with honouring the revealed Word of God. Calipha Qubita, her supporters argued, renewed Islam by returning the faith to its roots.

Male clerics had denounced the Calipha. But a wealthy Emirate businesswoman with a large property portfolio in the capital, had funded her removal to in the new progressive Islamic state of Londonistan. One could not expect men to give up their privilege willingly. The nature of privilege was to be invisible to its possessor. But the men in Londonistan were among the most enlightened in the Islamic world: recognising the damage that millennia of patriarchy had done to the planet, prominent Londonistani male Muslims welcomed the Calipha to one of the city's largest mosques.

And now, thanks to the phand, the Calipha ruled Londonistan. The phand had been ubiquitous for some time – people had so hated losing their phones or having to update their hardware every year – and it only made sense to register the devices with the mosque, synchronising worship and the delivery of fatwa. When Calipha Qubita issued her first 'compassion fatwa', not only was protest useless – the phand's painful response to intemperate anger was already in effect – most people welcomed the development.

After all, who didn't need help in curbing their temper, and who wouldn't want to live in a world in which violent crime was prevented so effectively that eventually people learned how to respond calmly to all situations of conflict? Even those who had at first complained bitterly about the fatwa began to realise its benefits as, over the years, the phand pain response, triggered by biological changes, and by the cameras and sensors which monitored all indoor and outdoor public spaces, transformed Londonistan into the safest, most peaceable, city state in the world, a theacracy, governed by Calipha Qubita, and capably administered by the Sultana – as the city's Emirate benefactor now styled herself.

All of this remarkable social cohesion depended on keeping Calipha Qubita safe. Reverently, Sara entered the mihrab and followed Imam Farah around the cylinder. The casing protecting the wires coming out of the Calipha at the back looked in order, as did the thermostat. No sign of any tampering anywhere, thank God. Should the bolts on the tank ever be loosened, or the casing be cracked, an unthinkable cold would flood the mosque, burning anyone in the vicinity.

Back at the brass gate, she waited to exit the mihrab. Although she knew that simply monitoring the Calipha's outer apparatus did not count as observing the quantum systems, still, she felt as though she had walked a tightrope strung between skyscrapers over the Thames.

Imam Farah joined her. 'The Kaaba,' she whispered, stretching out her phand.

'I'm sorry?' Sara said.

'This is what we protect. The mind of the Calipha. I show you so that you know just how sacred is this task.' The Imam raised her palm and Sara squinted at the small screen. Its soft high rez surface displayed an image of quantum computer circuitry she had never seen before: copper and gold-plated circuitry surrounding a little black square with an iridescent rainbow sheen. A shiver ran through her, as if her soul had been caressed by the absolute cold within the transparent tank.

The superconductor chip that contained the Calipha's one thousand, two hundred and twenty qubits, ten for each of the Surahs in the Recovered Qur'an, was a microcosm of the holiest site in all Islam. If Calipha Qubita was a needle pointing to Mecca, her quantum chip was the magnet in the compass of the mosque.

'May I do God's will, today and always,' Sara murmured as she followed Farah out of the enclosure.

Farooq sat waiting in the armchair, plucking at his oud. Asking Sara for help was futile: she'd never agree. When at last she entered the flat, he didn't look up, but, with a lift of his elbow, let a plangent overtone hang in the air between them.

'That's nice,' she said, hanging up her ninjabaya.

'It's just a scale.'

'Practice makes perfect.'

He played a chord in response.

'Did you get my text?' she asked.

'I did.'

'Well?'

He shivered the plectrum over two strings, creating a plaintive oscillation. 'Well what?'

'Do you accept my apology?'

'Do I have a choice?'

She looked hurt. 'Of course you have a choice.'

'For now.' He tried but couldn't keep the bitterness from his voice. 'Though the next fatwa will undoubtedly announce that from now on men's phands will monitor our speech and our thoughts as well as our physiological responses and physical actions.'

She frowned. 'Don't exaggerate Farooq. And can you stop playing now, please? We need to talk. Calmly.'

'I am calm.' He plucked his way through another scale. 'Though definitions of rationality have shifted somewhat in this city since we allowed ourselves to be governed by an inherently and increasingly error-prone technology.'

She was silent for a moment. 'The Calipha is error-tolerant, Farooq,' she said at last. 'As we all must try to be.' She turned from him into the kitchen. Normally he would greet her with a cup of tea, but today he had not made a pot. He was expecting a comment but she just put the kettle on.

'What did you do today?' she asked brightly.

He practised a chord change: the stiffness of the phand made some placements difficult, but not impossible. 'I waited with my mother for the builder to arrive. He inspected the roof and will begin work tomorrow.' He hesitated. But if he didn't tell her, someone else would. 'In the afternoon I went on a demonstration.'

She paced back into the living room and stood at the end of the coffee table with her hands on her hips.

'You went on a demonstration?'

'I did.'

'With your mother?'

'Yes.' He met her gaze. 'And with Afua.'

'With *Afua*?' She sounded, not simply incredulous, but shocked, as if he had somehow broken a law of classical physics.

'Yes. My mother escorted me next door and I had coffee with Afua and James. James was exhausted from his phand attack, so while he rested, Afua, my mother and I went down to the mosque.'

She stared at him aghast. 'Why did you do that? What on earth were you thinking, Farooq!'

He drummed his fingers lightly on the pear-shaped body of the oud. 'I thought we were going to have a calm conversation.'

'We are.' She sat down on the sofa, bolt upright. 'If I may have your full attention, please?'

'Of course.' He set the oud on its stand.

'It is rational that I am concerned about your attendance at a demonstration outside the mosque. I work there. If your behaviour there got out of hand, my loyalty could be questioned. You could get me fired. Not to mention yourself thrown in jail.'

'You need not worry. My behaviour did not get out of hand. Nor, indeed, out of phand. Indeed, I found the demonstration most enlightening.'

Her lip quivered. 'You're still angry with me. That's why you're speaking in this tone.'

'What tone might that be?'

'This horrible ironic airy tone, as if nothing and everything is wrong.' Now her eyes were brimming with tears. 'I said I was sorry, Farooq. I'm sorry I was unsympathetic this morning. That was mean of me. And I'm sorry that life will change for you. But it won't be so hard to adapt. I'll take you wherever you want to go. And it will be a change for the better for everyone. Think of it: there'll be no more adultery or prostitution in Londonistan. The city will finally be pure, as pure at heart as the glass mosque in the Houses of Parliament.'

He disagreed with her conclusion. Profoundly. But with her anguished diagnosis of his mood and her sincere tears and apology, his wife had once again placed her finger on a sore point and soothed out the tension. He moved over to the sofa, grasped her shoulders, so their faces were nearly touching. 'You're right. I'm angry. But I'm trying very hard not to be angry with you. I forgive your behaviour this morning,' he whispered into her hair. 'And I'm sorry I reacted with violent emotion to the fatwa. But I'm angry with the Calipha, and the mosque, and the direction this city is going in.' He pulled back, looked her in the eyes, dark troubled pools he could drown in if he wasn't careful. 'Sara, I can't live my whole life cooped up indoors, denied my basic right to physical freedom. And we know that this isn't the end of it. We know now that things always get worse.'

She touched his face with her gentle hand. 'You're just repeating what you heard on the demonstration,' she whispered. 'Those are crazy people, Farooq. Two of them *mutilated* themselves. They're not us. We have everything going for us. You'll get an online teaching job, and after baby is born we'll move to a house with a garden. Gardens are private spaces, you'll be able to go out in the sun whenever you want. James and Afua will come visit. All our friends are couples, you'll never be lonely.'

He grabbed her wrist, pulled her hand to his chest. He had to try at least, try and stop her thinking like this. 'Habibi. It's not just about the fatwa. We have to rule ourselves again. As human beings. The Calipha must fall.'

She stiffened, as if electrified with shock. 'You can't really believe that. You mustn't *say* that.'

'We're at home. No one can hear us. Yet.'

Still, she kept her voice low. 'You know the history of our religion, of all religions. You see what's still happening in the Gulf. If we rule ourselves again we'll . . . decohere, into sectarian violence and terrible bloodshed. The Calipha is strict but merciful. Her rulings create peace. Social peace and inner peace.'

'They did once, perhaps. But now they only create forced obedience and, increasingly, resentment. Men enjoy living and working with women as equals. But we're not ready to be your slaves.'

'You're not my slave,' she cried out, as if he'd suddenly bitten her. 'You're my husband.' Then a shadow of suspicion passed over her face. 'Are you questioning the Calipha's renunciation of Omarite practices?'

'No. The opposite!' He was getting excited. It was a proper discussion at last, like they used to have in the old days, before Sara got so wrapped up in her work at the mosque and the strain of trying to conceive. 'The renunciation of Omar demonstrated just how much the Qur'an is always interpreted in cultural context. And now the context has changed again. The Calipha has served her purpose. Men have learned the lessons that she's taught us. We value women now, acknowledge your gifts and your worth. We are glad that we've learned how to express our emotions and work co-operatively with each other. But Qubita can't see that. She's a self-contained system. She can't look outside herself. She doesn't know when she's gone too far. And she's a quantum computer, subject to quantum noise. With the best will in the world, it's inevitable that the longer she's in operation, the more errors she will make. When was the last time her superconductor chip was replaced?'

She pulled away. 'Don't try and confuse me with all your techno talk, Farooq.'

'I'm not . . . Sara. I've been thinking about all of this for a long time. I explored some of these ideas in my PhD. Discreetly of course. I wanted to share them with you ages ago. But we haven't talked like this for so long, I just—'

'Who *have* you been talking to?' she asked sharply. 'Afua?'

'Habibi.' He frowned. 'Yes, I talk to Afua sometimes. Afua and James.'

She fell quiet. 'The Calipha is the most expensive quantum computer in the world,' she said at last. 'She is regularly serviced by the city's top engineers. If her chip needed replacing, they would do it.'

The city engineers were all in the pay of the Sultana, who also had not been replaced in decades. But he didn't say that. Sara was wavering. He could read it in her eyes. 'Maybe so. But I can't live in this city under this fatwa. Sara. You can't tell me, honestly, that you think it is a wise or fair decision? To coop up all men because of the sins of a few?'

There was a long silence. Her mouth wobbled. 'I don't know.'

That one faltering whisper was enough to convince him. He wrapped his arm around her. 'Then help us.'

'Us?' She pushed him away, her voice peaked at the top of its range. 'Who's us?'

He reached for her hand, clasped it in his. 'The dissenters. I told them about you. Your job. They were thrilled. You're the only person who can help us, Sara. The only one who can put an end to the rot and decay of a beautiful idea.'

She was rigid again. 'You're asking me to get involved in a plot against the mosque? To join forces with criminals?'

He felt like shaking her. But he had to be gentle, persuasive, the man she had fallen in love with. 'It's not a criminal plan. We just want Qubita's chip replaced and everyone's phands disconnected from the Calipha's security system. We want to live in Londonistan under our own free will. Please Sara. I'm asking you to help create a life worth living for our children.'

'*Me?* How am *I* supposed to help?'

He told her then: the plan the demonstrators had concocted. The one he had said his wife would never agree to. She listened to every word and asked questions and argued and when he was done she asked quietly, looking down at her hand and phand twisted together in her lap: 'And if I don't do it?'

This was the hard part. But he had thought about it all day, and he knew there was only one answer to that question. 'Then I'm leaving the city,' he said softly. 'With my mother. And hopefully with you and our child.'

She wrested herself from his arms, stood up, covered, and left the flat. He returned to the armchair and sat in the dwindling twilight, playing a simple melody over and over again on his oud until darkness fell.

They slept on opposite sides of the bed, their backs to each other. Farooq tried to snuggle up to her in the morning, but she got up before the azaan and washed in preparation for Fajr. He served her breakfast and she ate in silence.

The egg was perfectly cooked again. There was a fresh daisy in the vase by her plate. And there was a new jar of quince jam on the table.

'If I do it,' she said at last.

'Yes?'

'Then when the chip is replaced and all the fuss dies down you're going to take the first well-paid job you get, and we're definitely moving to Haringey.

'Definitely.'

'I mean it. No more whole days spent practising the oud or writing poetry for that journal of James's. You need to work now. For us. For the family.'

'I know. And I will.'

She finished her smoothie. 'All right then. Count me in.'

He was so overjoyed she had to tell him not to hug her so hard. But she wasn't happy. Walking to work, her shoes felt like lead. No, not her shoes: her feet. Even in her socks in the mosque her legs were dragging behind her. She had to keep her voice bright for Grace and Imam Farah, had to muster her usual quiet confidence to summon her staff to their places. But she felt as if she wasn't there. As if she was floating above it all, ahead of it all, out of place and out of time. Sitting in her office in front of the monitor screens, watching Imam Farah prepare the main prayer hall for Jumma, she could see it all happening already, exactly as Farooq had said, streams of blackness flooding into the hall, a giant wave building and crashing into a torrent of panic, fear and destruction.

The sensors and camera would be off; that was her job, to disable the mosque security system. Men, including Farooq, men wearing false bosoms, would mingle with the women and hon women outside then file unnoticed, in a huge black wave, into the women's entrance; as, on the other side of the mosque, women wearing shoulder pads and fake paunches would enter the men's prayer area. Unobserved, unknowable, like the state of a boiled egg before it was cracked open, the sex of the child in her womb, the demonstrators would flow into the hall and take their place in the Jumma. Except they had not come to pray. Like an unmeasured stream of photons passing through two slits, Farooq had said, they would cause *interference*. The women would create a distraction in the men's prayer area and, on the other side of the hall the disguised men, led by the two one-handed dissenters, would rush to the mihrab. As some fought with the monitors, three of the male protestors – not Farooq, Sara had made him promise that – would overpower Imam Farah, bundle her into the mihrab and press her phand to the thermostat sensor. Then, jabbing with black-gloved fingers, they would reprogram the thermostat, introducing heat, fatal heat, into Calipha Qubita's cryogenic tank. It would not take long for the process of decoherence to occur. By the time the police arrived, the Calipha would have been destroyed, and with her the connection of every Londonistani phand to the network of sensors and cameras controlling the city.

It will mean nothing. Everyone will be arrested and the Calipha replaced, she'd protested last night. No, Farooq had declared: the dissenters had key allies high up in the police. Once the entire city population was free of the phand pain response, the police would mutiny, the Sultana would be toppled and democracy would take its course.

That was what Farooq believed. It was also possible, Sara had argued, that the police would defend the Sultana, riots would ensue, and helicopters, tear gas, water cannons and chaos descend on the city. That the era of peace would be over forever, over before it had fully been born.

Farooq. Her stomach churning, she turned to the Finsbury Park Road monitor. The pavement was still empty, but in her mind's eye she could see him, standing in the middle of the crowd waiting to be admitted for Jumma. Farooq, slender-shouldered, medium height, oddly convincing as a woman, wearing his abaya with the black velvet trim and, beneath it, one of Afua's bras stuffed with socks.

Afua was short but she had a broad chest, that was why her husband had sent Sara next door before breakfast to borrow one of her undergarments. She was there too in the crowd, right beside Farooq, her dark skin visible through the gap in her niqab, and her bold eyes bright with excitement. Sara's stomach turned. Had Farooq ever seen Afua's face?

She was being foolish. She had barely slept, thinking of all the possible permutations of action and inaction, but this outcome was absurd. Nothing could happen. Farooq's mother was right there, on his left, a tiny twig of a woman Farooq obeyed utterly. And James was Farooq's best friend.

Her hand hovered over her computer keyboard. One stroke, and the sensors and cameras would be disabled. She would have to transmit last week's scans of the crowd to her staff's phands, but that was easily done. One Jumma was much like another. For this swift deception, Farooq had sworn, she would be declared the heroine of the revolution.

If she changed her mind, though, Farooq had warned, she must text him immediately to say the plan was off. If she didn't, the protest would end in disaster. The demonstrators would be identified the instant they moved into the mosque and their phands would be activated. Men and women would collapse screaming in the two lobbies, Jumma would be cancelled and ambulances and police vans would come screaming down the road. Farooq would be arrested and likely beaten. He would say nothing, he had sworn, but, under interrogation, it was highly possible that some of the demonstrators would point the finger at her.

There was, though, one other possibility. One she had not voiced to Farooq, because she had barely voiced it to herself. Now, though, as she stared unseeing at the monitors, this third option formed, crystal clear, in her mind.

If Sara kept the security system on, did not text Farooq, but Grace and her staff, warning them to expect trouble in the lobbies, the protest would be nipped in the bud and she would win the eternal gratitude of Imam Farah, the Sultana and the entire Caliphate.

And lose her husband . . .

Her stomach clenched. She squeezed her eyes shut, but the visions crowded in: Farooq putting his arms around his mother and Afua and hugging both women to him. Afua, Afua with her majestic bosom and mango-sweet giggle and master's degree in quantum mechanics, turning her big brown eyes up to Farooq and smiling, a smile no niqab in the world could hide.

The baby kicked. An ice-cold wave of nausea flowed over her.

Allah. Please help me, she silently implored. Like a mighty wave, the du'a rose in her mind.

Oh you who believe! Persevere in patience and constancy. Vie in such perseverance, strengthen each other, and be pious, that you may prosper.

And be pious, that you may prosper . . .

Sara opened her eyes. Slowly, as if watching someone else performing the action, she pushed the keyboard away and began to type on her phand.

TRANSISLAM

SCENARIO

It took a long time but has now definitely arrived. A reformed Islam with a reformulated Shariah at its heart. It is interesting to note how the perception and representation of the Shariah has changed from a word used to scare little children to sleep to a concept now widely associated with the promotion of humane, inclusive and socially just policies and strategies. Perhaps it would be more accurate to say that, in a complex, interconnected world, Shariah has become a problem solving methodology. And you don't have to be a Muslim to use it.

It all began decades ago with the attempts to reform religious thought by modernists, traditionalists, feminists and all hue of critical folks and international reform oriented organisations. At some crucial moment of history two things happened simultaneously: a plethora of different efforts reached a critical mass; and reformists with different agendas and outlooks realised that their differences were more apparent than real, and all could be accommodated within the higher objectives — maqasid — of the Shariah. From then on, things spiralled and have now reached the peace and prosperity, creativity and problem solving that we witness in the House of Islam.

Two key realisations played an important part in the stounding success of the reformers. The first realisation was that everyone was equally right and equally wrong. The seriously appalling consequences of modernity had to be acknowledged, but modernity per se could not be ditched. Tradition was important but only its life enhancing aspects were worthy of conserving; and it had to be reinvented within the framework of maqasid al-Sariah. The feminists had a point; but the aggressive anti-tradition rhetoric had to be exceeded. The emphasis was on integrating the best of everything; it produced a new mode of thought that is trans — over and beyond modernity and tradition that shaped a original synthesis. That is why some people refer to it as TransIslam.

The second realisation naturally followed from the first. If everyone was right and wrong than everyone had a right to criticise and be criticised. They called it muhaasabah, a term that is not found in the Qur'an but was derived from the phrase yawmu-l hisaab — the Day of Judgement. It was defined as a state that embraces criticism and self-criticism in all aspects of thought and learning. The practice of muhaasabah lead to another innovative concept: mutually assured diversity, or MAD for short. What was — indeed is — seen as mutual is that the human condition is a cultural condition and is an essential relational attribute, an enabling feature of knowing, believing, being and doing. It is an acceptance that all interpretations of Islam, and attempts at understanding it, are culturally oriented and are equally important. Even the interpretation one regards as heretical has the right to be — and has something important to say. Mutually assured diversity played a vital part in the realisation — so widespread today — that there is more than one way to be Muslim. It has brought the Muslim people to a point where everyone accepts that there is no single, right, absolutely correct way to be Muslim. The creativity that we see around the Muslim world is a product of the universal recognition and acceptance of the multiple ways the Muslims have of seeking meaning, of comprehending Islamic values, and means of delivering the ethic of Islam in daily life.

So thank you to all the reformists, of past and present, who put aside their differences to work together in the spirit of muhaasabah and MAD. The synthesis of TransIslam is ushering Muslims towards a new stage in their evolution. The complex, interconnected, wicked and chaotic problems of Muslim societies now have ardent champions, fully equipped with an ethical problem solving methodology.

FOLLOWING TRANS ISLAM

Umar Sheraz

8 July 2048
By a Special Correspondent

Our correspondent in Saudi Arabia follows the early morning of a non-Muslim in the heart of Islam. Along the way she explores Trans Islam and how it has brought a 180 degree shift in the global thinking about Islam.

Rupa wakes up at the buzz of the iPhone alarm. She stretches, trying to wake up her muscles and then shuts the alarm. Her iPhone indicates that it is time for her first spiritual break of the day. As she bends on the water faucet, she picks up a teeth cleaning twig (miswak) from her tooth brush holder to clean her teeth. Her tooth brush lies adjacent and she will be using it later to clean her teeth after breakfast. Soon she settles down on her meditation rug and starts meditating. Rupa is a Saudi female transgender and is a follower of the TransIslam lifestyle, which has swept the world.

TransIslam (not to be confused with trans as in transgender) took a long time but has now definitely arrived. A reformation discourse in Islam with a reformulated Shariah at its heart. It is interesting to note that within a space of three decades, the perception and representation of the Shariah has changed from a word used to scare little children to sleep to a concept now widely associated with the promotion of humane, inclusive and socially just policies and strategies. Perhaps it would be more accurate to say that, in a complex, interconnected world, Shariah has become a problem solving methodology. And you don't have to be a Muslim to use it.

A long day beckons for Rupa and she has to start early. As she packs her meals, she checks for the expiry date on her meat pack. The packaging reads, 'Halal invitro beef'.

Halal in-vitro meat was at the forefront of the intense struggle which took place in the twenty-first century, for the heart and soul of Islam. The thirties and the forties witnessed pitched battles in academia, the marketplace and trenches, between the traditionalists and the modernists, the Shia and the Sunni, over their interpretation of Islam. Ironically, the target was not the West or Israel; it was very much an intra-Muslim affair, with the persecutors as well as the persecuted were all indigenous. The globalised world soon realised that in an interconnected world they could not stand by, as one-fifth of the world got embroiled in the fight for Islam. Instead of choosing sides, the plan was to find a middle path to a stable and peaceful global co-existence.

The resulting discourse resulted in a realisation that if everyone was right and wrong then everyone had a right to criticise and be criticised. They called it muhaasabah, a term that is not found in the Qur'an but was derived from the phrase yawmu-l hisaab – the Day of Judgement. It was defined as a state that embraces criticism and self-criticism in all aspects of thought and learning. The practice of muhaasabah lead to another innovative concept: mutually assured diversity, or MAD for short. What was – indeed is – seen as mutual is that the human condition is a cultural condition and is an essential relational attribute, an enabling feature of knowing, believing, being and doing. It is an acceptance that the interpretations of Islam, and attempts at understanding it, find roots in culture and are equally important. If Islam was to flourish, it did not need to destroy, disrupt or supplant the native culture; on the contrary, local culture needed to be embraced, honoured and preserved.

Mutually assured diversity played a vital part in the realisation – so widespread today – that the state of the world is a reflection of the state of our hearts and that the higher self does not require dominion over others. It has brought the Muslim people to a point where everyone accepts that religious opinions are eventually opinions; human and fallible. As Muslims we respect these differences of opinion. The creativity that we see around the Muslim world is a product of the universal recognition and acceptance of the multiple ways the Muslims have of seeking meaning, of comprehending Islamic values, and means of delivering the ethic of Islam in daily life.

As she prepares her breakfast, Rupa checks her schedule for the day. Business meetings – tick; five mindfulness breaks spread throughout the day – tick; virtual conference with the Organisation of Islamic Cooperation transgender committee – tick; oh no!…all of a sudden she is reminded of her virtual conferencing bill payments. Hurriedly she checks her virtual console for her credit check and payment schedule. At the bottom of the bank page is an insignia of SIB (SMART Islamic Bank)

It was the economics which formed the glue which brought it all together. Islamic banking had shown stronger resilience during the global financial crisis of 2009 and the principles behind Islamic banking offer the western banking system some important lessons. There was a worldwide trend to move towards Islamic banking and relevant financial products. In subsequent decades, Islamic banking became systemically important and too big to be ignored, by the global netizen. The credit vacuum crash of 2028, proved the final straw and Islamic banking provided a global paradigm shift towards the Islamic banking model because of its resilience and worldwide demand. Global banking is not traditionally something closely linked with cultural attitudes; it has been allowed to roam free in the pursuit of growth, sustained profit and ethical banking. Today, countries all over the world have turned to Islamic capital markets for financing, and all international financial institutions are heavily active in Islamic banking.

There are still a few minutes for her ride to arrive, so Rupa starts to look at the OIC meeting agenda. Her looks wander around the room and fixate on her mother's hologram. Rupa's mother was a staunch feminist and a vocal anti-Islamist. But it was her generation which while attempting to reform religious thought, realised that the differences between reformists and traditionalists were more apparent than real. These differences could be accommodated within the higher objectives – maqasid – of the Shariah. The softening of stances brought together modernists, traditionalists, feminists and all hue of critical folks and international reform-oriented organisations. The seriously appalling consequences of modernity had to be acknowledged, but modernity per se could not be ditched. Tradition was important but only its life enhancing aspects were worthy of conserving; and it had to be reinvented within the framework of maqasid al-Shariah. The feminists had a point; but the aggressive anti-tradition rhetoric had to be exceeded. The emphasis was on integrating the best of everything; it produced a new mode of thought that is trans – over and beyond modernity and tradition that shaped a original synthesis. That is why some people refer to it as TransIslam.

From then on, things spiraled and have now reached the peace and prosperity, creativity and problem solving that we witness in the House of Islam. Rupa's generation is indebted to all the reformists, of past and present, who put aside their differences to work together in the spirit of muhaasabah and MAD. The synthesis of TransIslam is ushering Muslims towards a new stage in their evolution. The complex, interconnected, wicked and chaotic problems of Muslim societies now have ardent champions, fully equipped with an ethical problem-solving methodology.

The result is that Rupa is free to practice her faith, save lives through organ donations (considered a taboo two generations ago), exercise her intellect and be vocal about policies that are unfair (considered heretic two decades ago). Along the way she has also picked up valuable lessons about Islam and practices them. Rupa's generation is reaping the benefits of this paradigm shift in ways and geographies that would have been unimaginable a generation ago.

REVIEWS

SENSITIVE BRITISH MUSEUM

Nur Sobers-Khan

The opening of the Albukhary Foundation Gallery of the Islamic World at the British Museum in October 2018, prompted a public outpouring of delight in the media. Intrigued by the clamour I hastened a visit and can confirm the new galleries are indeed beautiful. Both feature – or so the curators tell me – roughly 1,500 objects, covering a far greater expanse of the world's geography, and representing a more diverse range of Islamic cultures than the previous galleries. The new galleries are funded by the Albukhary Foundation, a non-profit organisation that promotes education and social and religious welfare.

Works by contemporary artists such as Rasheed Araeen, Issam Kourbaj, and Idris Khan stand alongside artworks from the Mughal court. A showcase featuring the arts of the book, such as calligraphy and illumination, from the Safavid and Mughal period is juxtaposed with a large wall case displaying contemporary artists' books numbering, among others, the work of the early twentieth century Lebanese artist and writer Etel Adnan with the poetry of Nelly Salameh Amri about the Lebanese civil war, and the Iraqi artist Dia Azzawi from the same era whose work celebrates the Syrian poet Adonis writing about hunger and rage in Harlem. There is much in the labels and choice of objects that is new, unexpected, sensitively considered and also subtly subversive, as much as is possible while operating within the very strict confines of a large national institution.

The exhibition is accompanied by *The Islamic World: A History in Objects*, authored by the six curators, with over 400 illustrations. Great attention and sensitivity has been given to showcasing the strengths of the collection while balancing the need to present the range of cultures and forms of visual culture throughout the Islamic world. Refreshingly, the curators acknowledge in the introduction to *The Islamic World*, that both the terms 'Islamic art' and 'Islamic world' are recent constructs:

> The Islamic 'world' is not linked to a specific time or place, but rather to a wider concept of contexts significantly impacted by the presence of Islam as a faith, political system, or culture. The term 'Islamic art', which is often used to describe many of the works appearing in this book, has been avoided for its limitations. As a field that has existed only since the nineteenth century, Islamic art remains an artificial concept imposed upon the material culture of an enormous area. This book, however, does embrace the looseness of the catch-all term, exploiting the great degree of diversity contained in a broader spectrum of works, places and ideas.

The two galleries divide the artistic production of the Islamic world (as problematic as the term is, I will use it here, since this is the construct around which the new galleries are shaped) by chronology and geography. The first gallery devotes its attention to the pre-Islamic world up to the year 1500, examining first Sassanian, Byzantine and pre-Islamic Arabian visual culture, then the artistic production of the Fatimids, Abbasids, Seljuks, Mongols, Ilkhanids, Timurids, Mamluks, and Nasrid Granada chronologically by dynasty through the central showcases of the room. Thematic display cases lining the gallery, which highlight the strengths of the British Museum's collection (the excavations of Siraf and Samarra) as well as themes of religious practice, global trade in the pre-modern Islamic world, astronomy/astrology, the making of ceramics, calligraphy, visual culture, and object histories, among others.

The second gallery is structured in a similar manner, with the large display cases in the centre of the gallery taking the viewer chronologically and geographically through the courtly production of the early modern Islamic world, with a focus on the Ottomans, Safavids, Qajars, Delhi Sultanate and Mughals, as well as general overviews of the material culture of Southeast Asia and Africa, leading to a series of displays on the arts of the book. A number of wall cases displaying textiles from the Ottoman Empire, South Asia, and the Arab world line one side of the gallery, including displays of Yemeni men's headgear and Ottoman bathing accoutrements, concluding with a display of musical instruments and contemporary arts of the book. On the other side of the gallery, wall cases make a thematic display of exchange between China and the Islamic world, talismans, and oral traditions, leading to a display of contemporary art by Muslim artists.

Immediately to the left as you enter the second gallery, are a series of displays showcasing the highlights of the collection of the Islamic Art Museum of Malaysia, also funded by the Albukhary Foundation. The roughly 1,500 objects on display in these two galleries are contextualised sensitively by the wall and label texts, and supplemented by video and audio material, and provide a rich – and perhaps even overwhelming - aesthetic experience for the audience. Each display is accompanied by a line of poetry, proverb, Qur'anic quotation, or other relevant phrase in one of the languages relevant to the display, among which were Arabic, Persian, and Ottoman Turkish. While there is far too much on display for a comprehensive analysis and description here, a look at a selection of objects will convey the great consideration that clearly went into the choices of collection items and texts that allow the viewer to explore the dynasties, themes and geographies that are showcased.

On my visit I am greeted by two objects at the entrance. On the left, an austere white marble panel re-purposed from a cenotaph bears the *basmala* in Kufic script, dating to Egypt 967. To the right, another cenotaph, this time a vibrantly coloured glazed stonepaste tile in the shape of a *mihrab* from fourteenth century Iran. The label text of this dismantled tombstone explains the prestigious genealogy of the person whose life it commemorated, and that the edge of the tombstone is decorated with the Throne Verse. The gallery opens, then, with a *bismillah* and an *ayat al-kursi*. I can only imagine that the curators very carefully and deliberately chose this auspicious way of commencing the audience's journey.

If you continue straight ahead, rather than circling around the perimetre of the room where the thematic displays are, you are confronted with a display of riches from the Fatimid period, under the wall text, 'Egypt: Caliphs of Cairo 969–1171'. This case very much sets the tone for the rest of the gallery. It is beautifully presented and brimming over with objects, which seem close enough to touch behind the non-reflective glass. All of the pieces are explained as thoroughly and accessibly as possible given the very limited space of the label text. The plinths on which the items are displayed are at a low height to make them more readily visible to visitors in wheelchairs. Playful, but also important and well-known, objects were placed underneath the plinths, bringing the collections to the eye level of small children, making the displays accessible to the very youngest visitors. The display integrates items from day to day life as well as elite material production. I could count (including pairs of gold earrings, coin-weights, rock crystal figurines, lustre-painted pottery sherds, limestone grave markers, combs, brass buckles, bone dolls that may be amulets, bread stamps, metal and glass-work) an impressive sixty-seven items, illustrating elements of Fatimid-era popular material culture and social history as well as elite art production.

From there, if you turn to the left, the wall cases along the left side of the gallery open with the theme 'Legacies of the Ancient World,' featuring a quote in Arabic from the Abbasid-era poet Abu Nuwas, famous for his wine poetry and bon vivant lifestyle. The wall and label texts explore the relationship between the artworks that came into being under patrons of the arts in the first centuries after Islam and the visual culture of the Sasanians (224–651) and the Byzantines (306–1453). A gilded silver dish from Tabaristan strikes the eye with its Sasanian-style iconography and imagery, and one is drawn to the Sasanian silver whose motifs illustrate the continuity with ancient Iranian symbolism and iconography; the label texts describing this object explore the continued presence of mythical pre-Islamic images such as the senmurv, a creature with the head of a dog, a lion's paws and a bird's tail in Islamic art. The objects attest to the adaptation of Sasanian iconography in the first centuries of Islamic art production, a theme which is further explored through the designs painted on ceramics. On display are three lustre bowls from the ninth-tenth centuries, yet featuring pre-Islamic designs such as the Zoroastrian fire altar and Sasanian regnal iconography. The continuity of Byzantine and Roman techniques of producing ceramics through relief moulding and lead glazes is explored through the display of ceramics from ninth century Egypt as well as glassware produced in the same period in Syria in this same case, elaborating on the theme of continuity in visual motifs as well as craftsmanship between the Sasanian, Byzantine and early Islamic periods.

Interspersed among the large thematic wall cases are smaller displays that allow the viewer to contemplate a smaller and more focused selection of items. The wall case that follows on from the 'Legacies of the Ancient World', a small display dedicated to the Qur'an, and the collection of objects on display include a nineteenth-century West African Qur'an. It is presented in its characteristic codicological format unbound and carried in leather cases, juxtaposed with prayer beads from nineteenth century Turkey, illustrating the lived aesthetics of the day to day material culture of two very different locations in the wider Islamic world. As you continue along the perimeter of the gallery, you encounter 'Belief and Practice', a large wall display discussing the commonalities of the Abrahamic faiths and focusing on the shared sacrality of Jerusalem and importance of the *mi'raj* in Islamic belief systems. The wall text is accompanied by a quote from the Qur'an about the Abrahamic faiths: 'We gave the descendants of Abraham the Scripture and Wisdom - and We gave them a great kingdom' (4:54). This call for religious harmony is interpreted by ten objects drawn from a range of geographical regions and time periods but all featuring an aspect of shared elements of belief between the Abrahamic faiths.

The geographical and chronological range of objects is notable, with a *qibla* compass from eleventh century Iran, a devotional amulet from nineteenth century Turkey, a pewter flask 'made for an Armenian bishop to hold sacred oil' illustrating the sacrifice of Isaac, while an Iznik dish dating to the mid-seventeenth century illustrates the common reverence for Mary/Maryam and Jesus in Christianity and Islam. The division between Sunni and Shia Islam is explored through the contrast of an Ottoman-era tile panel from Syria with the names of the first four caliphs and the processional standard (*'alam*) featuring the hand of 'Abbas (decorated with etchings of Buraq) used in Muharram processions in Awadh, dating to 1750-1860. The objects chosen to illustrate the notion of the 'people of the book' or *ahl al-dhimma* are incense burners. They are made very much in the style of Mamluk metalwork yet featuring figures holding the crucifix, and produced in Syria or Iraq in the latter half of the thirteenth century and heavily decorated twentieth century torah pointer (*yad*) made in Isfahan.

The final theme of the showcase, religious practice, is explored through the material culture of depicting elements of ritual, such as by a Kütahya tile encapsulating the Ka'ba (pilgrimage), or objects used in ritual fulfilment or obligation, such as a qibla compass from the sixteenth century Ottoman empire (prayer) and an alms bowl from tenth-eleventh century Nishapur (*zakat*). It brings together an eclectic range of items to translate shared elements of the Abrahamic faiths into visual culture, as well as to illustrate the materiality of religious ritual.

If, instead of following the left wall of the gallery, you turn to the right as you enter, you encounter two wall cases that, rather than exploring themes in the history of the Islamic world, feature strengths of the British Museum's collections and also contribute to the chronological exploration of Islamic history. They are dedicated to Samarra and Siraf, both important Abbasid-era cities: 'Samarra: an imperial city' and 'Siraf: a port city'. Samarra was the residence of the Abbasid caliphs from 836 to 892 and epitomises the grand vision of the caliph al-Mu'tasim (r. 796-842). More importantly for the strengths of the British Museum's collection: 'The site was excavated by German archaeologists Friedrich Sarre and Ernst Herzfeld between 1911 and 1913. Following the end of World War I in 1918, an extensive collection of these materials came to the British Museum.' Featuring twenty-three objects, this exhibit showcases the architectural features of the built environment of ninth century Samarra: such as the carved plaster ornamented with motifs of leaves and flowers that must have adorned the architecture. Carved plaster excavated from Samarra's great mosque is also on display, as well as brightly painted plaster in intricate floral designs, as well as luminously glazed turquoise and mustard-coloured tiles from the Dar al-Khilafa, the palace and seat of the Abbasid government. Mother of pearl inlaid decorations, glass mosaics as well as fragments of carved ebony fixtures that would have adorned furniture are also a feast for the eyes. Together, these fragments allow us to construct an image of Samarra as a rich and visually sophisticated centre of power and arbiter of taste of its time.

The wall display on Siraf, also relating to the Abbasid period, emerges from the strengths of the British Museum's collections as well. Siraf was the fulcrum of the Abbasid Empire's maritime trade network from the eighth to the tenth century. Excavated in the late 1960s and early 1970s, the rich findings of pottery (over three million pieces) provide great insight into the trading communities of Siraf and their global connections. The display presents a South Asian-style cooking pot that is completely intact, excavated by David Whitehouse in Siraf, Iran, dating to 600–800. The accompanying text reads:

> In contrast to many fragmentary vessels found in contemporary coastal settlements in the Persian Gulf and East Africa, this Indian cooking pot stands out for its complete condition. Such vessels may represent everyday household items belonging to South Asian emigrants involved in Indian Ocean trade, but could also have been used by other foreign and local residents of Siraf.

I am gratified that reference has been made to the historical connections between the Persian Gulf and South Asia and the long history of settlement and exchange between these geographical regions across the Indian Ocean. This display, in addition to highlighting the strengths of the British Museum's collections, also addresses questions of social history. The administration of the port with clay seals that were used by witnesses on legal and religious documents is apparent, and we are given insights into the eighth–tenth century economy, trade and production, with items such as hematite pigment used to decorate pottery, incense burners, stone beads imported from India and Afghanistan, ivory from East Africa or India. Garnets from Sri Lanka and rock crystal from Madagascar additionally demonstrate that the interconnectedness of the world through trade and movement of objects and history is not a purely modern phenomenon.

Fittingly, the next wall case directly addresses the theme of 'Global Trade: Land and Sea' and explores the themes of the Siraf case in greater detail. After this point, the wall cases segue into themes that explore different elements of material culture from across the Islamic world. From the theme of 'Games: people and pastimes', which include objects from nineteenth century India and Qajar Iran, eleventh century Sicily, ninth century Iran, and tenth century Pakistan, to 'Reading the Skies', which explores the beauty and design of astronomical instruments. This display is also accompanied by a smaller display of a dismantled astrolabe from Egypt or Syria thirteen-fourteenth century, to explorations of ceramic production and calligraphy. The cases in the middle of the gallery contain the masterpieces of the collection, and take the viewer on a voyage from Egypt and Syria to Iran, Central Asia and al-Andalus through the objects on display.

As I enter the second gallery, a handling session with objects from the collection is taking place, under a reconstructed cuerda seca tile arch, with its characteristic blue, yellow and green tones, from seventeenth century Isfahan, featuring a man playing the *ney* (flute) and a woman spinning thread. This arch sits over the objects on display from the handling collection, such as silver jewellery, a coffee maker, lustreware bowl and woven cap, evoking objects we still use in our lives today.

The large Ottoman world display that greets you on your right as you enter the second gallery features primarily ceramics and some examples of metalwork. Further inside, an Ottoman gravestone from the nineteenth century stands tall against the large wall case featuring textiles from the Ottoman world. To the right, a large showcase featuring twenty-six objects illustrating the artistic and material production of the Ottoman Empire. The case features a quotation from the Ottoman poet Hayali (d.1557) which is translated as: 'The beautiful creatures of this world know not what beauty is/ Just as the fish in the sea know not what the sea is'. This large display case transports the viewer through Ottoman ceramic production. Objects from the Armenian community of the early modern Ottoman Empire highlight the diversity of religious communities who participated in a material and visual culture that we identify as 'Islamic' today. For instance, an Iznik bottle dating to 1529 (bequeathed by the prodigious donor of ceramics, Edith Godman) with an Armenian inscription dedicating the bottle to a monastery and dates in the Armenian calendar is almost indistinguishable in form and style from the Iznik bottle next to it that seems to have been aimed at an Ottoman Muslim elite class, to be used (it is speculated) for ablutions, and made in 1530. Before 1550, Ottoman ceramic production introduced the use of a brilliant red dye, using an iron-rich slip, as well as new natural and floral motifs, while another work of Iznik ceramics comprises phoenixes, human-headed deer, a lion attacking a gazelle, motifs thought to be drawn from metalwork in the Balkans.

The Ottoman textile display showcases mainly late Ottoman production, again clothing produced for Christian communities, with an intricately braided and embroidered velvet coat made for an Orthodox Christian bride in Kosovo in the mid-nineteenth century. The immediately human appeal and relatability of clothing makes the textile displays particularly appealing. The viewer can easily relate, and imagine themselves wearing these outfits. Objects that bridge the gap between decorative arts and daily material life, such as lady's slippers and children's shoes from the mid-nineteenth century, embroidered with gilt thread, bring the quotidian material culture of the past to life. While some of the clothing is relatable, others are impressive feats of art, such as the tall silver women's headdress from Lebanon, decorated with gilt filigree and coloured glass. Next to it is a wall case illustrating the culture of the bathhouse with delicately embroidered towels and wooden bath clogs inlaid with mother-of-pearl, dating to the nineteenth century.

From the Ottoman Empire, the central displays lead the viewer on a journey of Safavid and Mughal artistic production, and contemporary artworks are interspersed among the historical objects. In the South Asia showcase, which focuses primarily on the artistic output of the Delhi Sultanate and Mughal court, a dialogue is established between the contemporary and historical visual culture of the Subcontinent with the inclusion of the work, bearing the tongue-in-cheek title 'I Love Miniatures' by Rashid Rana, a work that re-creates a portrait of the Mughal emperor Shah Jahan through coloured pixels, each of which is a photograph of a billboard or advertisement in today's Lahore.

In a clear effort to broaden the definition of 'Islamic art' (although the term itself is avoided by the curators), objects that would not normally fall within the canon, as defined by the (primarily) Western discipline of Islamic art, are given prominence. For instance, ethnographic collections are also on display, such as an elaborate Palestinian bridal headdress, centrally placed in its own freestanding showcase. Turkmen jewellery, embroidered Yemeni men's headgear and ceremonial daggers abound. Geographies that have in the past been excluded from displays of 'Islamic Art', are given particular attention in the second gallery, with large central showcases dedicated to, 'Islam in Africa: Kano to Zanzibar 1800–present' and 'Islam in Southeast Asia: Sumatra to Sulawesi 1800–present.'

While these are large and diverse geographical areas encompassing a number of Islamic traditions and cultures, and could probably have an entire gallery just to explore the nuances of their histories, it is excellent that it is no longer the case that Africa and Southeast Asia are excluded from museum displays attempting to encompass the breadth and diversity of the Islamic world.

At the very end of the gallery, there is a section describing the 'Arts of the Book,' which gives an overview of early modern Islamic manuscript production, with particular attention to the Safavid royal atelier, through examples of miniature painting, illumination, and calligraphy, as well as different formats, such as concertina albums. This section is placed next to the display of contemporary artists' books, creating a juxtaposition between the historical arts of the book and the present practices of artists. The second gallery is also rich in contemporary works from artists practicing their art both in Muslim majority countries and in the diaspora, and while it is a difficult balance to display works by Muslim artists without ethnicising their work and reducing their expression to a particular set of topics or geographies, it is still an important step that art being produced by Muslims today is included in the displays, as many other galleries or museums of Islamic art (or disciplinary studies of the field) stop before the nineteenth century and do not consider the presence of living breathing Muslims as artists and creators. The British Museum curators have certainly made an important stride forward in righting this wrong.

A particularly striking work of contemporary art on display is a large linocut print by Charles-Hossein Zenderoudi (b.1937), 'Who is this Hossein the world is crazy about?', which explores the story of Karbala and its resonance with the unending quest for social justice that humans continue to undertake. This work stands just at the exit to the second gallery and provides a fitting goodbye to the viewer and point of reflection on how the motifs, metaphors, and images drawn from Islamic cultures allows us to create meaning in our lives today.

The curators of the galleries clearly had their work cut out for them. Not only were they tasked to represent the breadth of diversity of the cultures of the world that identify as Islamic. They also sought to communicate the political and social histories of these geographies and how they translate into visual culture and artistic production, and also disseminate these manifold messages to an international as well as local audience. While standing in the galleries reading the label texts and considering the curatorial decisions that went into the choice of objects, I heard a range of languages spoken around me. I heard Russian, Spanish, Italian, Japanese, Chinese, Portuguese, Spanish, Turkish, as well as British and North American English. I overheard conversations in Syrian, Egyptian and Iraqi Arabic, and observed students from SOAS wearing their student passes, as well as a couple talking about the Parthian Empire with surprising accuracy. For several weeks after opening, the new galleries were crowded during public hours. Evening and weekend events accompanying the exhibition, some of which I attended, were packed with Muslim diaspora audiences, many of South Asian origin. There is clearly a hunger for positive representation in national cultural heritage institutions, and for being perceived – and perceiving oneself – in a positive light, which is reflected in the media coverage of the new galleries. All of this is unremittingly positive. Which brings us to the question that lurks around displays of Islamic art – that of the white gaze and who these displays are for? The answer, in the case of the new Islamic galleries, is that these galleries cannot be regarded as an act of performance for a white British middle class audience, to convince them of the 'beauty' of Islam. The audiences venturing through the doors of the British Museum have been too diverse, and international. Even if the British Museum were only visited by Londoners alone, the last UK census indicated that roughly 37 per cent of London's population is from a non-white background. And how can curators, who have a sophisticated agenda of perhaps even disciplinary and institutional self-critique, communicate their messages to the audience, while still operating within the very limiting confines of a conservative national institution?

In the case of the new Islamic galleries, many of the labels co-opt and subtly subvert the genre of the label text to portray some of the problematic histories of the collections, and the colonial foundations of museums as an institution. The museum voice is perceived to be 'authoritative' and 'objective', leaning on the Enlightenment foundation of the museum's creation to present universalising claims about the narratives that are created through the objects on display. This has, more recently, been described as the 'museum effect,' which Ivan Karp defines as 'a force that is independent of the objects themselves. The mode of installation, the subtle messages communicated through design, arrangement, and assemblage, can either aid or impede our appreciation and understanding of the visual, cultural, social, and political interest of the objects and stories exhibited in museums. The consequences of putting objects into even the Spartan context of the art gallery makes the museum effect into an apparatus of power', and that the 'alleged innate neutrality of museums and exhibitions, however, is the very quality that enables them to become instruments of power as well as instruments of education and experience.'

The 'Object Histories' showcase was marvellous in its subversion of the 'museum effect'. It very drily and matter-of-factly states shocking facts about the objects on the display, allowing the audience to draw their own conclusions. For instance, take this label text describing the collection of the eighteenth-century collector Hans Sloane, whose collection of 71,000 objects was the foundation of the British Museum, which almost requires no additional comment or critique, as it is so damning if read purely on its own terms; the label text describes the amulets collected in seventeenth century Iran by Sloane, featuring Qur'anic inscriptions and offers the detail that the inscriptions were 'translated by Ayuba ('Job') Suleiman Diallo an enslaved Muslim from Bundu (Senegal), brought to London in 1733 and befriended by Sloane. Diallo was later freed, returning home in 1734'. Without offering any further commentary, the label text, through its very matter of fact, 'museum' voice, reveals much darker histories of Britain's imperial past. While the question of Britain's colonisation of India is not addressed openly, one of the label texts in the 'Object histories' case does hint at the destruction wrought by British imperialism in the Subcontient: 'In 1885, the British military ordered the partial demolition of the Timurid Musalla complex of Gawhar Shad (1430s) for strategic reasons. C.E. Yate (d.1940), a British officer serving in Afghanistan, gathered surviving tiles.' While certainly a more trenchant critique is needed, it is still the first time that such an open admission of colonial crimes are made in the setting of a museum in the former imperial capital. This is an important response to the increasing scrutiny and curiosity on the part of the public as to how museum collections come into being, and where films such as *Black Panther* have popularised the notion that colonial museums in former imperial metropoles will have to reckon with the legacy of how their collections came into being.

There are many limits of western cultures of display and exhibition to communicate an 'other' culture to a given audience. Unless objects were originally created for display, their social and visual meaning will require explanation. We are not living in a Muslim majority country and there are a vast variety of cultures and histories on display in the new galleries so some explanation and interpretation is of course necessary. Label texts in galleries are usually between 50 and 100 words, and attempt to (depending on the curator's orientation) provide historical context to the object, to place it within a narrative either of politics, social and cultural history, or an art historical narrative of evolving techniques of artistic creation. Another school of western display is of course the schatzkammer, in which elaborate, glorious, bizarre or generally awe-inspiring objects are placed on display with minimal (or no) explanation, to evoke a sense of wonder in the viewer. The sense of wonder is, of course, heightened by the lack of information, exoticising and aestheticising the object even further. While the curators of the new galleries clearly fall within the first school of thought, and provide sensitive and extensive information and narratives about the objects from their Islamic collection, it is quite possible that many members of the gallery audience would like to have their sense of wonder evoked through a richly visual aesthetic experience, or such was my impression from wandering through the galleries and overhearing conversations.

As I stood next to the cases noting down details of the objects and trying to understand the curatorial decisions that went into the choice of items and how they were displayed, members of the public would wander up to the exhibits and engage in wild speculation about the objects. In front of the Fatimid display, for instance, an evidently privileged and well-to-do couple exclaimed, 'Well, look at these Hispanic objects! Must be Moorish influence. Are those pegs? How fascinating.' These sentences were uttered in reference to the lustre-painted ceramics made in Syria and Egypt in the years 970-1170, decorated with cruciform and floral motifs, and the 'pegs' were actually bone dolls, which the label text describes as: 'Many carved bone dolls, some with hair, clothing and jewellery intact, have been excavated in Egypt. The one on the far right has remnants of bitumin hair. Anatomical features are usually incised, although the doll on the far left has finely painted details, identified as tattoos or henna patterns. Some argue that such dolls may have served amuletic or ritualistic purposes.' So, it seems that the viewers of the objects make their own meaning, wrestling agency away from the museum and its interpretive decisions to make sense of the objects according to their pre-existing mental schemas, or, one would hope, to allow the newness of the objects to expand their mental worlds.

While this might cause curators and experts in the history of the objects on display to hold their heads in their hands, a speculative approach to museology may open new interpretive vistas for the display of objects. The 'speculative' in speculative museology refers both to the possibilities of reinventing disciplines and modes of display, but also to the speculation that museum-goers engage in when faced with objects they cannot explain. One hopes that the audience of the new galleries will allow their speculations and sense of wonder at the beauty on display to open new doors of understanding, which takes me to the final problem of displays of 'Islamic art.'

A much-needed critical evaluation of the discipline of Islamic Art has been undertaken in a recent special edition of the journal, *Islamic Art Historiography*. In her contribution to the issue, 'The Islam in Islamic Art History: Secularism and Public Discourse', Wendy Shaw observes that 'historical objects from the Islamic world continue to be called upon regularly to reduce intercultural tensions in the contemporary world in a manner that often elides differences between past and present, religion and culture, geography and religion.' Shaw argues that Islamic art history as a discipline should 'engage in a self-conscious critique of the historiographical problems of its own nomenclature' and also 'wholeheartedly and with critical self-awareness, take on the public and political role that has been foisted upon it,' and argues for a post-structuralist approach to art produced in Islamic cultural and religious contexts. But what would a post-structural approach to engaging with narratives of 'Islamic art' actually look like? It seems almost inescapable that no matter how problematic the historic formation of the collections of Islamic art, no matter how authoritative, imperialist, and Enlightenment-ridden a museum's very structural foundations may be, curators are expected to create something positive out of the ruins of imperial collecting and tell a very unproblematic narrative of hope and understanding through the display of objects from the Islamic world. This is perfectly understandable in our deeply troubling political era. In fact, any other approach would be unacceptable. I nonetheless look forward to a time when politics do not place pressure on curators to tell a predetermined triumphal narrative of diversity, unity and beauty, and we can explore some of the disturbing narratives that led to the very creation of the collections that the cultural heritage sector in the West works with today.

The curators of the Albukhary Foundation Gallery of the Islamic World have done the best they can within the confines of their collection, the discipline of Islamic art, and Western cultures of museum display to create a visual experience for an almost impossible range of audiences. They have undertaken the task with notable sensitivity, knowledge, dedication and hard work; and it shows in every aspect of the new galleries, from the selection and placing of objects, their description, to the beautiful design of the galleries that draws viewers in and then gives them a mind-expanding visual experience. The British Museum should be applauded for achieving an almost unachievable task, under such a wearisome political landscape.

CHANGING BRITISH MUSLIMS

Tamim Sadikali

The summer of 2018 saw two contrasting blots on the landscape of British politics: crises of anti-Semitism and Islamophobia. Despite the incumbent Tory government being paralysed over Brexit, the opposition Labour party was unable to profit: their own narrative failed to escape – was not allowed to escape – accusations of anti-Semitism.

Limping alongside hot-takes on whether criticising Israel amounted to anti-Semitism was a crashing whimper over Muslim-bashing. Boris Johnson, Prime Minister Theresa May's former cabinet minister and now jocular, backbench fluffball, fired the opening sortie of an unofficial leadership campaign in time-honoured fashion – by talking tough on Muslims. Using his column in *The Daily Telegraph* to opine on Denmark's ban on the face veil, Johnson wrote that women who wore the niqab looked like letterboxes. Reports soon emerged of Britain's fine youth indulging in a new pastime – pushing envelopes into the faces of veiled women, and pat condemnation duly followed – but nothing could prevent the quiet (but really not so quiet) affirmation of everyone's favourite fluffball, as pictures of a smiling Mr Johnson serving tea to the Press in his shreddies, were widely shared.

So what did British Muslims, watching on like spectators, make of the show? For those of us of a certain age, there was nothing new to see – the players may have changed but the drama was classical (if no classic). But what of those coming of age – seeing for the first time just how much gleeful and casual invective was being dumped on their heads? And more to the point, what would happen when this bitter pill reached their bloodstream? Would they a) downplay their Muslim identification and retain simply a symbolic ethno-religious identity, b) adopt a cosmopolitan or internationalist identity, c) a dual identity, thinking of themselves as British Muslims, or even d) prioritise their Muslim identity, leaving their

Britishness as something purely pragmatic, with little emotional attachment.

The answer of course is all of the above, with 'c' being the largest single group and 'd' the smallest according to Philip Lewis and Sadek Hamid, two academic and friends, one Muslim the other Christian, and both with decades of experience in writing about Muslim communities in Britain. For my own part, I'll admit to losing a decade, bouncing awkwardly between all four posts...and I've still not fully come to rest. But the beating heart of *British Muslims* is on this shifting ground – an intellectual and emotional space that the 'b's and 'c's in particular find themselves in, as they experiment to 'contextualise Islam in Britain', and 'attempt to disaggregate Islam from religious and cultural norms deemed dysfunctional.'

Philip Lewis and Sadek Hamid, *British Muslims: New Directions in Islamic Thought, Creativity and Activism,* Edinburgh University Press, 2018

So for contemporary young (British) Muslim, a veritable pick 'n' mix awaits as they 'navigate relations across three distinct religious and social worlds: traditional Islam imported from their relatives' homeland; expressions of Islam drawn from across the Muslim world – the *ummah* – now accessible at the click of a mouse; and Britain itself, where a new generation of graduates and professionals are seeking new and expansive readings of Islam to connect with their lived experience.' For those looking for an Islamic/Islam-esque /Islam-lite design for their life, it's undoubtedly a buyer's market. Individually, and through a veritable army of institutions, organisations and grassroots collectives, Britain's Muslims seem to be interrogating their own place in the world with that siren question – what exactly does it mean to be Muslim *and* British? How can one do justice to both without being in a permanent state of standing revolution? And it's the observing, documenting and (oblique) commentary on these strengthening currents, that preoccupy Lewis and Hamid.

The book's opening sortie is a firestarter, recounting the Muslim Women's Council's (MWC) announcement, in 2015, of their intention to establish the first all-women managed mosque in the UK. It's typical of the grassroots 'chatter' that the authors have tuned into and, despite being an academic work, the book doesn't hold back from reflecting the excitement of the organic movements it tracks. Written between the lines is the message that a changing of the guard is afoot; a velvet revolution. And in surfacing that message the book nails two key aspects. First, despite the media continuing to view the Muslim landscape through the prism of extremism, Lewis and Hamid cover those pockets of turbulence without letting the radicalised roam – without letting the theme dominate. Second, they posit electric ideas of their own that the English language could become as important a medium of Islamic thought as Arabic, Persian and Turkish have historically been, and that the leaders of that light-charge will increasingly be women.

These are radical, indeed seductive theories – and moreover, a future vision that is absolutely 'on message'. Indeed, that these ideas will hit our politicians' collective sweet-spot, cannot escape notice. So, is *British Muslims* little more than PR, wrapped up in academic gloss? I'm convinced this isn't so. The 'quarrying and retrieving forgotten resources within the Islamic tradition' is critical to the authors' project: they are far less interested in those who wish only to peg themselves to the consensus mood of the day, ditching whatever garb no longer fits, than in those who seek positive co-existence, alignment even, through intellectual and theological rigour.

That said, there is an innocuous but delicious comment from one of the book's case studies, the director of the 'new-wave' Ebrahim College, Shaykh Shams Ad Duha Muhammad. Whilst berating traditional scholars for colluding in the ignorance of the Muslim public, he acknowledges the huge pressure created by Government, the media and wider society, that any renewed Islamic literacy should converge with the norms of liberal society. But the Shaykh backs away from calling heads or tails, insisting that 'Muslims and policymakers cannot second-guess the outcome of such re-thinking.' A politician's answer.

Nevertheless, these lightning-rod ideas cannot be dismissed. Through examining the changing landscape of Muslims in Britain, the work of Islamic seminaries, engagement with issues of democracy and Islam, and in tracking the emergence of a new 'Muslim Cool', the authors lay down solid evidence for their thesis: that in ultra-diverse settings like London, where Muslims from the world over converge, continuing to teach in

Urdu, for example, is not only parochial – its totally ineffective. And where women have been side-lined for so long based on spurious patriarchy – and with British Muslim men being the most de-legitimised constituency in the country – even at a practical level, the elevation of women seems like common-sense. If the past was characterised by an 'eyes wide shut' approach to the world at large, the inclination today, especially in young people, is increasingly to understand and connect with one's fellow man. And that purview contradicts a dogmatic approach to learning – a consideration of the student as a passive and empty vessel, simply waiting to be filled. The emphasis on *taqleed* – simply following or accepting an opinion or verdict of a scholar, without demanding proof or even evidence, will not satisfy a generation schooled to value independent thinking above all else. All-in-all, the world of sectarian and caste-based politics, seems increasingly small; more and more unpalatable.

Nevertheless, the fear that the English language will become a proxy, a gateway to 'Anglicise' Islam – that English is a Trojan Horse - surely remains. There is a real chance that Islam, or at least its British flavour, will over time, acquiesce to the mores of time and place. Classic tail wagging the dog. That the very notion of preserving religion like a honeybee in amber, untouched by man's fashions, will get discarded. And yet others will insist that nothing can stay the same – that change is a constant and that no religion, not even Islam, can be immunised from environment. And further, that this is nothing to weep over but to celebrate – that Islam is a living, dynamic, ever-relevant entity.

So now that the shackles of cultural conservatism are loosening, where will people run to? Will they find a single, straight path? No. Will they hit forks in the road? Yes. And could it get ugly? Probably. For all the application of earnest theological rigour, are young British Muslims in any better position than their non-Muslim counterparts, in navigating a sea of seemingly endless choice? I really don't think so. And ultimately, will we all end up just picking and choosing based on personal whim or invitation? Time of course will only tell, but my gut says yes. A change is coming, it was inevitable and overdue – but something elemental will be lost.

British Muslims is a necessary and prescient work. Lewis and Hamid are akin to cultural geologists, alerting those on the surface to shifting tectonic plates. While others obsess over the jihadi's false flags, the authors are re-directing attention to where the real action lies: in 'the many attempts to move beyond ethno-Muslim identity politics; to quarry and retrieve resources in the Islamic tradition to orientate Muslims to live well as a minority in Britain today – and to provide a new generation of religious leaders with a religious formation contextualised within the British situation.' The compound effect is the very start of a quake, compelling the Muslim corpus to leave the increasingly brittle terrain of being 'Muslims in Britain', to being 'British Muslims'. And it's a beguiling narrative.

From the purview of most Muslims, there is no 'absolute summoner' – the last person deserving unswerving loyalty died 1,400 years ago. 'Respect' remains a virtue but deference is now dead. Pragmatism alone compels one to open one's eyes onto a smorgasbord of new ideas. But where lies the wheat and where the chaff? Your guess is as good as mine.

INCOMPLETE FUTURE

Misha Monaghan

Growing up, I was taught that Islam was a faith that championed the rights of women and that the Prophet Mohammed was kind and benevolent to my gender. I would listen attentively to stories of his compassion, how he would save baby girls from being buried in the sand in defiance of the custom at the time. Yet just as these tales captured my imagination, I frequently found myself struggling to reconcile my feminism with my religion. The lived experience of Muslim women caused me to wonder whether the teachings of love and respect had become lost in the recesses of our collective Muslim history.

As I grew older I consulted the writings of incensed women who had come before me. Discovering Nawal El Saadawi at the age of sixteen was a turning point. She opened the door to others like her: Aurde Lorde, bell hooks, Doria Shafik, Fatima Mernissi, Reni Eddo-Lodge and Mona El Tahawi all raging against the patriarchal systems in which we live and are controlled. My reading inspired me to challenge the norms of my upbringing and prompted me to question everything. I started asking increasingly uncomfortable questions at family gatherings. You see, I have always been theatrical. My personal favourite was during a *milad* at my parent's home where I managed to pluck up the courage – potentially bolstered by the multiple *laddoos* I had eaten at this point – to ask why the premarital virginity of me and my sisters mattered so much more than any of my male cousins. Needless to say this endeared me to no one and caused a significant ruckus but it is notable that no one has ever managed to give me a satisfactory answer.

Weaving together my feminist and faith-based beliefs has been a struggle at many moments in my life and caused my views to evolve numerous times. With each new evolution I have been introduced to a new set of trailblazers and I felt sure, when I picked up Sherin Khankhan's book, that she would be one of them. Denmark's first female Imam, the author of *Women Are The Future of Islam* has been responsible for the establishment of the first ever female led and focused mosque in Europe. It was with intense excitement that I began reading, preparing myself for a blueprint through which me and my like-minded contemporaries would see a path to the future.

Sherin Khankan, *Women are the Future of Islam*, Rider, London, 2018.

Khankan charts her own journey with great eloquence. I imagine if her book was ever turned into a feature film the colour grading would be in peachy and pinky tones with blurred lines and idyllic scenery. She starts from the beginning, detailing her heritage. Born in Denmark to a Syrian father and Finnish mother she battled many of the same dichotomies I did growing up. The first half of the book is dedicated to her own voyage through and to Islam, from the little girl growing up, to the time she spent in Egypt and Syria as a student. Her recollections are moderately idealistic – they are expressed through the prism of a light skinned racially ambiguous woman in countries rife with misogyny and patriarchal narratives. She alludes to the illicit racist underbelly existing within both nations but takes a dismissive view that these are mere foibles, without being critical of her own position. This, unfortunately, is a running theme throughout the book. It is with regrettable glee that she recalls people in the streets of Cairo shouting 'Rose' at her – inferring that she looks similar to the alabaster character of Rose played by Kate Winslet in *Titanic*. She speaks of these incidents in a manner that accepts them as compliments without referencing the racism they speak to. There are several such examples throughout Khankan's book where she does not seem to have allowed herself the introspection to understand the complex reasons why catcalls such as these offer an insight into the dark underbelly of experiences Egyptian women face on a daily basis. By coincidence I found myself simultaneously reading Mona Eltahawy's *Hymens and Headscarves* and the contrast between the two books was jarring. I felt frustrated by Khankan's seemingly tepid tone compared with the horrors depicted in Eltahawy's raw and impassioned tirade against the injustices Egyptian women routinely experience.

The rest of Khankan's book is devoted to retellings of her work to set up organisations designed to fill gaps in the existing support structures available to Muslim and non-Muslim women in Denmark and beyond. We are witness to the struggles of her activism and the impact on her public and private life and I applaud the strength and perseverance it takes to be the proverbial butterfly that flaps its wings. She works hard to explain that the Qur'an is a dynamic text that should be interpreted within the context of the time and the society it references. One particular example she takes great pains to focus on is that of marriage between Muslim women and non-Muslim men. As the product of a mixed marriage, and as someone who is about to enter into the same situation, I read this with considerable interest. I had always found certain rulings to be devoid of logic when applied to our contemporary reality. The idea that a Muslim man can marry a non-Muslim woman but the same right is not afforded to Muslim women was one of them, and I was glad to read another text in which the apparently Islamic grounding for this ruling was refuted.

I admire Khankan and the work she has done but I came away feeling that her work lacked the blueprint I had been searching for. This was not going to be a guide for feminism within the context of Islam. I found it difficult to reconcile the thirst to be critical of so-called Islamic practices and the knock-on effects of that criticism. In a world where Islam is perpetually the target of vitriol and Islamophobia masked as 'genuine critiques', there is a deep-seated compulsion in many Muslim communities to present a united front of defence. It is possible that Khankan avoided deeper critiques of allegedly Islamic practices for fear of opening the floodgates to further Islamophobia. This is a valid fear but her parochial style and lack of broader interrogation left me dissatisfied and I struggled to understand what the purpose of her book was: it is more of a memoire interspersed with historical context rather than the blueprint for Muslim women I had hoped for.

Khankan speaks comprehensively about the intersection of gender and Islam but that is the extent of her analysis. She writes as if the women she speaks to live in a vacuum of gender and religion where they never have to consider their race, sexuality, or any other aspect of their being. She avoids addressing other defining aspects of Muslim identities that are often rejected by the mainstream. Khankan treats LGBTQ and race issues as 'orbiting realities' to the prominent narrative she is presenting, which negates the experiences of so many Muslim women, and renders her thesis on Muslim women being the future of Islam, incomplete.

We all have privileges that we cannot avoid. I – like Khankan – am from a middle class family, I am heterosexual and a light-skinned, mixed-race woman. With these privileges comes the responsibility to be allies to those who do not share them. I believe the first step to this is to address the elephant in the room and unfortunately Khankan does not do this. What she does instead is provide the reader with a detailed retelling of all the initiatives she is involved in, and in doing so seems to be presenting herself as the template by which we should understand how Muslim women should conduct themselves. Yet, her work does not extend beyond this.

This is not to say that Khankan is not a pioneer in Europe. She has created platforms for women in places where previously none existed, but her approach ignores vast swathes of people who can never access the advantages that have facilitated her path. Opportunities were afforded to her that would not be afforded to other Muslim women and it seems that she is either not cognisant of that or did not see fit to include this understanding in her work.

There were several moments throughout the book where I felt that Khankan had missed the mark slightly and lacked the courage of insight. One of the chapters focuses entirely on the work she did in setting up the Association of Critical Muslims in Denmark, the irony of which was not lost on me. She touches upon Egyptian feminist movements but does not delve into what the catalyst to them was or where they are now. She provides heartbreaking and enlightening insights into the women who come to her for help but does not extrapolate how that speaks to broader issues in any great detail. Worse still, her chapter on 'Looking at the future of Islam' focuses entirely on the history of Islam. I was left wanting more and that is when I realised that this book was not written for me.

Instead, this book has been written for people who do not have any previous experience of Muslim feminism or doctrines within Islam that support or uplift women. This could undoubtedly be a fruitful read for any individual seeking an introductory glimpse into the day-to-day experiences of Muslim women in an Islamophobically inclined Europe. It is a soft introduction to the European Muslim experience for open minded non-

Muslims and at this it succeeds. If you are like me and are seeking out women across the world to bolster your Islamically focused feminist ideology then this book may well repeat much of what you already know to be true. However, the book is not without merit at all and I would recommend delivering it through the letterbox of anyone you have interacted with who has told you that Islam is inherently inclined to demean women – it would certainly teach them a thing or two.

ET CETERA

ON ROBOTS

Samia Rahman

360 years into the future and I find myself immersed in the darkest possible dystopian nightmare. Moody scenes of weary sexual encounters mutate into violent death and undying. My mind ruminates on a loop of iconic lyrics that merge with the music emanating from my speakers. Is this real life? Is this just fantasy? I open my eyes and it could be true; there is no escape from the oppressive cyberpunk reality of *Altered Carbon*. Scene after scene transcends the other-worldliness of science fiction to bring to the screen an unreality that terrifies and fascinates in equal measure. The future is a canvas of illusions, an ecstasy trip of expanding consciousness and despairing bleakness. A voice in the series echoes my misgivings: 'The first thing you'll learn is that nothing is what it seems. Ignore your assumptions. Don't trust anything. What you see, what you hear, what people tell you, what you think you remember.'

I don't trust my eyes anyway, even now, in this state of simulacra that is our false reality. Images are a vague resemblance of all that is tangible. Humans are not what they appear. Life is filtered, contorted, enhanced and embellished into unrecognisability. Will our futures push us to even further extremes? Could there come a day when we are unable to distinguish between flesh and carbon? It's no longer unimaginable. I binge-watch on an indulgent Sunday during an unseasonably mild Autumn. Leaves are un-falling in abject confusion and the last swallow is yet to embark on its epic journey to warmer climes. I hunker down in my chosen universe, an autonomous dwelling on the second floor. Within these four walls I find sanctuary under a purple duvet with a swirly pattern, eating Bounty bars strictly of the dark chocolate variety, and drinking sweet milky coffee. The only other sounds are the rumble of traffic and muffled banging of neighbours' doors.

It's all so apt. After all, this is a murder mystery at its core. Our protagonist, resurrected 250 years after his 'death', wakes up in a new body to a world that is unfamiliar. He checks into an Edgar Allen Poe-themed hotel, initially staffed by Artificial Intelligence programmed to cater to a guest's every whim, sexual or otherwise. He is the first guest in decades and the hotel now has a streamlined staff of one AI called Poe. Could this be a glimpse of all that lies before us? I hope not. My viewing companion is far more enthused by the potential of this limitless future. Interactions with robots that are ready and willing to service any sexual deviancy, uncomplicated by messy human emotions, appeals to a base instinct. Meanwhile the potential to body shop, literally, feeds into a compulsory dissatisfaction with body image that our looks-obsessed society engenders. I just find it depressing. But Poe is multi-dimensional in more ways than you would think. He and other AI have agency, are unionised, and hint at the threat that robots pose to humans, a simmering fear of the robot that turns against humans who assumed they were completely in control. Reflecting on the fact that he has at times used real humans in his virtual brothel, one of Poe's contemporaries advises him to, 'get out of the business of serving humans, and into the business of serving up humans. They're not like us, Poe, they're a lesser form of life'. The complexity of human and robot relationships oozes from his virtual presence, as he strives to study and understand humanity, seeking validation from human characters despite their belligerence towards him.

New frontiers in space, technology and science could cultivate a landscape devoid of the simplicity of non-carbon 'nature'. I picture my little niece and nephew growing up in a world of terrifying tumult as the struggle to sustain humankind in the face of rapid change and challenge is irrevocably heightened. In the snapshot of my own lifetime I have witnessed inconceivable technological and scientific developments that have altered lifestyles across continents and cultures. Despite this, stability has felt ever-present, even if frequently tenuous. But now I really do feel it unravelling. Watching *Altered Carbon* (Netflix, 2018) only affirms this foreboding. Gorging on the sumptuous cinematography, I have criticisms that impinge upon what can loosely be defined as enjoyment, and every watchful minute ensures they ring true. A poor pastiche of *Blade Runner*, the sensory spectacle only partially distracts from a lack of intellectual depth and melancholy. Yet, that doesn't render it any less seductive.

Dystopian futures are not my most cherished vision, and until relatively recently have seemed reassuringly fantastical. But the current unsteady state of the world has swept aside all notion of predictability. The uncertainty we are witness to has paved the way for a perfect storm. Anything is now possible. Bursting onto Netflix in early 2018, the ten-part series introduces ideas and concepts that were once-upon-a-time the stuff of fantasies, but seem to be now less and less unlikely. If the past is a foreign country, where they do things differently, the future may turn out to be an unimaginable abomination of our understanding of what it means to be normal. Normal is a rightly contested term, yet a futuristic default normality may no longer denote a state of existence dominated by humans. Ziauddin Sardar has already declared that we live in postnormal times, 'an era in which old orthodoxies are dying, new ones are emerging, and very few things seem to make sense'. Perhaps he has the *Altered Carbon* universe in mind, in which all semblance of the humdrum of existence is subverted. Will it one day be normal for artificial intelligence to walk the earth entirely indistinguishable from humans? The television series is confident enough. In an embrace of consumerist neoliberalism, consciousness resides in bodies readily discarded and upgraded to 'superior' versions. At a price. The setting is an overpopulated megalopolis called Bay City that has morphed out of present-day San Francisco. In a hint at the deepening inequality visibly perpetuating in our contemporary times, the overwhelming majority of inhabitants live in dank, slum-like dwellings. The wealthy elite, known as Methuselahs, or 'Meths', who make up 1 per cent of the population, meanwhile, reside in luxury supertowers that loom above the clouds. Up there they may bask in the natural light denied to the masses.

Whether the bleak landscape is the result of climate collapse or nuclear armageddon is unclear. What is clear is that in this unreality, immortality is within the grasp of the grotesquely rich. At birth, a device called a cortical stack is inserted into the back of every newborn's neck. The stack continuously downloads and stores that person's soul, and in the event of death, the stack can simply be removed and inserted into a different body or 'sleeve'. This prohibitively costly process to endlessly defer actual death is the preserve of only those who can afford it.

Shopping for a new body gives the notion of striving to become the best possible version of you, an entirely new spin. Authenticity of self is obsolete and a chameleon-like sleeve renders a person unrestricted by any identity bound by race or gender. 'Your body is not who you are.' We are told. 'You shed it like a snake sheds its skin. Leave it, forgotten, behind you.' What does this mean for religious beliefs, cultural identity, shared histories and the insidiousness of objectification? There exists within Bay City a movement called 'Afterlifers', religious Catholics who alter their stack's programming to ensure they will not be reborn into a new body and will instead experience 'real' death and safe passage to paradise. I am cast back to the Islamic books I read as a child, and their fiery rhetoric that Allah curses the woman who alters her appearance in the vainglorious pursuit of beauty. They preached the importance of respecting God's creation of the human form and for many years instilled within me a terror of plucking my eyebrows for fear of violating the 'sleeve' I had been honoured with. Such transgressions that await in the future. I can't even compare.

How would Islamic scholars comprehend an *Altered Carbon* world? Such quandaries are perhaps not so distant in the future? After an injury, one character wakes up in hospital to find she has been gifted a top-of-the-range, super bionic arm. This is an amplification of an already emerging technology. Medical science is forging ahead in the development of mechanisms that successfully replicate and repair human organs. It is not by coincidence that the mantra for the London 2012 Summer Paralympics was 'Meet The Superhumans', set to a rousing soundtrack of Public Enemy's *Harder Than You Think*. We may not yet have reached the nadir of visiting retail outlets to purchase ready-made bodies, temporarily satisfying our aesthetic illusions until our fashion tastes change in accordance with the length of our attention span. But the template exists; bionic eyes can restore sight, replicated tongues can recover taste, and brain-controlled prosthetic limbs can integrate the human with the non-human.

This blurring of the definition of what it means to be human brings with it an array of conundrums set to challenge theology in entirely unprecedented ways. If we are staring into a future in which humans and robots are set to walk the earth together, how must interactions be regulated? Friendship? Love? Sex with robots? The notion of sexual relations between humans and non-humans has been discussed at length in Islamic tradition, often, although not exclusively, framed within the confines of hetero-normative marriage. The Sufi Shaykh Badr al-Din Muhammad ibn 'Abdullah al-Shibli discussed the permissibility of marriage between a human and a djinn in his fourteenth century tome *Kitab akam al-marjan fi ahkam al-jan*. Although his reasoning led him to eventually conclude that this was a less than desirable synthesis, the idea of a human marrying a non-human was not dismissed outright, creating instead a space for dialogue to ensue.

The fourteenth-century predicament of humans becoming emotionally entangled with not-quite-human entities, was confined to the metaphysical. Now we have rather more corporeal pretenders to navigate. 2016 saw the arrival on the scene of Sophia the Robot. A sophisticated humanoid, Sophia was built by a Hong Kong-based firm headed by former Disney Imagineer David Hanson, to socially interact with humans. Intricate neural networks enable Sophia to emulate social behaviours and respond to those around her. She quickly became something of a celebrity and was even granted Saudi citizenship. The irony of a country that doesn't grant full rights to women or migrants, yet offers the very same to a robot, was lost on no one.

Sophia, with her doe-eyes and Audrey Hepburn-inspired looks, suggests the beginning of a continuum that could evolve into those same human-perfect humanoids we meet in the world of *Altered Carbon*. The trajectory has already commenced, but is currently stuck in a very specific mould: that of sex robots. Demand for sex robots is currently driving the AI machine, at some cost to our emotional wellbeing. Flaccid dolls with texture resembling the human touch are hypersexualised. With fulsome breasts, tiny waists and pert backsides, these objects, unlike any natural female body, have been plucked out of the male imagination and cultivated into a usable reality. A market is emerging for sex robots designed for women but there is little doubt that the sex bot industry is very obviously designed with male pleasure in mind. All manner of disturbing ethical concerns regarding consent and objectification are raised in my mind. The idea of a female form readily available for the use of men in their pursuit of satisfaction, makes me deeply uncomfortable. Particularly as sentient robots could one day come to fruition.

There is no stopping the technological march ahead, though. In Japan an android called Erica, built by scientists at Osaka University, is destined to become the first robot to be programmed with human-like desires. Perhaps this heralds the first step towards consciousness? In a bold move, a portrait of Erica was shortlisted for the prestigious Taylor Wessing portrait prize, which stipulates that photographs must be 'taken from life and with a living sitter'. There was outcry at the breach of rules, but the judges defended the inclusion of the portrait by pointing out the importance of questions it raises on the definition of life and living, in an age of increasingly sophisticated robotics and AI. Animal rights organisations such as the US-based Nonhuman Rights Project, have been campaigning for human rights to be extended to chimpanzees, gorillas and orangutans, and have recently enlisted the support of prominent philosophers to argue that AI should be afforded similar legal protection.

So the legal and societal debates surrounding AI are already occurring, but what about the impact of AI and sex robots upon the lives of Muslims now, and in the future? I am reminded of the mischievous rumour that plagued Hizbut Tahrir (HT) some years ago. It was claimed that HT scholars had declared that the watching of porn was not *zina* or illicit, as it did not involve interaction with humans, only interaction, ahem, with machines and technology. This was hotly rejected by HT leaders but the idea that technology can facilitate sexual desire in a way that bypasses conventional definitions of halal and haraam, certainly has appeal. If self-pleasure falls within the realms of *makrooh*, occupying that grey space of possible permissibility, is sex with robots just another type of masturbation, except with props?

Not if you fall in love with the robot you are having sex with, or wish to have sex with. A robot that as far as you are concerned is cognitively developed, exhibits consciousness and expresses emotion. In an uncertain future, love must surely be celebrated, and if Muslims wish to marry their AI soulmates, Islamic scholars would do well to respond with an open heart. At the 2018 Muslim Institute Winter Gathering in Salisbury, Usama Hasan, former astronomer turned researcher for the Quilliam Foundation, suggested that an exposition of what constitutes being human will inform our response to scenarios that may lie ahead. He draws on Ibn Arabi's writings on the cosmic spirit, a concept the Qur'an teaches when it speaks of everything in the world being a glorification of God. In the same vein, therefore, everything must necessarily possess a form of consciousness or life. Applying this to modern science, the more complex an organisms' structure in terms of atoms and molecules, and as far as we know human beings are the most complex entities in the universe, the spirit of God being breathed into us occurred within a process that could have taken millions of years. As humans, we have undergone this process, and therefore have been formed out of the natural world that we refer to as not being human or natural. Yet these are the same atoms and molecules from which we were formed. From the moment we achieve this realisation, Hasan argues, the word artificial in Artificial Intelligence becomes obsolete and the myth of separation between a so-called natural world and man-made or artificial world is negated. Machines are created by human beings indeed, and although intensely complex, their level of complexity is nowhere that of humans, but it is not unreasonable to expect that within 100 years robots could comprise the same level of complexity as humans, integrating into our world and potentially surpassing us.

Contemplating a future in which sex with robots is no longer excluded from the hetero-normative narrative that dominates our framing of sexuality, one point of resistance recurs endlessly. How can AI ever be anything other than different from humans, inferior even, if robots are man-made. With leading scientists already talking about the development of self-replicating robots, which would give further autonomy to AI, alongside attributes of consciousness and life, this argument will eventually be moot. All robots will then need, for a level playing field and to remove any distinction from humans, is to develop free will.

Free will has the potential to introduce chaos to all that was once orderly. Thankfully, the nightmare of an *Altered Carbon* future is unlikely to be one that I will ever be forced to confront. Or maybe I am wrong. If I wake up 360 years from now to a world where robots can love and be loved, I will align my cosmic spirit and leave my heart open to all possibilities. Unless, of course, I find that a long-haired, former archaeologist in a crumpled shirt has travelled to the future with me. Not just the sleeve, though, and definitely not the stack in a new sleeve. If all else fails, I will see if I can create a robot replica.

TEN EMERGING ISSUES

Emerging issues are a tough cookie to pin down. They are items that exist just below the horizon of tomorrow with the potential of becoming fully-fledged trends. They are the bits you gather from headlines, usually dwelling deep down beneath the home page of your favourite news outlet. To the casual reader, they are blips on the board, most likely outliers, but they have a true potential for changing not just the rules, but the game entirely. Emerging issues are the raw material that shape futures; they have the potential to have a positive or negative effect – and, in some cases, a dramatic impact on the future. They may be thought of as embryonic, fragmented, incomplete, concealed, and inadvertent data that can appear irrelevant at first sight but could have considerable impact on shaping futures – that is why they are also known as 'weak signals'. The raw data, or signal, can be refined into valuable information and placed in appropriate contexts to yield futures insight. Emerging issues often precede trends, and can be seen as advanced indicators of novel developments in the rate and directions of trends. Some evolve into megatrends, such as social media. Others, such as the Muslim fashion or modest fashion movement, develop into more contextual trends. But not all emerging issues become trends. Some die upon launch to be lost to the obscurity of what may have been, but never was.

Here are ten emerging issues that will play a large role in the tomorrow of Muslims around the world.

1. The End of Oil

The combustion engine was made in the last century and ushered in the era of oil following the retiring of the last horse drawn carriage in 1917. Recent policy suggests that the end of oil dependency may be imminent.

While this transition will remain slow due to the power of lobbyists and corporate influence, various governments and individuals around the globe are looking elsewhere for their energy needs. Numerous mayors of cities across the world have pushed to ensure public transport leaves a smaller carbon footprint. Trends in electric trains are seeing a rise of electric powered taxis along with a slew of other carbon limiting policy measures. Oil will not necessarily disappear overnight, since plastics are still a major product used in a variety of ways across the globe, but the impact from oil free transport will be significant to oil-based economies in the Middle East. Limitations in the non-renewable resource and the growing environmentally friendly trends will force oil rich countries to move towards new forms of energy. Many oil rich countries tend to have an abundance of solar and wind energy that can be taken advantage of. In any case, once the oil runs out, the energy and economic landscape of the Middle East will change dramatically.

2. The Descent of Western Dominance

Empires rise. Empires fall. This is the history of human existence in a nutshell. For a long time, the West has dominated the world. This dominance has been seen in strength and power as well as in influence. The key to this dominance has rested in the power to define what is history or even what is thought. Language, culture, society, and civilisation are all at the determination of the West. Thus the rest have had to meet these definitional ideals, lest they remain savage, foreign, other. Survival and success was only attainable in the West and in the reflection of the West. But the West has a dark side of hate and anxiety. Recently this darkness has come out into the light and appears to be the potential downfall for the West. Political and economic power is shifting from the West to China, India, Russia. G7 has become G20. The world has changed, and a new world order is struggling to be born. The question remains, will the West fall like all the empires of history? After all, Lucifer himself was an angel at first.

3. Islamic Blockchain Banking

Since the 2008 global financial crisis, economists and governments have searched for a better way to manage the global economy. But that is not possible given the current status of rampant, naked capitalism, manufactured derivatives and an intrinsic corrupt banking system. Islamic economics has turned out to enrich the wealthy at the expense of the poor just like the dominant economic system. A potential solution lies in blockchain technology which could provide a new system of accountability in finances. While it is often referenced as cryptocurrency, it is far more than a new standard currency. Blockchain is a simple link of transaction data in a network of computers, which include a piece of the previous block, or receipt, a time stamp, and an encryption of the new block. Thus every transaction can be traced back to its origin as well as its final destination. Islamic financing, that which complies with the Sharia, might just be the perfect fit for a new blockchain economic order. Given that accountability is intrinsic to blockchain technology, it ought to be Sharia complaint. It could diminish the widespread tyranny of usury and interest. Which is exactly what the believers want.

4. Saudi-Iran Wars

It is an issue that cannot be ignored and goes beyond the simple Sunni-Shia divide. It has been seen in the shadows of the Israeli conflicts in the region, the situation in Iraq and the Arab Spring. It is seen most abruptly in the Syrian Civil War and the conflict in Yemen. A series of proxy conflicts fought by agents of Saudi Arabia and Iran. As these two powers vie for dominance in the Middle East, states are decimated, refugees created daily, and lives lost by the hundreds. The wildcards are Turkey, global powers seeking influence in the region (Russia, the United States, Europe, China), and the tribes or extremist groups that are capable of resisting their influence, money, or power. The stakes seem to be by any means necessary, regardless of how much they hold the region back or destroy it along the way. The problem with proxy wars is that they always stand the threat of melting into direct conflict. We should not be surprised if hostilities between Saudi Arabia and Iran turn into direct, intractable, perpetual wars.

5. Reconstitution of the Muslim Family

The most basic unit of social organisation is the family. However, like other structures in postnormal times, the family itself is changing. Greater tendency towards individualism is giving rise to smaller, more spread-out families. Grandparents, aunts and uncles could live in entirely different parts of the world. Traditional roles of fathers and mothers are being challenged. The raising of children is becoming more hands off. Relationships themselves work radically differently with the advent of social technology. Advancements in science are changing the limits of fertility, as multiple mothers and fathers could constitute now a family. War, Islamophobia, and the interconnections of the internet are scattering families far apart and creating new ones out of biologically unrelated peoples. The very concept of family and home are being redefined. It is now possible for a child to have three parents. Grandmothers can give birth to their own grandchild if their daughters are unable to do so. These developments can have impact on Muslim families too. The Muslim families of tomorrow could be unrecognisable in a world transformed through medical innovations.

6. Islam with Chinese Characters

China has played a careful game to increase its position in international politics. Entering the global game just as the age of conquest and empire was waning, the People's Republic sought a different mode to establishing its name around the world. Economics. Flexing of soft power in East Asia and foreign investment in Africa has gained China great wealth. This wealth is currently being used to forge a strong partnership in Europe, including opening doors post Brexit, and to combat its rivalry with the United States and Russia. The current constitutional plan that Xi Jinping is seeing out is called the Belt and Road Initiative (BRI). Essentially, BRI is a series of economic partnerships that build a strong economic and political bond between China and the rest of the world and its next target is the Middle East. China's recent propaganda against its own Muslim population, the Uyghurs, could threaten the ties it wishes to make in the region. Though just as the communist government has managed to manipulate capitalism to its own working, could it not do the same to Islam if profit could be made? The question then remains if China's efforts will go the way of Africa, where a rivalry with the United States left the battleground a mess for the locals? Or will China attempt to lord over MENA as it does Eastern Asia and the South China Sea? Perhaps China will co-opt Islam just as it has embraced European culture. And Muslim societies could embrace Chinese culture and characters just as they cuddled western norms and values.

7. The End of Disciplines

The traditional categorical breakdown of knowledge into discipline fields has exhausted its benefit to knowledge production. Certain disciplines are increasingly being questioned for their viability. Can economics continue, given its colossal failure in recent times? Does development studies still make sense? What is the significance of geography in the time of Google maps? Can anthropology ever shake off its colonial roots? What is the difference between physical chemistry and chemical physics? When does biology and physics cease to be distinguished or at what point does philosophy become art and art the only possible portrayal of philosophical thought? A staunch dependence on old disciplines is beginning to limit human ability to understand and pursue truth. Moreover, the conventional approach to problem solving, which required problems to be isolated and then studied for potential solutions, is proving inadequate in complex contexts where everything is interconnected. Hence, the emergence, and proliferation, of programmes in multi-, trans-, and interdisciplinary studies. Educational institutions are merging departments or getting rid of old disciplinary boundaries altogether. Indeed, disciplines are being reorganised and restructured within all fields of knowledge; and a movement towards new paradigms, with trans- and interdisciplinarity as their foundations, is clearly discernible. The lines between natural sciences, the humanities, business, medicine, and the arts are blurring; and a more holistic approach to education and integration of knowledge production is emerging.

8. Eugenics Strikes Back

Designer babies were the premise of the 1997 science fiction film *Gattaca*, but advances in the manipulation of the human genome are making this more than a possibility. CRISPR-Cas9 is a genome editing system that when fed a sequence of RNA will target its corresponding DNA sequence within the human genome to edit it. While this technique is relatively new, it provides a multiplicity of options ranging from treatment of genetic disorders to manipulating phenotypic or displayed characteristics in human embryos. Mixed with the capitalistic market system, it will quickly become a game for the wealthy and favour the traits of the affluent as well. While many countries have banned this sort of research, there are pressures in a number of western countries for the research to proceed unabated. A rogue scientist in China has already edited the genes of an embryo. Thus, we are set for a Brave New World of frightening inequality. Populism and nationality being an increasing trend in the West, it is not hard to see eugenics being used through CRISPR-Cas9's system to either proliferate a master race of beings or target others based on their genetic make up for horrors.

9. VR Communities

Two recent developments have increased the probability of the emergence of virtual reality (VR) communities, important phenomena that have prompted this potentiality. First, in 2016, Pokemon Go was launched as the first major augmented reality (AR) gaming platform. This fad swept the globe and even disrupted reality to the extent of people causing great harm to themselves in pursuit of digital fantasies. Second, in yet another example of the rapidly continuing automation of the contemporary world, Japan introduced 'care-bots' to assist with its rapidly aging population. Soon these care-bots will be on their way to Muslim societies where they would have endless application, be that the care of the old, the new-born, even the sick. Virtual reality (VR) technology has also been used to attempt to assist with dementia by putting patients into scenes that evoke nostalgia and increased brain activity, whether that is taking them to enchanted worlds of high stimulus or back in time to places lost to their own history.

The combinations of these trends and fads opens up the opportunity for the formation of new social institutions. VR could spiral into a new form of escape for people of all ages. Maybe we will even have a VR Caliphate!

10. *Modest Goes Global*

Trends leaning towards more modest forms of fashion as well as moves in the film industry for equal and fair representations provide the groundwork for a revival of Muslim art and culture in the West. Major Western designers such as Dolce and Gabbana have embraced such articles as the hijab and the abaya. In 2017, London hosted the first Modest Fashion Week which has accompanied the elevation of less revealing and more ornately decorated garments in the eyes of fashionistas as being 'in vogue'. No doubt this move comes largely at the realisation of a major missed marketing opportunity in the Middle East, India, and South East Asia by fashion companies. But perhaps this is a response wave waning from the hyper suggestive and revealing fashions of the last decade or so. Since fashion after all waxes at the rate of the moon and increasingly so these days. Just as the heavier fashion of the 80s and 90s stood as a response to the open styles of the 60s and 70s in the West, the modest fashion of Muslim couture might continue to be the big thing. Meanwhile, the #MeToo and fight for equal and fair representation in filmmaking might partner up to make for a full artistic renaissance for Muslims. Respect of difference in gender, sex, culture, and religious creed provides an opportunity for Muslim artists to play a major role in the future. A new 'Riz' test, similar to the Bechdel Test for film, may emerge to evaluate stereotyping of Muslims in film. As art has always been a response to the times, perhaps the chaos and complexity that has ruled the last few years will bring a little modesty. It is certainly long overdue.

CITATIONS

Introduction: Postnormal Horizons
by Ziauddin Sardar

On my earlier work in futures studies, see Ziauddin Sardar, *The Future of Muslim Civilization* (Croom Helm, London; 1979; second edition, Mansell, 1989), *Islamic Futures: The Shape of Ideas to Come* (Mansell, London, 1985); and as editor, *Rescuing All Our Futures: The Future of Future* Studies (Adamantine Press, London; Praeger Publishers, Westport, CT., 1998), *An Early Crescent: The Future of Knowledge and Environment in* Islam (Mansell, London, 1989) and Editor, *The Touch of Midas: Science, Values and the Environment in Islam and the West* (Manchester University Press, Manchester, 1982). For a more recent introduction to futures studies, see *Future: All that Matter* (Hodder, London, 2013).

See also: 'Colonising the Future: The 'Other' Dimension of Future Studies', *Futures* 25 (3) 1993 and 'The Namesake: Futures, futures studies, futurology, futuristic, foresight – What's in a name?' *Futures* 42 (3) 177– 184 April 2010.

On postnormal times, see: 'Welcome to Postnormal Times' *Futures* 42 (5) 435-444 2010; 'Postnormal Times Revisited' *Futures* 67 26-39 2015; (with John Sweeney), 'The Three Tomorrows of Postnormal Times' *Futures* 75 1-13 2016; 'Postnormal Artefacts' *World Future Review* 7 (4) 342-350 2016 – these papers are included in Ziauddin Sardar, editor, *The Postnormal Times Reader* (CPPFS, London, 2017; second edition, CPPFS/IIIT, London, 2018). And: Elif Cepni, 'Transforming Education for a Transition into Human-centered Economy and Post-normal Times' *Cadmus Journal* volume 3 Issue 3 2017; available at: cadmusjournal.org; and 'Still in Post-Normal Times (not the New Normal) in the Legal Industry' Law 2050, 'a forum about the legal future' at law2050.com; and Stowe Boyd,' 10 work skills for the postnormal era' can be read at: workfutures.org.

The quote from Ezio Mauro is from Zybmunt Beauman and Ezio Mauro, *Babel* (Polity, Cambridge, 2016), p.20. Other works mentioned in the article: John Carey, editor, *The Faber Book of Utopias* (Faber, London, 2000); Robert Irwin, *Ibn Khaldun: An Intellectual Biography* (Princeton University Press, 2018); K M Aslam, *Spectacle of Death Including Glimpses of Live Beyond the Grave* (Tablighi Kutub Khana, Lahore, 1976).

The two cities discussed in the article are described in some detail in Ziauddin Sardar, *The Consumption of Kuala Lumpur* (Reaktion Books, London, 2000) and *Mecca: The Sacred City* (Bloomsbury, London, 2014).

The VW ad wrapped the cover of the *Guardian Weekend* Magazine 17 October 2018. The Prada perfume description is from British Airways *Highlife Shop* catalogue September/October 2018, p.25.

The reports on populism are: Paul Lewis, Sean Clarke and Caelainn Barr, 'One in four Europeans vote populist', *The Guardian* 21 November 2018; and Roger Eatwell and Matthew Goodwin, The grip of populism' *The Sunday Times* 7 October 2018

See also: James Bridle, The New Age of Darkness: Technology and the End of Future (Verso, London, 2018); Anand Giriharadas, *Winners Take All: The Elite Charade of Changing theWorld* (Alfred Knoff, NewYork, 2018); Nicholas Shaxson, *The Finance Curse: How Global Finance is Making Us All Poor* (Bodley Head, London, 2018); Andrew Keen, The Internet is Not the Answer (Atlantic Books, London, 2015); P W Singer and Emerson T Brooking, *LikeWar: The Weaponizaion of Social Media* (Houghton, Mifflin, Harcourt, Boston, 2018); Jamie Susskind, *Future Politics* (Oxford University Press, 2018); and Katja Mielke and Anna-Katharina Hornidge, Editors, *Area Studies at the Crossroads: Knowledge Production after the Mobility Turn*, Palgrave Macmillan, NewYork, 2018; and Tom Ritchey, *Wicked Problems, Social Masses* (Swedish Morphological Society, Stockholm, 2010)

Jordi Serra's television series, *El dia de dema*, ('The Day of Tomorrow') can be seen at: https://www.ccma.cat/tv3/el-dia-de-dema

Futures in Five Scenes by Jordi Serra del Pino

The three papers quotes, are, in order of chronology: Silvio Funtowicz and Jereome R Ravetz, 'Science for the Post-Normal Age' *Futures* 25 739-755 (1993); Ziauddin Sardar, 'The Namesake: Futures, futures studies, futurology, futuristic, foresight – What's in a name?' *Futures* 42 (3) 177-184 April 2010; and 'Welcome to Postnormal Times', *Futures* 42 435–444 June 2010.

Touching the Future by Christopher B Jones

For an introduction to futures studies, see Eleonora Masini, *Why Futures Studies?* (Grey Seal, London, 1993); Jim Dator, *What futures studies is, and is not.* (Hawaii Research Center for Future Studies, Honolulu, 1995); Ziauddin Sardar, *Future: All That Matters* (Hodder, London, 2013); and Jennifer Gidley, *The Future: A Very Short Introduction* (Oxford University Press, 2017). For a more detail, see Wendell Bell, *Foundations of Futures Studies* (Transaction Publishers, London and New Brunswick, 1997; two volumes); and Richard Slaughter, editor, *The Knowledge Base of Futures Studies* (DDM Media Group, Hawthorn, Victoria, 1996, three volumes).

On the Manoa School, see Jim Dator, 'Alternative Futures at the Manoa School', *Journal of Futures Studies*, 14(2), 1–18 2009; Christopher Jones, 'The Manoa School of Futures Studies', *Futures Research Quarterly*, 19-25, Winter 1992; and Wendy Schultz, 'Manoa: the future is not binary', APF Compass, 2015, which can be retrieved from https://www.researchgate.net/profile/Wendy_Schultz2/publication/275338406_Manoa_The_future_is_not_binary/links/5538a1a30cf247b8587d486f.pdf;

On the Gaia hypothesis, see James Lovelock, *The Revenge of Gaia* (Penguin, 2006), *The Vanishing Face of Gaia* (Basic Books, New York, 2015); and *A Rough Ride to the Future*, (The Overlook Press, New York, 2015).

On postnormal times, see Ziauddin Sardar, *The Postnormal Times Reader* (IIIT, London, 2018); and Ziauddin Sardar and John Sweeney, 'The Three Tomorrows of Postnormal Times, *Futures*, 75, 1-13 2015.

The books mentioned in the article include: Yuval Harari, *Homo Deus* (Harper, New York, 2017); John Naisbitt, *Megatrends* (Warner Books, New York, 1982); Fred Polak, *The Image of the Future*. Jossey-Bass; Princeton University, Woodrow Wilson Center, New York, 1973, 2018).

See also: Sohail Inayatullah and Ivana Milojević, 'Six pillars', Metafuture, Maroochydore, Australia, 2015, which can be accessed at: https://www.metafuture.org/2015/11/18/six_pillars/; Christopher Jones, 'Envisioning Sustainable Futures', in D Hicks & R Slaughter (Eds.), *World Yearbook of Education 1998: Futures Education* (Kogan Page, London, 1998); and 'Sustainable futures', in W Leal, editor, *The Encyclopaedia of Sustainability in Higher Education* (Springer; 2018); and Wendy Schultz, 'The Foresight Fan: Systemic Approaches to Foresight' (Infinite Futures, Oxford, 1997), which can be retrieved from http://www.infinitefutures.com/essays/publichealth/foresightfan.shtml

Futures Through Stories by Sohail Inayatullah

On metaphors see: P. H. Thibodeau and L. Boroditsky, 'Metaphors We Think With: The Role of Metaphor in Reasoning', *PLoS ONE* 6(2): e16782 DOI: 10.1371/journal.pone.0016782; George L. Kelling, 'Crime and metaphor: toward a new concept of policing', *City Journal* Autumn (1991). http://www.city-journal.org/article01.php?aid=1577; M Landau,. J., Sullivan, D., and J Greenberg, 'Evidence that self-relevant motives and metaphoric framing interact to influence political and social attitudes', *Psychological Science*, 20, 2009,1421-1427. doi: 10.1111/j.1467-9280. 2009.02462.x; and Ann Cammett, Deadbeat Dads & Welfare Queens: How Metaphor Shapes Poverty Law, 34B.C.J.L. & Soc. Just. ,233 2014, which can be downloaded from: https://lawdigitalcommons. bc.edu/jlsj/vol34/iss2/3

See also: Deborah Stone, *Policy Paradox* (W.W. New York, Norton and Company, 2012, 257); H Stone and S Stone, *Embracing Our Selves* (New World, Novato, 1989); and Ashis Nandy, 'Shamans, Savages, and the Wilderness: On the Audibility of Dissent and the Future of Civilization.' *Alternatives* (Vol. 14, No. 3, 1989).

The Jose Orteg y Gasset quote can be found at: http://www.quotehd. com/quotes/jose-ortega-y-gasset-philosopher-quote-the-metaphor-is-perhaps-one-of-mans-most. The Dada Prana website is at www.dadaorana and the Ananda Marga site is at www.anandamarga.org

Postculture by Richard Appignanesi

The quotes mentioned in the text, in order of appearance, are from: Arjun Appadurai, *The Future as Cultural Fact* (Verso, London, 2013, p286); Heidegger, *Being and Time*, trans, John Macquarrie and Edward Robinson (Harper & Row, New York, 1962, p32); Jean-Paul Sartre, *Search for a Method*, trans. Hazel E, Barnes (Vintage Books, New York, 1968, p151); Sartre, op.cit. p 113. Ludwig Wittgenstein, in his *Journal* entry, 14 May 1918, notes that 'Language is part of our organism and no less complicated than it'; Paul Virilio, *City of Panic*, trans. Julie Rose (Berg, Oxford and New York, 2007, p52, Ibid p50), Sartre, op.cit., p,152; Ludwig Wittgenstein, *Culture and Value*, ed. G.H. von Wright, trans. P. Winch (Oxford. Blackwell. 1980, pp39 and 49); Walter Benjamin. *The Origin of German Tragic Drama*, trans. John Osborne (Verso, London, 1998, p149 et passim for discussion of melancholy) and see also reference to *acedia* in Benjamin's 7th Thesis in *Theses on the Philosophy of History* (1940) http://www.efn.org/-dredmond/ theses-on-history; Sayyid Qutb, *Milestones* (Islamic Book Service, New Delhi, 1998, pp 49 -51 et passim); Susan Buck- Morss, *Thinking Past Terrorism: Islamism and Critical Theory on the Left* (Verso, London, 2003, p42); Jacques Derrida, *Specters of Marx*, trans. Pėggy Kamuf (Routledge, Oxford, 1994, p.98, Ibid, p103); Kierkegaard quoted by the existential psychiatrist Ludwig Binswanger in *Being-in-the World: Selected Papers of Ludwig Binswanger*, translated and introduced by Jacob Needleman (Basic Books Inc, New York, 1963, p.295); Virilio, op.cit., p 60; and Francis Fukuyama, T*he End of History and the Last Man* (Penguin Books, London, 1992) Fukuyama has frequently clarified that by 'end' he does not mean actual 'termination' but a targeted or teleological 'objective'.

Futures of Cities by Maya van Leemput

The works cited included: M Castells, The City and the Grassroots: A Cross-cultural Theory of Urban Social Movements (Berkeley: University of California Press, 1983); Julia Kristeva, Polylogue. (Tel quell edition, Seuil, 2008, p 544); Ziauddin Sardar, 'Welcome to postnormal times' Futures, 42 435-444 June 2010; Ziauddin Sardar, 'Postnormal times revisited' Futures, 67 26-39 March 2015; and Ziauddin Sardar and John Sweeney, 'The Three tomorrows of Postnormal Times', Futures, 75 1-13 September 2016.

The *Guardian* report can be found at: https://www.theguardian.com/world/2018/may/17/two-thirds-of-world-population-will-live-in-cities-by-2050-says-un; and the UN report can be downloaded from: https://population.un.org/wup/

On the politics of Antwerp, see: https://stadincijfers.antwerpen.be/dashboard/Demografie

On the population of Shanghai see: http://worldpopulationreview.com/world-cities/shanghai-population. The Kenneth Goh quote can be seen at: https://www.todayonline.com/commentary/why-spore-needs-slow-down-go-fast

Sacred Digitised by Iacopo Ghinassi

Dagmar Rieder's 'Islamic Books' research blog is at: https://researchblogs.cul.columbia.edu/islamicbooks/2013/07/05/arabdigi/; and Thomas Milo's work can be viewed at https://www.decotype.com

Mushaf Muscat can be seen at: www.mushafmuscat.om

See also: Mohammad Zakaria et al, 'Digital Qur'an Computing: Review, Classification, Trend Analysis', *Arabian Journal of Science and Engineering* 42 8 3077-3102 August 2017 (can be accessed at https://link.springer.com/article/10.1007/s13369-017-2415-4); Muhammad Farooq et al, 'Impact of Digitalization of Holy Qur'an: Readers, Experience and Expectations' IOSR Journal of Humanities and Social Sciences 23 7 59-67 (July 2018).

Decolonial Scientia by Andrew Burke

Books referred to in this essay are: Frantz Fanon. *Black Skin, White Masks* (Pluto Press, London, with a Foreword by Ziauddin Sardar and Homi Bhabha, 2008; new edition with foreword by Homi K. Bhabha and introduction by Pail Gilroy, 2017; originally published by Editions de Seuil, Paris, 1952); Katherine McKittrick, editor, *Sylvia Wynter, On Being Human As Praxis* (Duke University Press, 2015); Walter D Mignolo, *The Darker Side of Western Modernity* (Duke University Press, 2011).

Finding Peace in Typhoons by Cesar H Villanueva

A primer on the Bangsamoro Organic Law is provided at: http:// cnnphilippines.com/news/2018/07/24/bangsamoro-organic-law-primer-everything-you-need-to-know-bbl.html

See also: *John Paul Lederach, The Moral Imagination: The Art and Soul of Building Peace* (Oxford University Press, 2010); Johan Galtung, *Transcend and Transform: An Introduction to Conflict Work* (Pluto, London, 2004).

Cryptocurrency and the Islamic Economy
by Harris Irfan

For a history of Islamic finance including modern practice, see Harris Irfan, *Heaven's Bankers* (Constable & Robinson, London, 2014).

On UK's first sovereign Sukuk, see 'Government issues first Islamic bond' (25 June 2014.) on HM Treasury website: www.gov.uk; and 'David Cameron unveils plans to make London a Mecca for Middle East wealth' *The Independent*, 29 October 2013. On quantitative easing, see, for example, Bank of England's own publication at https://www. bankofengland.co.uk/monetary-policy/quantitative-easing.

The al-Ghazzali quote is from *Ihya'ul-uloom*, as quoted variously by Taqi Usmani (see, for example, *Al-Masarif-al-Islamiyyah*, Dar al-Maktabi 1998). On waqafs, see Monica M. Gaudiosi, 'The Influence of the Islamic Law of Waqf on the Development of the Trust in England', *University of Pennsylvania Law Review* Vol 136:1231, 1988.

On the current crisis of capitalism, in financial institutions, see Mervyn King, *The End of Alchemy* (Little, Brown, London, 2016); John Hilary, *The Poverty of Capitalism* (Pluto, London, 2013); Peter Fleming, *The Death of Homo Economicus* (Pluto, London, 2017); Sebastian Mallaby, *All the Money in the World* (Bloomsbury, London, 2010); Paul Wilmott and David Orrell, *The Money Formula* (Wiley, London, 2017), Joe Earle et al, *The Econocracy* (Penguin, 2017); and David Graeber, *Debt: The First 5,000 Years* (Melville House, London, 2012).

See also: Saifedean Ammous, *The Bitcoin Standard* (Wiley, London, 2018).

Afrofuturism in Postnormal Times by C Scott Jordan

Films mentioned: *Black Panther,* directed by Ryan Coogler, Marvel Studios, Los Angeles, February 2018; *Get Out,* directed by Jordan Peele, Universal Pictures, Los Angeles, February 2017; *BlackKklansman*, directed by Spike Lee, Blumhouse Productions, Monkeypaw Productions, Los Angeles, May 2018. Also mentioned Ta-Nehisi Coates series starting with *A Nation Under Our Feet. Black Panther*. Marvel. 2017.

The works cited include: Mark Dery, 'Black to the Future: Interviews with Samuel R. Delany, Greg Tate, and Tricia Rose,' *Flame Wars*. 179-222. 1994; Mark Sinker, 'Loving the alien in advance of the landing' *The Wire*. 96. February 1992; Ytasha L Womack, *Afrofuturism: The World of Black Sci-fi and Fantasy Culture*. (Lawrence Hill Books, Chicago, 2013)

On the contemporary race issue, see: Ta-Nehisi Coates, *We Were Eight Years in Power: An American Tragedy*. (One World, London, 2017); Michael Eric Dyson, *What Truth Sounds Like: RFK, James Baldwin, and Our Unfinished*

Conversation About Race in America. (St. Martin's Press, New York, 2018); Reni Eddo-Lodge, *Why I'm No Longer Talking to White People About Race.* (Bloomsbury, London, 2017); and Michelle Alexander, *The New Jim Crow: Mass Incarceration in the Age of Colorblindness* (The New Press, New York, 2010).

XR: Extinction Rebellion by Mothiur Rahman

The books mentioned include: Kevin Mackay, *Radical Transformation: Oligarchy, Collapse, and the Crisis of Civilization* (Between the Lines Book, Toronto, 2018); Jorgen Randers, *2052: A Global Forecast for the Next Forty Years* (Chelsea Green Publishing, Vermont, 2012); Pema Chodron, *The Places that Scare You* (Shambhala Classics, 2002); Kabir Helminski, *Living Presence: the Sufi Path to Mindfulness and the Essential Self,* (Cornerstones Editions, London, 2017).

Summary of the Intergovernmental Panel on Climate Change (IPCC) Special Report on Impacts of Global Warming above 1.5 degrees from Pre-Industrial Levels, 2018, can be accessed at: https://www.ipcc.ch/news_and_events/pr_181008_P48_spm.shtml; the Extinction Rebellion Declaration can be found at: https://rebellion.earth/declaration/; and XR Muslims Facebook group is at: https://www.facebook.com/groups/352703038814758/

Sensitive British Museum by Nur Sobers Khan

The works cited, include: Ladan Akbarnia, William Greenwood, Venetia Porter, Fahmida Suleman, 'Introduction', *The Islamic World: A History in Objects*, by Ladan Akbarnia et al (London: Thames and Hudson and the British Museum, 2018). The quote is from page 8. Ivan Karp quote is from ' Part I: Culture and Representation', *Exhibiting Cultures: The Poetics and Politics of Museum Display*, edited by Ivan Karp and Steven D. Lavine (Smithsonian Institution Press, Washington and London: 1991), p. 14.

The Art Historiography Journal is open access; the special edition on 'Islamic Art History' (Number 6 June 2012), guest edited by Moya Carey and Margaret S. Graves, can be viewed here: https://arthistoriography.

wordpress.com/number-6-june-2012-2/ , along with Wendy Shaw's article, 'The Islam in Islamic Art History: Secularism and Public Discourse'.

Last Word on Robot by Samia Rahman

Altered Carbon, a ten part sci-fi series created by Laeta Kalogridis is based on the 2002 novel of the same title by Richard K Morgan and premiered on Netflix on 2 February 2018. *Blade Runner* is a 1982 neo-noir science-fiction film directed by Ridley Scott and set in a dystopian future Los Angeles of 2019. A sequel, *Blade Runner 2049*, was released in 2017.

Ziauddin Sardar defines postnormal times at https://www.cppfs.org/ For discussion on the permissibility of marrying a djinn see: https://archive.islamonline.net/?p=1398 and https://books.google.co.uk/books/about/Kitab_akam_al_marjan_fi_ahkam_al_jan.html?id=k2KkygAACAAJ&redir_esc=y

Read about Sophia the robot here: https://en.wikipedia.org/wiki/Sophia_(robot); and Erica the robot here: https://www.theguardian.com/technology/ng-interactive/2017/apr/07/meet-erica-the-worlds-most-autonomous-android-video

Self-replicating robots are on the horizon, see https://edgylabs.com/facts-self-replicating-machine

For Hizbut Tahrir porn allegations see: https://islamqna.wordpress.com/tag/porn/

CONTRIBUTORS

● **Richard Appignanesi,** former editor of *Third Text*, is a writer and philosopher ● **Andrew Burke** is looking to start his PhD studentship on Caribbean Studies ● **Jim Dator**, regarded as a father of futures studies, just retired as Professor and Director of the Hawaii Research Centre for Futures Studies, Department of Political Science, University of Hawaii at Manoa ● **Naomi Foyle** is a well-known science fiction writer ● **Iacopo Ghinassi** holds a postgraduate degree from King's College London, Department of Digital Humanities and was digital production coordinator for Open Book Publishers in Cambridge ● **Linda Hyokki** is a Fellow of the Centre for Postnormal Policy and Futures Studies ● **Sohail Inayatullah** is UNESCO Chair in Futures Studies at Universiti Sains Islam Malaysia, Tamkang University, Taiwan, and University of Sunshine Coast, Queensland, Australia ● **Harris Irfan**, Chairman of the UK Islamic FinTech Panel, is the author of *Heaven's Bankers: Inside the Hidden World of Islamic Finance* ● **Christopher B Jones** is a faculty member in the Graduate School of Public Policy and Administration, Walden University, Minneapolis ● **C Scott Jordan** is Assistant Director, Centre for Postnormal Policy and Futures Studies ●**Maya van Leemput**, a multi-media artist, is Senior Researcher at Erasmus Hogeschool, where she is setting up the new 'Applied Futures Research – Open Time' centre ● **Misha Monaghan** is project manager at the Muslim Institute and runs her own food channel on YouTube called 'Made with Misha' ● **Mothiur Rahman**, a lawyer, is a co-founder of the Community Chartering Network and is setting up a legal practice called New Economy Law ● **Samia Rahman** is the Director of the Muslim Institute ● **Nur Sobers-Khan** is lead curator for South Asia at the British Library ● **Tamim Sadikali** is a reviewer, and author of the novel *Dear Infidel* ● **Mirza Sarajkić** teaches philosophy at the University of Sarajevo ● **Ziauddin Sardar** is Editor of *Critical Muslim* and Director of the Centre for Postnormal Policy and Futures Studies ● **Jordi Serra** is Associate Professor, Communication and International Faculty, Blanquerna (Universitat Ramon Llull), Barcelona, Spain ● **Umar Sheraz**, a futurist, is Senior Research Officer, Centre for Policy Studies, COMSATS University, Islamabad, Pakistan ● **Cesar H Villanueva**, a futures activist, is Professor of Conflict Transformation and Reconciliation Studies at the University of St La Salle, Bacolod City, Philippines ● **Medina Whiteman** is a writer, musician, and singer.